Recovery Experts Applaud Upc

"In her book, *Breaking Through Betrayal*, Holli Kenley creates a fresh look at self-betrayal or relapse through a compassionate lens. The reader is given the opportunity to embrace the process with empathy and understanding. This books gives the reader a road map to move through self-betrayal or relapse to a deeper level of self-discovery. Holli shares her insights about relapse in a distinctive manner with clearly defined concepts and activities to engage the reader and further their learning. Betrayal and Relapse [Section IV] is a must read for anyone experiencing relapse."

Cathy Taughinbaugh, Certified Parent Coach

"Holli Kenley is on a mission to heal the pain and shame associated with relapse. Whether you are recovering from years of self-betrayal or substance use, through her professional insights and personal experience Holli will gently guide you to a place of healing and understanding. I can't think of a more qualified person to walk with you on your journey back from the heartbreak of relapse. If you are ready to embrace the gift of self-discovery, *Breaking Through Betrayal: And Recovering The Peace Within* was written for you."

Dawn Clancy, Writer & International Speaker
Founder & Creator of Growing Up Chaotic

"The Second Edition of *Breaking Through Betrayal* offers an empathic, insightful and compassionate look at the universal pain of betrayal and relapse. Like an experienced wilderness guide who can skillfully navigate treacherous terrain, Holli Kenley points out the steep cliffs and the quicksand, while gently encouraging each traveler to claim their own unique vistas and hidden treasures on this journey. The process outlined through narrative and activities includes restorative practices that lead to increased hope and resiliency. Like its author, this book is a wise companion on the journey."

Rajani Venkatraman Levis, LMFT, PPS, CTS
Psychotherapist & Certified Trauma Specialist

"Holli Kenley shares her comprehensive approach to a situation most of us experience at least once in our lifetimes – betrayal. As a former therapist, I appreciate the author's ability to take a complex topic and turn it into an uncomplicated and well-organized read, including easy-to-follow exercises at the end of each chapter. This book is an important resource for anyone experiencing grief and loss as the result of betrayal. Read it and "recover the peace within."

Janet A. Hopkins, Editor-in-Chief, *In Recovery Magazine*

Therapists Praise *Breaking Through Betrayal*

"This volume deals with the subject of *betrayal*, and is appropriate as a self-help aid for clients. It also contains useful suggestions for therapists dealing with those who have experienced betrayal of trust of several kinds: interpersonal, familial, sexual, and financial. The steps in the healing process are well outlined and make clear that relapse is to be expected. Overlap with loss and the grief process is also well discussed."

Lucy R. Ferguson, Ph.D., Member, AFTNC
Faculty Member and Dean Emerita, CSPP, Alliant University

"Holli Kenley brings to light aspects of betrayal with passion and storytelling, clarifying its phases and processes' complexities and resolution. She gives perspectives on work with this tangled, distressing and often missed theme in therapy, reaching out to people with tools and resources to work through the pain of betrayal."

Lani B. Stoner,
Marriage & Family Therapist

"With an all-encompassing definition of betrayal, Holli Kenley provides support and guidance through conflicted relationships of all kinds including institutions and destructive natural events. She helps us with empowering cognitive-behavioral methods to examine numerous losses and wounds that are often minimized or denied. She is able to guide us through the pain of awareness and feelings with compassion and insight, and develops solutions, hope and growth that is needed to go beyond the victim and survivor roles. An excellent read and powerful workbook for unresolved feelings and losses that need to be addressed in the treatment of addicts/alcoholics (and their loved-ones) in order to examine relapse triggers and will contribute to long-term sobriety."

Melissa Yarbray, MA,
Marriage & Family Therapist, Chemical Dependency Counselor

"Holli Kenley's *Breaking Through Betrayal* makes a complicated issue of dealing with betrayal easy to understand and more importantly strategies that really work to recover the peace within. Everyone has had to deal with one form of betrayal; rejection and abandonment to violations of trust or a truth that becomes a lie. Ms Kenley's experience as therapist and her openness to share her own feelings will help anyone to move past their pain to peace."

Gary Jeandron,
Marriage & Family Therapist

"Holli Kenley's *Breaking Through Betrayal* is useful for anyone caught in self-blame, shame or repeated victimization. Though almost the antithesis of my inner-transformation approach, this empowering 'in-control' approach can help readers take charge, assess injury, gauge healing and find excellent strategies to protect themselves from future trauma when relating to one's betrayer."

Beth Hedva, Ph.D.
author of award-winning *Betrayal, Trust and Forgiveness*

"Are you ready to heal? Have you experienced trauma, violence, or abuse? Most of us can answer 'yes' to the questions above—*Breaking Through Betrayal and Recovering the Peace Within* can be the answer. This healing workbook is filled with guidance, sacred empathy, self-analytical exercises, and directional steps to help one begin their path to recovery from being betrayed. Holli Kenley's book offers its reader a journey which travels from self-acknowledgement to self-forgiveness and reframing instruction to elicit creative healing. Reading *Breaking Through Betrayal* is a gift, read it for yourself or gift it to someone who is reaching for freedom from the pangs of betrayal."

Barbara Sinor, Ph.D., author
Gifts From The Child Within and *Tales of Addiction and Inspiration for Recovery*

"This book amounts to an in-depth (possibly the first such) study of betrayal in a variety of situations and as the root cause of numerous mental health conditions and disorders. As a 'background' emotion, it is often overlooked by practitioners and well-meaning laymen alike. Betrayal is pernicious and all-pervasive. The author's use of a strong vocabulary ('dark', 'cancerous') to describe it is justified: betrayal comprises the entire gamut of rejection and hurt. Nor is betrayal limited to the interpersonal realm; one can and is often betrayed by bosses, political leaders, pillars of the community, and institutions.

This book is the outcome of the author's own experiences as a marriage and family therapist and as a person who has been betrayed by a member of her family. When auto-biographical epiphany gives rise to intellectual rigor, we usually have a winner and this book is no exception: as promised by the author, it is a riveting, well-written tour of hitherto largely uncharted waters, replete with numerous case studies, a systematization of the emotional and cognitive components of betrayal and its consequences, a plethora of self-help measures, and self-evaluation questionnaires. About half the book is dedicated to recovery from betrayal. It belongs in the libraries of mental health practitioners, people who suffer or have suffered from betrayal (and who hasn't?), and those who monitor intriguing and promising emergent ideas in psychotherapy and clinical psychology."

Sam Vaknin, author *Malignant Self-love: Narcissism Revisited*

HOLLI KENLEY, MA

MARRIAGE & FAMILY THERAPIST

Breaking THROUGH *Betrayal*

AND RECOVERING THE PEACE WITHIN

2ND EDITION

New Horizons in Therapy Series

Loving Healing Press

Sarah ~
With Wellness...
Holli Kenley

Second Printing February 2016

Author photo by Julianna Calin

Learn more about the author at **www.HolliKenley.com**

From the New Horizons in Therapy Series

Library of Congress Cataloging-in-Publication Data

Names: Kenley, Holli, 1951- author.
Title: Breaking through betrayal : and recovering the peace within / Holli
    Kenley.
Description: 2nd edition. | Ann Arbor, MI : Loving Healing Press, [2015] |
    Series: New horizons in therapy series | Includes bibliographical
    references and index.
Identifiers: LCCN 2015036067| ISBN 9781615992850 (pbk. : alk. paper) | ISBN
    9781615992843 (ebook)
Subjects: LCSH: Betrayal.
Classification: LCC BJ1500.B47 K46 2015 | DDC 158.2--dc23
LC record available at http://lccn.loc.gov/2015036067

Distributed by Ingram (USA/CAN), Bertram's Books (UK/EU)

Published by
Loving Healing Press
5145 Pontiac Trail
Ann Arbor, MI 48105

www.LHPress.com
info@LHPress.com
Phone 888-761-6268
Fax 734-663-6861

Loving Healing Press

Contents

Table of Figures

In Loving Memory
David Joseph Miller (1987-2009)

~ The goodness in David, simply and beautifully,
brought out the good in everyone ~

Acknowledgements

There is one person with whom I have always openly shared my own betrayal experiences and whose heart has always responded with unconditional regard and respect. There is one person to whom I first unveiled the ideas and thoughts behind the curtain of betrayal recovering. There is one person who listened patiently and tirelessly to every word that I wrote, again and again. There is one person whom I trusted to be brutally honest with feedback, editing, and revision, and who did so with untold precision, compassion, and insight. There is one person who has always been my strongest cheerleader, my most loyal companion and friend, and the love of my life—my husband Dan. Thank you, sweetheart, for sharing this journey with me!

There is another person from whom I probably inherited my right-brained abilities and from whom I learned to risk putting that creativity down on paper. There is one person whose perseverance and whose polished performances in all aspects of life taught me to respect my craft and to deliver the best I had to give. There is one person whom I trusted to read the first complete draft of my manuscript and whose keen eye I knew would scan for clarity, coherence, and quality of work. Thank you, Dad, for the hours of reading and editing and most importantly, for putting your paternal print on my work.

Lastly, there are so many amazing people who have come to mind during the writing of this book and for whom I have untold admiration and respect. These are people who were willing to trust their pain in the hands of another and who were willing to take the recovery journey by embracing a path of wellness and wholeness. These were everyday people who made the decision to leave the bitter taste of betrayal behind them and to better themselves because of it. For all my former clients and for those of you yet to come, I acknowledge your good work and I acknowledge you.

Preface

> "The first wealth is health."
>
> —Ralph Waldo Emerson

A Note to the Clinician/Counselor

In *Breaking Through Betrayal: And Recovering the Peace Within*, I approach "betrayal" as a singular entity—a presenting issue with a therapeutic approach tailored specifically for recovery from it.

From my many years of practice in the areas of abuse and trauma, "betrayal" often came into the room. However, time and time again working with a multitude of presenting disorders, as the client and I peeled away the layers of pain and shame, we came face to face with "betrayal". As I became more aware of betrayal's ubiquitous and insidious nature, I entertained a theory of causation and challenged my recovery thinking around the idea of "it all boils down to betrayal".

As I have continued to grow my thinking around "betrayal", I am not suggesting "betrayal" serves as a catch-all or substitute for any disorder or presenting issue. As is the case in many professions, health care professionals are constantly being challenged by new ideas and approaches with the intent of raising the standard of care, increasing successful outcomes, and improving the lives of our clients. As a former English teacher, I remember the "waves of change" (often referred to as "fads" among educators), which were marketed as the new promise for educational reform. Many of these movements would come and go, making little or no difference on student achievement or growth. From my experience as a teacher and as a therapist, it is wise and necessary to embrace change and remain open to new ideas. At the same time, I believe it is unwise to say, "This is *the* cause or *the* remedy", or "This is a panacea for recovery." Therefore, when stating "it all boils down to betrayal," I am not suggesting we should all jump on the betrayal bandwagon and discount physiological and/or psychological factors of causation and/or issues of co-morbidity.

Quite the contrary, what I am suggesting is for "betrayal" to be given some well-deserved attention. It is time to widen our lens, viewing "betrayal" as a universal experience by comprehensively examining its connotations and applications as discussed in Chapter 1: What is Betrayal? It is an opportunity to increase our understanding of betrayal's anatomy which manifests in three distinct *States of Being* as thoroughly analyzed in Chapter 2: What Am I Feeling and Why? And in Chapter 3: To What Degree and How Long Will I Feel This Way?, it is the uncovering of distinct critical "underlying principles of betrayal" which affords us the opportunity to increase our awareness as to why some clients remain stuck in their betrayal experiences and why others do not.

Further, what I am suggesting is when the waters of pain are calming down within our clients or perhaps during their personal storms, clinicians and therapists take another look underneath the surface. "Betrayal" is frequently embedded within other presenting disorders or issues such as depression, addiction, grief/loss, anxiety, and anger. Because we, as health care professionals, are anxious to see our clients experience some degree of relief, we address what is in front of us—a crisis situation, a disorder ravaging an individual's life, a relationship/family being torn apart. Of course, we must continue to do so, and yet at the same time, let's challenge ourselves to look deeper.

Have our clients mentioned the word "betrayal"? Have we asked about it? If it has been brought into the room, have we missed it or dismissed it? And, if we have confronted "betrayal", what have we done with it and has that been enough? Do we really know what to do with betrayal's three deeply debilitating *States of Being*—Confusion, Worthlessness, and Powerlessness—and their accompanying dark destructive manifestations? And, do we possess the courage and the compassion to guide our clients through the process of "righting themselves" when their betrayal experiences tell them otherwise? Most importantly, have we acquired the knowledge of specific therapeutic strategies to do so effectively?

We can't afford to wait any longer. Our clients are waiting to begin "Breaking Through Betrayal: And Recovering *their* Peace Within".

Come join me. Let's find out how. It is time.

Preface to the Second Edition

The Second Edition of Breaking *Through Betrayal* now includes a brand new section about the timeless issue of relapse as a form of self-betrayal. Although the word "relapse" has most often been used in the addiction literature to refer to a return to substance abuse, we expand upon its definition and application to include all forms of self-betrayal. In the new chapters 12 through 15, we connect with multiple meanings of self-betrayal and uncover its debilitating emotions, self-deprecating life messages, and the masks of denial, disguise, and detachment. In chapters 16 through 18, our discussion continues as we move out of self-betrayal by recognizing areas of vulnerability as well as releasing the restraints of relapse, positioning us in a place of renewal and rediscovery.

"When it is dark enough, you can see the stars."

—Charles A. Beard

Introduction

This is a book about betrayal, a dark human experience that is uninvited, unwanted, and most commonly unexpected. It is a timeless, costly, and ever-reaching experience. Almost no one is exempt from its infectious fabric. Its historic infamous fibers weave their way back even as far as the Greek gods and goddesses. The Greeks' rich elaborate myths, based on their pantheon, are filled with tales of deception: Zeus betraying Hera, Hera betraying Zeus, Zeus along with the aid of Poseidon casting Odysseus (from Homer's *Odyssey*) out to a ten-year exile from his homeland for betraying them. The Greeks at once feared and revered their gods, never knowing how, when, where, or why their loyalties to them may be tested.

The timeless myths are just as relevant today as we read them and tap into the common emotional fabric of deception. Through the threads of time, we continue to see that even Jesus was not left unscathed by betrayal, not just by a vast army of Romans or, more personally, by his own people, but more intimately by one of his loyal disciples—Judas. Those of us who know the story are both sickened and moved by its outcome and implications. Sadly, most of us can relate to the story because we have come face to face with this cancerous emotion. It can rear its ugly head at any time, in any place, and with anyone. And if it doesn't infect us, it is probably targeting someone we know or know of. There is no sanctuary from betrayal; it touches every aspect of our lives: spiritual, relational, political, environmental, behavioral, and the list goes on.

As I write this book, the word "betrayal" is being thrown around every day, on almost every news story. Populations in the United States and around the world face both internal and external injustices being waged against them by forces out of their control. Tragically, on a daily basis, the fallout from these betrayals is seen and heard in the lost visions of its peoples.

- "We were lied to by our leaders, again. Their abuse of power is unconscionable. We are not better off than before; things are much worse."

- "No, you are the one who is disloyal. You need to stand by the decisions made. By not doing so, it shows others we are weak and vulnerable."

This is not a book about who is right and who is wrong, but about the depth and prevalence of betrayal in our society and about its implications for us.

- "We don't feel safe living here anymore. Who is going to stand with us? Who is going to help us?"

- "I don't know who to trust anymore. I have always believed that we were a government for the people and by the people. But when I don't believe that my voice or my vote matters, I don't see much hope anymore. We have every right to feel betrayed. Where do we turn? Who can we believe?"

Political, social, and economic violations exemplify the vast scope of betrayal, those deep dark injustices and injuries rebuking all reasoning. Betrayal is an emotional *state of being*, commonly felt and yet uncommonly dealt with. When betrayal is expressed, it is heard and then in the whisper of a moment, it is dismissed. It is uncomfortable and unsettling; we are uneasy to confront it. But it swarms around us daily, not just in our political and financial lives, but in our personal, relational, and professional ones as well.

- "My husband was just diagnosed with inoperable lung cancer; how could this happen to me? We are so young!"

- "My dear friend's son was killed in a tragic car accident over the weekend. I can't make sense out of it; he was just beginning his life."

- "My best friend went behind my back and started dating my boyfriend. How can I ever trust anyone?"

- "I gave this job the best ten years of my life, only to be looked over for the promotion—again!"

- "The justice system did it again! That 'scum of the earth' walked after assaulting more young children! I've lost all faith in our legal system."

- "If he hits me one more time, I swear, I'll leave. In the meantime, I'll try to be a better wife, or maybe he will change."

From the vast political arena to the personal scope of our relationships and encounters, betrayal penetrates through our barriers and boundaries. Sometimes, we don't know what is festering within us or even what to name it. And even if we do name it, we don't know what to do with it. What we do know is that it doesn't just go away. We hold onto the darkness and the darkness holds onto us.

How this book came about

I am a Licensed Marriage and Family Therapist (LMFT) in the state of California. Although I have been treating clients since becoming an intern in 1998, it wasn't until the fall of 2003 that the issue of betrayal really began to tug at me. I was practicing in a counseling center that had been established at a large church in my community. Over a period of two years, I counseled with a steady stream of clients (mostly women) who, even though they were working through their respective recovery programs, remained stuck. As their therapist, I felt frustrated that these intelligent, successful, dynamic women were debilitated, to varying degrees, by the rejection, violation, and abandonment of their unfaithful spouses. They could not fully climb out of their pits of betrayal. They were surviving, but certainly not thriving.

In the fall of 2005, I moved into private practice. In addition to my regular client load, I facilitated a codependency group. It was a closed group of women only, all of whom had experienced infidelity in their marriages and had been or were in the process of separation/divorce. During the six-month duration of the group as well as in the follow-up sessions, their anguish resurfaced time and time again.

- "How could he? Why would he choose her over his family?"
- "Don't his children matter?"
- "I gave him everything—doesn't that count for anything?"
- "I 'now' realize it was all a lie."
- "And to make it worse, he blames me!"
- "I just want to hear him say he is sorry—or just explain why."

Betrayal, betrayal, betrayal—the dark emotional presence penetrated the room like thick tule fog on a cold winter night. These remarkable women couldn't get through it or past it. Betrayal remained the noose around their neck; at times, it choked them. It suffocated them. And because they couldn't find peace or make sense out of their pain, they couldn't fully heal. Thus, these women remained vulnerable, continuing to feel betrayed and even re-betrayed by their ex-spouses' actions, words, and behaviors, or lack of them.

As their therapist/facilitator, I pulled out all the stops. In addition to the group process work, I gave them homework: journal assignments, grief work, anger management exercises, letters to write (to send or not), emotive-creative work—such as collages of themselves and their feelings (past and present and future)—"twelve-step" assignments (where appropriate), bibliotherapy and cinematherapy, and many other cognitive / behavioral tools that seemed timely and therapeutic. There was some degree of release and relief from the betrayal. It varied on an individual basis. Overall, I remained frustrated; they remained fragile and their spirits fragmented. The group concluded in the summer of 2006.

Throughout the ensuing year of July 2006–August 2007 of private practice, I continued to work with clients presenting a myriad of disorders. As an LMFT, I work under the umbrella of "relationship issues". My areas of specialty include trauma/abuse (especially sexual abuse), mood and anxiety disorders, addiction and codependency issues, and spiritual and faith issues. Most of my practice is comprised of counseling individuals and couples; periodically, I work with families. Believing strongly in, and working from primarily a Cognitive Behavioral therapeutic approach (where the therapist functions in a coaching role), I have been privileged to witness clients embrace the therapeutic process and their treatment plan. And because clients were committed and worked hard, many experienced a change in their thoughts, feelings, and behaviors. Their relationships evolved into healthier ones; they experienced a well and more vibrant life.

At the same time, it was during this period of time that I witnessed, over and over again, clients plateau in their recovery. They reached a level of relief and well-being and then got stuck. In some cases, clients regressed and worked their way back. Others regressed and remained in their dark place.

I examined their respective treatment plans. I moved into therapeutic approaches of family-of-origin work, transference work, object-relations work, and tapped into Rogerian as well as Gestalt principles, where appropriate. I reminded myself that all this was normal—a part of the therapeutic process. I kept telling myself, "clients proceed at their pace—what is safe, what is comfortable, what their egos can handle." But was I missing something? I thought I was, and it began to haunt me.

As I continued to reflect, think, and process the missing piece, I tapped into a personal struggle of my own. During the winter months of 2006–2007, I was deeply wounded by a family member. It was a relationship comprised of complex and complicated twists and turns. Over many years, it was strained, broken, bandaged, and then damaged again. In February 2006, it took its final turn, spiraling downward. It shook me to the core. I felt like a knife was rammed into my gut and twisted. My insides felt numb, yet nauseous. I carried around this anchor of despair inside the pit of my soul. For weeks, every day I would awake and feel the dark weight filled with anger, sadness, despair, confusion, and what-ifs. There were no answers, no remedies, just a debilitating state of being—*betrayal*.

Revisiting this experience allowed me open my mind and to feel the feelings again. The emotions were quick to surface as I replayed many of the exchanges in the relationship. Perhaps, this was "it"—the missing piece—betrayal. I logged the insight into my memory box. It seemed so important; I didn't want to forget it. I didn't have to worry; the "found" piece wouldn't let go of me.

One late, cool evening last spring, I began straightening up my office after finishing with my client. I was exhausted. I was frustrated. Yet, I remained determined and intrigued. Over the past two weeks, I had seen a dozen or so clients presenting with various disorders/issues:

- Depression
- Bipolar
- Abuse and trauma recovery (especially sexual abuse/assault)
- Anxiety disorders
- Substance abuse and dependence
- Codependency issues
- Relationship issues: infidelity, anger management, communication problems, parenting problems, blended family issues, separation/divorce
- Grief and loss issues

Again, most were progressing well. Presenting symptoms were relieved; cognitions were more realistic and in-check; behaviors changed and were continuing to become healthier. But there was a void; there was a hole. There was a residual darkness that dwelled in the depths of some clients. Every now and then, I got a glimpse of it, or maybe I inadvertently overlooked it. Perhaps the client felt it was gone, dealt with, and in the past. Embarrassed or reluctant to speak up, it was still there, like a shadow lurking in the dark. My mind began to reel through the Rolodex of past clients. I had seen it, heard it, and been witness to it so many times. I had listened, empathized, reflected feelings, and processed pain, but it wasn't enough.

I gathered up my belongings and stared at the soft white loveseat where individuals and couples had nestled themselves among the lavender suede throw pillows. Their faces were etched in my mind—their smiles, their tears, and their unresolved pain. I reached over and turned out the last light. The room was dark. I stood in my doorway, almost in a daze. I walked over to open the blinds on the large window across the room to let the moonlight in. But I decided against it. The room remained completely dark. For a moment, I felt lost. I found my hands feeling for the loveseat, the pillows, for things familiar and safe. As I sat down on the loveseat, I remained in the emotion and in the feeling of darkness. My mind went to my injury, the family member who had scarred my soul. The feeling became a thought, a deep and haunting thought: "This is what my clients are feeling; it is what dwells within their deepest recesses. Someone or something has injured them, injured them to their core. Darkness has penetrated their being." I sat for several minutes as tears of release and relief made their way down my cheeks. Taking a deep, relaxing breath, I slowly made my way to the door again. I relished a sweet moment of understanding and revelation. The swirling thoughts from moments before settled down like calm water after a crashing wave. I locked my office door, went down the elevator, and then out of the building into the cool desert night. I looked up at the silky moon and the stars spoke my very mind: "Underneath the intricately and uniquely formed layers of your clients' feelings—*it all boils down to betrayal.*"

The purpose of the book

The purpose of this book is to address the issue of betrayal and to give it some much-needed attention and investigation. To the say the word is no longer enough; it needs to be fully named, explained, and proclaimed! We, clinicians and clients alike, need to know what it looks like, feels like, and what to do with it. We need to explore it and examine it. We need to take apart its anatomy, educating ourselves about its meaning, prevalence, manifestations, sources, and impact on our lives. We need to get comfortable with getting acquainted with our enemy. Knowledge is the conqueror of fear; we need not to be afraid of our betrayal or betrayer anymore and what it has done or is doing to us.

The purpose of this book is to take you, the reader, on a journey—an invitation into uncharted waters to become intimately acquainted with your own experience with betrayal. At times, the process may take some real digging. The betrayal may be buried, repressed, or residing underneath a myriad of emotional and behavioral camouflage. We need to know how and when to get to it, and then what to do next? Through a series of exercises and activities at the end of each chapter, I encourage you to make your journey an interactive process, no longer sitting on the sidelines of the playing field. One thing I have learned as a therapist, teacher, and a betrayed person, is that betrayal does not just go away or heal by itself over time. While betrayal takes residence within your soul and spirit, it disrupts and interrupts your quality of life. I have witnessed hurt people who have become cynical, resentful, and bitter; others become more vulnerable, self-doubting, and thus easily re-injured; still other injured persons resort to unhealthy, destructive means to cope. And sadly, some pain-filled people invite additional harm to themselves after becoming less resistant to debilitating physical and mental illness.

Some time ago, during a counseling session, a young married mother of two sat across from me with tears streaming down her face. We had spent months working together. She was a survivor of childhood sexual abuse perpetrated by her older brother. She had endured the unimaginable for years; she had worked tirelessly on her recovery to become a more vibrant and whole woman. She thought she was navigating on safe ground. But recently, her mother, who had never believed the abuse took place, betrayed my client, again.

> "I thought that after all this time and all the trouble my brother had had with the law, my mom would believe me. I mean, my brother has just been arrested again, after sexually abusing his girlfriend's daughter. My mom still thinks he is innocent! She is putting up his bail money and paying for his attorney. I told her he is sick! He is guilty! I told her he did the same thing to me! All she said was to 'get out'. She wants nothing more to do with me. How can this happen…what is wrong with her?"

My client dissolved in front of my very eyes. Betrayal had engulfed her, suffocated her, and sucked the life out of her. At this moment, the bundle of benign scar tissue that dwelled within her began to explode, fueled by the most recent injection of rejection. Clearly, our work was not done and, if left unattended, this client would succumb to the malignancy of despair.

This book is for anyone who has known betrayal and who has been left scarred from its acquaintance. My intention is, at the very least, to give your heart a rest and your spirit a repose. At the very most, I intend to provide you with knowledge and insight about the issue of betrayal along with validation of your feelings and experiences. And, I intend to provide you with tools and strategies to enable and empower you to move into a healthier, peaceful place of release, relief, and recovery.

Come join me now as we begin this journey. Get ready for a rocky but rewarding ride. Get comfortable in a soft cozy chair and grab a soothing cup of tea. Let's dig into the first layer of betrayal and find out what it is. Let's identify this cancerous culprit and move ahead armed in the knowledge of betrayal. It has known us far longer than we have known it; it is time to change that!

Section I:
Knowledge and Awareness

1   What is Betrayal?

"Betrayal is the only truth that sticks."

—Arthur Miller

Definitions and Explanations

I find that with my clients, as well as with myself, there is almost always a small degree of relief when I understand what I am feeling. When I can give a client a diagnosis, an explanation, a reason for why he/she is feeling the emotions or symptoms being experienced, there is a level of comfort that allows for further investigation and intervention. If we can define our pain, we can explain our feelings and not just feel like we are going crazy!

After researching specific definitions/explanations for betrayal and finding hundreds of interpretations as well as applications, I have decided for our discussion to narrow down the definitions/explanations into three categories. These three categories are based on my work with dozens of clients whose personal stories and their manifestations of betrayal seemed to lend themselves to one of the areas. Although there is some overlap in their respective explanations and implications, there is enough disparity among them to give each one attention.

As you read through them with me and learn about them, you may find that you can relate to more than one explanation. There is no problem with this. The important thing is that you can connect with at least one of them and that you have the opportunity to experience that what you have been feeling and/or are feeling is real. You will be able to say to yourself, "Yes, that is what I went through; that is how I felt; I now know why I am feeling the way I do!"

I also suggest at this point that you grab a notebook or journal. There are times where I encourage you to write down some thoughts and feelings. And, there might be moments where you need to unleash or unravel your emotions. Or, perhaps you may just want to note something for more investigation at a later time. In any case, have some writing materials ready for whatever the need may be.

Here are the three areas we will be investigating:

- An investment into someone or something met with rejection and/or abandonment

- A profound trust in someone or something which is profoundly violated
- A truth that becomes a lie/ a belief that is shattered

1. An investment met with rejection and/or abandonment

This area of betrayal is extremely common. As healthy human beings, it is natural for us to give and invest into our relationships, into our work, and into those arenas of life that bring us meaning and value. Some of us are taught at an early age that it is "better to give than to receive" or that "the reward is in the giving", and so on. There is certainly truth in these statements. However, when the investment is lost or when it is not received in the manner in which it was intended, we feel the pain of rejection or abandonment, or at the very least we do not feel appreciated. This wounds us because our intentions or actions become meaningless; we become valueless. And it is we, not they, who are left holding the bag of betrayal.

Several years ago, a couple came in to see me. Their marriage was on rocky ground. In years past, it had survived an affair, and now, the same issue had resurfaced. Although the female had every right to be angry with her unfaithful spouse, I sensed there was something more to her pain. I suggested that she and I spend some sessions together. Over a period of time, I learned that this woman lived under a blanket of betrayal. Each and every investment that she had made into those whom she cared about had been met with rejection and/or abandonment.

> "My mom died when I was about ten. We were so close; she was my 'protector'. She was the only person who made me feel safe. I loved her and she left me... My dad was an abusive alcoholic. As a little girl, and even now, I have always tried to please him. But I was never good enough, and I couldn't do anything right. When I tried to reach out to my siblings, they taunted and abused me—verbally and physically. I was even bullied at school because of my weight. When my dad remarried, I did everything possible to make my step-mom like me. She hated me, and I was forced to leave home as soon as I graduated from high school. When I married, I thought it would be 'forever'. I gave selflessly to him, to our children, and to our home. I thought I had finally found someone who loved me and cherished me, only to be discarded, again!"

This illustrates an extreme case of multiple betrayals—one that left the client with deeply embedded scars. The common denominator is that each betrayal involved her investment into someone, each one leaving her emotionally cheated and depleted. Although this client was layered with wounds of betrayal, she worked tirelessly on her recovery. Over a period of several months, she was able to experience a much needed level of healing.

With this definition of betrayal, there is no set time period required for the investment or for the feelings of rejection or abandonment to present themselves. The investment may be short or long term; it is quite individual. However, I tend to find that the longer the investment has transpired or been left unattended, the more severe the manifestations of betrayal, and thus, the recovery work may need to be longer or more in-depth.

It is important to point out that this explanation of betrayal includes the investment into *something*. This covers a myriad of meanings, but the one that I most commonly have addressed with clients involves their work or professions. Because most adults work in or outside of the home, there is opportunity to come face to face with betrayal. It spans the spectrum from being unappreciated, to being over-looked for a promotion, to outright being laid off, fired, demoted, or phased out! This kind of betrayal tends to wreak havoc on one's self-esteem and worth. Many times, its consequences are far-reaching, affecting families' financial security and their faith "in the system".

Several years ago, I worked with a client who recently had taken on a new position in a large prominent organization. Although we were working on a separate issue, he began to struggle with the dynamics of personalities within the organization. Although his evaluations over a significant period of time were superior, his work ethic and performance professional, and his product impeccable, he was abruptly asked to tender his resignation. This amazingly strong individual crumpled up in my office. This tower of strength fell before my very eyes. His endless hours of commitment, quality work, and perseverance were met with the reward of rejection. Pain was his only payoff.

Therefore, as you are reading through this explanation of betrayal, think not only of your investments in people, but also in any relationship or thing.

Other examples might also include:

- A romantic relationship
- A friendship
- A family relationship or dynamic
- A marriage or partnership
- A job, career, or profession
- An educational opportunity or position
- A personal ability, talent, or gift
- A business relationship or partnership
- An organization or group involving people of common interests, beliefs, or abilities
- A faith-based organization
- The death of someone or the demise of something

Before we leave this area of betrayal, I want to highlight two of the above examples because I witnessed so many clients struggle in these arenas, and their deep seated feelings of inadequacy were often dismissed or minimized by well-intentioned friends or family members. First, let's take a closer look at the personal ability, talent, or gift. Being a former high-school teacher where I worked with juniors and seniors applying to colleges as well as a therapist working with adolescents and teens, I was deeply moved by young vibrant students who had invested so much of themselves into their education, their sports, their theatre/ music, and so on, only to be gravely disappointed by college rejection letters or by talent scouts and the such. Some, at the very least, felt misled by the system; others felt outright crushed as they watched their dreams fade into the dust. Comments such as these are etched into my memory: "It was all a waste; why did I even bother; I would have been better off just enjoying high school more like most of my friends; instead, I gave all this up and for what?" This type of betrayal is so common, especially among young people, and it is devastating. Because they have spent so much time investing into their identity which has been shaped and transformed by their respective achievements (academics, athletics, talents/gifts), they internalize the rejection and suffer with deep wounds of self-doubt and lack of worth.

The other example that needs mentioning is that of investing into an organization or group involving people of common interests, beliefs, or abilities. To evolve and grow as human beings, many of us choose to belong, join, or support certain organizations. For the most part, these experiences can bring us much personal satisfaction and fulfillment. Selfless humans feel the intrinsic rewards as they serve in their respective places of worship, service clubs, and/or non-profit organizations. Others raise countless amounts of money through their charities and foundations of choice, and in turn, reach out to help thousands in need. Others give of their time, their influence, and their own personal resources with the sole motivation being improvement in the welfare of others. Although there are numerous implications of betrayal in this type of investment, it typically occurs when an investment into someone or something is not received with the same intention or spirit with which it was given. It is not honored as it was meant to be, causing injury and injustice for the investor.

Many years ago, I was working with several clients who attended a large church in our community. Each of them was an active member of the congregation who gave of his/her time and resources, each in their unique ways utilizing their respective talents and gifts. When a scandal occurred which led to the downfall of the pastor which then prompted an investigation into the business dealings of the church, each of these clients felt terribly betrayed. Their eagerness and willingness to serve, along with their varying venues of generosity, had been misused, mishandled, and misdirected. What shattered these clients the most was that they were misinformed; they were led to believe their investments were of a worthy nature, never thinking they would be treated as worthless by another.

Sadly, each of us can probably think of at least one person, if not ourselves, who has experienced this deep sting of betrayal. Because our intentions are of the purest nature and our investments are of such personal sacrifice, the absence of regard for them leaves us blindsided and bewildered.

As we leave this definition of betrayal, I would like you to spend a few moments thinking about your past and with experiences that may connect with this explanation.

- Was there someone or something where you freely and openly gave of yourself—emotionally, physically, intimately, sexually, financially, professionally, intellectually, and/or spiritually?

- Was that investment of yourself (your personal as well as external resources) met with rejection, abandonment, or utter disregard for the value of the giver?
- Were you left feeling bankrupt from the experience?
- Were you left broke and broken, navigating through a fog of shattered emotions?

Although it is hurtful to recall these memories, I encourage you, for now, to log this experience (and any others that connect with this explanation). Writing it down is a good idea (notating it in a journal or notebook). We will get back to it later in the *activity section* of the chapter.

2. A profound trust in someone or something that is profoundly violated

This second definition may seem, at first glance, all too similar to the first one. However, I have chosen to separate it from the first because I believe there are some significant differences. The premise from which we want to work from with this explanation is that *one* component of a healthy relationship is trust (but there are other components as well). Some believe that trust is the only basis of a relationship; without it, there is not much to build upon or that the two are entirely intertwined. For the purposes of this book and our study on betrayal, I am suggesting that we examine trust as a separate entity but with two important considerations.

Trust as an innate emotion

In some of our encounters, relationships, dynamics with people and things, trust is *not* a seed lying dormant in a relationship which is then nurtured, fostered, and matured by the development of the relationship. Instead, it is a natural innate emotion. It is a preconceived bond, an almost supernatural current within us and/or between us. This kind of trust comes with the entitlement shared by the title of the trustee and the trustor.

Let us take a look at an example of this kind of trust issue, and it will become clearer. Perhaps, you will be able to connect to this explanation, or perhaps you know someone who does. Some examples that I want to share with you cover extremely fragile and tender territory. Please know that this can be difficult for some readers. So take your time, pace yourself, and keep a pulse on your emotional responses. This area of betrayal carries with it deeply embedded wounds, ones that can be easily reopened and re-injured.

One of my areas of experience and competence in my work as a therapist is in the field of abuse, in particular, sexual abuse recovery. Tragically, this kind of abuse (as well as with other kinds) is frequently perpetrated by someone whom we trust—fully, completely, and most uniquely—innately. Fathers, mothers, step-parents, grandparents, brothers, sisters, cousins, aunts, uncles—our closest relations break that inbred bond of safety and security. They misuse and abuse the "entitlement" of trust bestowed upon them by their very title. This profound violation of trust is indescribable, immeasurable, and inconceivable; its tentacles of damage far-reaching.

The following vignette is all too common, all too tragic, and an example of violation at the purest level of entitled trust—a child and a parent. A young married mother of three small children came in to see me. Recently, she had been feeling anxious, irritable, and at times, rage-filled. Slowly and tenderly, we navigated through her childhood. Gingerly, we pulled down the blanket of betrayal to expose the wounds. As she unveiled her past, she dissolved into a mass of liquid pain.

> "My stepfather was the only father I knew. He met and married my mom shortly after I was born. My biological father left my mom when she got pregnant. I loved my step-dad so much...why would he hurt me... ? So many years of abuse—so many broken pieces. I was just a little girl—maybe seven or eight. I trusted him! I was scared! I didn't know what to do! He told me not to tell anyone—it was *our secret*! Now, look what that *secret* has done to me!"

As my client recalled and revisited her years of sexual abuse, there was even yet additional betrayal. As a teen, she was able to muster up the courage to tell her mom about the abuse, only to be shamed, blamed, and disclaimed. And not just by her own mother, but also but other family members who were told and who rallied around the stepfather, the perpetrator.

Where was trust? Where were the security blankets of childhood? Where were the safety nets of adolescence and teen years? Where was the protective provision endowed upon those who were responsible for her care and well-being?

Sadly, this kind of profound violation is also common in other inherent bonds of trust: a close family friend, a teacher, a coach, a person of faith/leadership, a therapist or counselor, or any person whose title or role lends itself to a position of non-refuted respect and responsibility.

Several years ago, a middle-aged couple came in to see me. Although there were some minor issues that needed attention, the male was clearly suffering in more intimate and personal ways. After many sessions working together individually, he shared his private pain.

> "I was a little boy and she was a grown woman! A nun at the private school I attended!! She was to watch over me after school—to protect me, to make sure I was safe!! Years and years of using me as her toy—exploiting me in ways I did not understand! How could she when I was so young? Why? Why would someone like that want to hurt me? She ruined my life! I have left a trail of broken people, promises, and places wherever I go. I can't get rid of the shame, guilt, and at times, rage. I can't trust anyone—even myself...."

In bonds of this kind, trust is assumed; we walk blindly into it and with it. We don't question it; we don't give it a second thought. We shouldn't have to; it is inherent, it is natural, and it is pure. And so, when the veil is blown off and we are slapped around by the winds of treachery, we fall and we fall hard. The profound violation of our profound trust keeps us face down in our quicksand of betrayal, sucking us under. No wonder we struggle to find our way; no wonder life seems so hard and harsh.

There is a very strong possibility that some readers may be hurting right now. The vignettes shared may have triggered repressed and extremely painful memories. Some may be experiencing flashbacks, panicky feelings, or other reactions to the discomfort of the recall. Please take some time to calm yourself and to soothe your reactions: take some deep breaths; put the book down and walk into another room and sit down and relax; make yourself a cup of tea and take a short break. If needed, take a short walk or listen to some music. Please, do not read on until you are ready. The last thing we want to do is to betray ourselves by not listening to what we need to do to take care of bodies and minds. When you are ready, let's move on to the second area of trust.

Trust without the relationship component

The second trust issue is similar to the first; however, there is an important difference. We can have/feel trust in people and things *without* the relationship component. Through our knowledge (or lack of) about someone or something, we then form a perception about that person or thing. We then decide to trust or to presume there are grounds for trust.

This kind of trust violation may sound less injurious than the others, but it is not. We can go long periods of time and not be affected by this kind of violation, but when it does hit us, we are often blown over and trampled upon. We feel as though an emotional tsunami has struck. There is vast devastation.

Again, because I work in the areas of abuse and trauma recovery, I have experienced this kind of profound violation with many of my clients. Many years ago, I was doing an internship in a battered women's center. As a professional organization, the center provided legal advice and assistance to women who needed help or protection. Although in most cases, women and their children were given safeguards and tools in order to live healthier lives, there were many instances where the legal system failed to provide for the safety and security of these victimized women and children. Their trust in the justice system failed them; at times, it mocked them.

We only need to turn on the TV, read the newspaper, or turn on our computers to see the injustices that abound in our society. Tragically, even if we have escaped this kind of devastation, most of us know someone who has lost someone or something due to the selfishness, greed, manipulation, or evil of another person or thing. Every day, we see or hear about victims of crime—innocent men, women, and children—whose lives were savagely scarred or taken from us. We count ourselves fortunate when we hear of others who have lost everything—victims of scams, scoundrels, and sinister misrepresentation. In these instances, the trust that we have decided to put into these people or things has been, for the most part, our choice based on the information we have, our perceptions, and the level of trustworthiness we assign to it. Most of us motor along with a somewhat false or fragile sense of security, but a level of security none-the-less. We are whipped into a whirlwind of confusion and despair when the violation rips away our sense of safety, security, and sanity.

About a year ago, an elderly couple came in to my office. They had recently experienced a drastic financial loss and it was taking its toll on both of them—physically, emotionally, and thus, in their marital relationship. These two extremely vibrant and intelligent human beings were diminished to two floundering souls, wondering whom to trust, how to go on, and where to turn. In their own words, they had been taken to the cleaners; their financial security blanket pulled from underneath them. As the gentleman spoke, his despair filled the room.

> "I researched this investment thoroughly and completely. I spent five years doing my homework, leaving no area in question, leaving no stone unturned. I was convinced this was a solid way to go because the other investors and backers were people I knew and trusted."

His wife wiped her tears and added, "We've always believed that if we do everything right, if we are fair and just, things will work out. Of course we know there are risks no matter what we choose to do, but we had no reason to doubt the integrity or intension of the people at the helm of the organization." This lovely fragile woman wilted in my presence. "I am afraid, for the first time in my life. Now, we have nothing left and we are too old to start over, nor do we have the strength to do so."

Sadly, and all too tragically, this scenario and others similar to it are occurring repeatedly in our society. People, of all ages, are losing their personal retirement funds, their pensions, their health insurance, their homes, their jobs, their investments, and so on. Responsible intelligent people have chosen to put their trust in someone or something on the basis of their knowledge about that person or thing. It appeared to be the right thing to do, the smart thing to do, the wise thing to do, only to be overshadowed by its haunting devastation.

Financial ruin is one aspect of this violation of trust. Along with the financial fallout (or aside from it), many people suffer from the professional plummeting that can occur. We are taught at a young age to put our trust in the system. Work hard, play the game, do what you need to do, and the rewards will come. This kind of trust violation does not just apply to young people, but to anyone at any age who has put in the time, moved up the ladder, proven his/her loyalty, only to come face to face with indifference—the violation mask.

A young man in his early thirties sat in my office several years ago. He came in to deal with his depression after being referred by his physician. After just a couple of sessions, his story explained his situational onset of sadness. After obtaining a college education with an advanced degree, he started out on his journey, a road that had been clearly laid out for him by his mentors and program advisors. He trusted the plan for his life. The experts had given him the blueprint for advancement and he would follow it. Only, the roadblock came before the freeway opened up. His voice quivered and quaked as he relayed his violation.

"I did everything I was supposed to. I spent time in each area of the organization. I did 'hard time' in one office that no one could or would take. As my mentors put it, 'Go in and clean up this office; do whatever you need to do and we will back you all the way'. And so I did—I took the heat, but that was my job. I was told to stay there until the 'right opening' came up; advancement was right around the corner. With my eyes on the top position, I waited. Then, one day, a rumor came across my desk—the bosses were looking outside the organization to fill the position. There was no one on the inside who qualified. Spinning with disbelief, I made a few calls to find out the truth. This had to be a mistake! In a few sentences I was told:

'Times have changed. We need someone with different credentials and experience. We need to stay on the cutting edge of what other organizations are doing, and you are not the person with those qualifications or experience. You are most effective right where you are.'

Nothing or no-one could have prepared me for this. I trusted the system and the system failed me. I bought into the plan and the process; my payoff short-changed and my purpose cheated. Recently, I can't seem to pull myself out of this slump. I keep drifting downward, flirting with bouts of anger and blame. I'm not sure if I'm more upset with the powers that be or with myself for trusting a life map that guided me to a dead end."

Does this story sound familiar? Was your life map drastically altered or changed? Does either of these two scenarios bring up a past of pain and of broken promise? These violations can be difficult to recall and relive, even if it is just for a few moments. As with other places in this book, if you need to put your reading aside, do so. Give yourself the time to sift and sort through any emotions; however, I do encourage you to minimize any self-blame. When you feel ready, begin again. Please, continue to pace yourself and your responses.

As you think about your experiences and this aspect of trust, some areas to consider, as you take your own inventory, are the following:

- The legal or justice system
- Financial investments, organizations, accounts
- Political causes and leaders
- Marketing and advertisement campaigns
- Governmental procedures and policies
- Charities, foundations, fundraisers
- Professional organizations (of any kind)
- Leadership positions (of any kind)
- Healthcare systems and practices
- Environmental causes/issues

As we conclude with this section on betrayal, it is important to remember that *trust* is at the core of the explanation. Whether it is profoundly inherent within our bonds with one another or whether it is profoundly tethered by choice to another individual or thing, its profound violation pulls us into the depths of despair. The feelings and realities of loss are vast. Erosion of our spirits and souls is common place. We try to hold on to the fragile rope of hope, one day at a time.

Again, spend a few moments reflecting on this definition of betrayal and its implications with trust. Do any of these examples tug at you? Can you feel the uneasiness of a past experience nudging you? If so, jot it down in your notebook or journal (just briefly). At the very least, log it into a mental compartment to be addressed at the end of the chapter.

3. A truth that becomes a lie / A belief that is shattered

How many times have you heard the words—"How could you not know?" "Didn't you see it coming?" "Wow, you would have to be blind not to have known that!" "Are you *that* stupid—were you born yesterday?"

Probably all of us have heard these kinds of comments at one time or another. And, it surely does not make us feel better!! We already feel enough hurt and shame, at the very least, self-doubt. In this section, it is my intention to give your truth or belief validation as well as discuss its relevance to our discussion on betrayal.

One of the very first principles that I share with my clients (if appropriate and therapeutic) is that *your perception is your truth* (or belief). Our perceptions are based on what we experience and what information we gather from our relationships and daily interactions. How we perceive these exchanges or dynamics is through our own individual filters—filters that are layered with emotion, reason, and logic, as well as linguistic intricacies. Therefore, how each of us has viewed, interpreted, or understood someone or something to be true or believable should not be questioned, at least when it comes to the issue of betrayal.

Therefore, when examining this definition of betrayal, we will work under the premise that your truth or belief was based on your perceptions of the person or thing. And, your perceptions were well-founded and grounded in your experiences and interpretations of them. That is why violation is this arena is so painful; we have trusted ourselves. We have relied on our thoughts, our analysis, and our explanations. We have chosen to trust what we know—our truth or our belief. And, we are shaken to the core; we are made fools of; we become our worst critics, filling ourselves up with self-loathing and condemnation when this type of betrayal cuts us to the core.

Although there is some crossover with the two other definitions and explanations of betrayal, again, I think it is important to give this third interpretation some attention because of the aspect of self-blame. Two cases come to mind of clients who struggled with this kind of betrayal, clients who trusted their truths and their beliefs.

Several years ago, a client in her golden years came to see me. She had been married to a pastor for over forty years. She was (in her words) a dutiful wife—a model pastor's wife, mother of several children, a perfect home-maker, and in her spare time, a career woman as well. She explained how she compromised herself in many ways through the years, but felt it was her role to do so. My client believed this was the right thing to do. She believed that someday it would all payoff and she and her husband would enjoy their retirement years together. This woman trusted in her husband, in her faith, and in the commitment that she had given so many years earlier. One day her husband came home and spoke the unspeakable:

> "I am leaving you. I want a divorce. There is someone else who loves me and cherishes me like you never did. I've stayed this long and I can't live this *lie* any longer. I don't know if I ever loved you."

This woman's life was turned upside down within seconds. A few words were spoken and a lifetime of beliefs was dispelled and shattered. Decades of truths were redefined as lies. Golden years turned into tarnished, tainted, meaningless memories. And, as is the case with this kind of betrayal, the pain this client felt watching her husband walk out the door was no match to the brokenness within this woman, for the recrimination in allowing herself to believe in this man.

Another example that is all too common in this kind of betrayal involves cases where substance abuse or dependence is an issue. Ask anyone who has had a friend or family member who has struggled with addiction—was their trust tested? Were their beliefs in the person and his/her recovery broken? At the very least, did they experience disappointment in putting their faith in their loved one?

A middle-aged couple came in to see me a number of years ago. Their twenty-two-year old son was abusing drugs again. Their beliefs in him and in the recovery process were dispelled. As the father spoke, his brokenness spilled out:

> "We believed our son was on the right track. He has been clean and sober for over a year. He got a job, moved into his own apartment, and was finally making it on his own. Then, we started to catch him lying and we started to watch things fall apart".

As this loving father's words tapered off, his wife sobbed at his side. Her fragile spirit spoke a few words:

> "I thought that this time we had done everything right—stepping back, setting boundaries, staying strong with 'tough love'. I wanted this to work. I wanted to believe he could do it. I wanted to trust him, one last time. He is lying, stealing, hiding again. We don't even know where he is…it's the same behavior, over and over. I don't believe anything about him that he tells us. His life is a lie."

These two examples demonstrate the devastation in two different kinds of relationships. However, this third definition of betrayal—a truth that becomes a lie/ a belief that is shattered—covers a wide range of experiences. As you are thinking about this explanation and how it may have impacted your life, consider the following applications (along with a couple of examples for each one).

- A belief or trust *that* someone or something is who he/she/it represents him/her/itself to be—but is not.
  - a loving friend or boyfriend/ girlfriend breaks off the relationship
  - a secret about someone/something which is exposed—revealing revisions to the truth

- A belief or trust *in* someone or something—an expectation, a standard, a quality, a principle which proves false or less significant.
  - a hero, role model, or parent who *falls from grace or falls short of set standards*
  - a law or regulation which is meant to protect or to help proves ineffective and/or worthless

- A belief or trust *about* someone or something—based on fact, history, research, or experience that is later negated.
  - scientific DNA evidence reverses pre-existing claims and judgments
  - over time and with new evidence, historical truths become misguided stories or myths

Unfortunately, most of us come face to face with these situations on a daily basis. We feel let down and disappointed, but we are able to put it behind us and move on. However, there are circumstances the affect us and infect us covering a gamut of feelings, from discouragement and despair to those of devastation and disillusionment.

Working as a high school teacher and then as a therapist, I was witness to the highs and lows of young love. Although I had a front row seat to the blossoms of newly found love as well as the discarded buds from an abrupt breakup, no story moved more than that of a teen client who was brought in by her parents to see me. These parents were beyond frustration. They were frantic, and they had every right to be. After a recent breakup with her boyfriend, this gregarious, positive, and extroverted daughter was riding a tidal wave of self-destruction: she was losing weight by causing herself to throw up; she was shutting everyone and everything out; she was hiding behind closed doors, entertaining thoughts of suicide (information shared by her friends); and they had recently discovered that their beloved daughter was self-mutilating. After the necessary referrals were made and crises intervention steps put into place, this fragile and fragmented young lady and I began to work together. Her words of betrayal were piercing and poignant:

> "It all started after my boyfriend broke up with me. We were together for over a year—he said he 'loved me'—that 'we would always be together'. We were even making plans of how we would see each other after we both went away to different colleges. I believed *everything* he said—especially his promises."

This tender teen began to melt into a pool of pain, disclosing her deepest despair.

> "I wanted to wait to have sex, but I didn't. I loved him and he said he loved

me. For some girls, it is not that big of a deal, but for me it was. I wanted to wait; it was really important to me. A few months after we started having sex, he started to lose interest in me: stopped calling or texting, pulled away, and then he told me the unthinkable—he had feelings for someone else. Being desperate, I compromised myself in ways I would never have thought of, all just to hold on to him! But it didn't get us back together. It only pushed him further away!"

I listened as this confused and tormented teen asked about her bonds of betrayal.

"How could he say one thing one minute and then do the opposite the next? How could he love me—make love to me—and then toss me away like trash? Didn't I mean anything to him? Didn't it matter that I gave myself completely to him? Was I such a fool to believe him and to trust him? I see him going on with his life, moving on. And all I can do right is try to hold on, feeling myself slipping away piece by piece. Not believing any more, in others and in myself."

As this vignette illustrates, broken promises dispel our beliefs—in people, in their intentions, and in their representations. Sadly, as in the case of this teen, many of us have believed in the words spoken to us, taken them to heart, and acted upon them accordingly. It is our human nature to do so. What we are not prepared for is the shattering of our spirits that comes with the puncturing of the promise, and being left to reel in the remnants of our lives, if we can.

As with the other explanations of betrayal, spend a few moments reflecting on this area and your experiences. I encourage you not to diminish or to negate any betrayal you might feel, blaming yourself instead or making it your responsibility. Who or what misrepresented him/her/itself to you? Who or what did you put your trust in or belief in, only to be left with feelings of foolishness and futility? Lastly, after feeling that you really knew someone or something and that your truth was supported by fact, when did you feel blindsided by your shattered realities? As you revisit these experiences, again, keep your pulse on your reactions. Take some time to soothe your soul and calm your spirit. When you feel ready, continue.

As with the other areas of betrayal, note these experiences in your journal or make a mental note. As painful as this is, it is the first step to healing the wound of being wronged. It is the critical beginning to opening up the bag of betrayal, releasing its hold on you, and offering comfort to you.

Activities – Chapter 1

Please choose one of the following activities below.

1. If you have not already obtained a journal or a notebook, please do so. Take a piece of paper and divide it into three columns (see next page). If you have already noted some betrayal experiences while reading chapter one, place them in the columns where they fit. If there is crossover, put it down in more than one column. Do not second-guess any level of betrayal; write any and all down. If you have a few written down, and more come to mind, add them in. Pace yourself and keep a pulse on your emotions. Take a break if needed and return when ready.

2. If you have not already written down any experiences, use the chart on the next page and the instructions above to notate them. I encourage you not to minimize or disregard any occurrence with betrayal.

3. If the chart feels unnecessary, or too rigid, then "free write" your experiences with betrayal. For now, just briefly listing them is fine. We will go into more detail later. The important message is that you validate these violations and that first step comes with this process. As with #1 or #2, pace and protect yourself.

A truth that becomes a lie / A belief that is shattered	A profound trust in someone/ something which is profoundly violated	An investment into someone/ something met with rejection and/or abandonment

2   What Am I Feeling and Why?

"Pain. We all know what it tastes like. Whether its source is physical, emotional, mental, or spiritual, its interruption in our lives disrupts and reshapes. It intercepts our hopes and plans; it rearranges our dreams. It always leaves a mark."

—Tim Hansel

States and Truths

In chapter one, we got acquainted with the frightening faces of betrayal; we examined their formidable features. I asked you to recall and revisit your painful places, and I asked you to spend some time reflecting and writing about them. This process was to create knowledge about betrayal so that you could have a deeper understanding and validation of your own experiences. In Chapter Two, we are going to take a look at what we feel and how those feelings manifest when we experience betrayal. We will also normalize and affirm those feelings/symptoms as we gain an understanding as to why we are feeling such treachery, turmoil, and trauma. When we can talk openly about our feelings or symptoms, and when we can understand why we have those feelings or symptoms, we experience much needed relief and release. And perhaps more importantly, knowing that others feel as we do brings us well-deserved comfort and calm.

Time and time again, as I listened to clients who were betrayed, there was always a common theme—feelings of exasperation and desperation.

- "I feel totally lost! I don't know where to go, what to do, or who to turn to!"
- "My head is spinning with disbelief! I feel like I am on a roller-coaster—aimlessly going on and on—headed nowhere.
- "I can't catch my breath. When I think of what they did to me, I start to suffocate. How do I come up for air?"
- "What can I do? I can't get the answers I need, but then, are there any answers?"

These words from wounded clients represent just a tiny fraction of the myriad of emotions that manifest when we are betrayed. Do any of them sound poignantly familiar? Have you found yourself reeling from thoughts such as these when you have encountered the unimaginable beast of betrayal? Please know that you are not alone. These plaguing pangs of uncertainty go hand in hand with the bondage of betrayal. Let us now unravel the ropes that bind us, let us free ourselves from its grip, and let us move forward empowered by another layer of knowledge and understanding.

Many of you are probably familiar with the term *stages* in reference to explaining a particular pattern of recovery or diagnosis. We often think of stages when we talk about grief recovery or of the severity of an illness such as cancer. In these stages, we typically move from one phase to another or from one level to another; and there can be movement back and forth from stage to stage. For our discussion on betrayal, I am suggesting that we experience three *states* of being. The difference is that we do not necessarily move from one level to another or from one phase to another which is usually indicative of a degree of wellness, of recovery, and/or of relapse. With betrayal, we are in a particular state for a period of time and while in a particular state, we experience a myriad of manifestations. There can be overlap of the states because of re-injury or re-occurrence of betrayal. However, movement from one state to another in not an indication of recovery or lack of; it is knowledge of what we are feeling during that period of time and why.

Let us now take a look at the three states of being that we experience when we are betrayed. I have found that they typically present in the order that they are listed, and they each are accompanied with a range of manifestations.

- State of Confusion

- State of Worthlessness

- State of Powerlessness

As we begin this next part of our conversation on betrayal—what are we feeling and why are we feeling this way—I would again encourage you to keep your notebook or journal with you. There will be opportunities to identify your feelings and to connect them to the underlying truths of betrayal. It will also serve as a tool for reflection and for release.

1. State of Confusion

When clients, who have been betrayed, come into my office, they are in a complete state of confusion. Thoughts are racing and minds are spinning. Life in general feels foreign, frantic, and frightening. Chaos reigns as feverish feelings take over rational reasoning. The foundation from which one was functioning is fractured, fragmented, and forgotten. Life as one has known it, grown with it, and trusted in it is forever re-landscaped. And, there is one daunting and haunting question that each and every person asks—why?

It is the very struggle with the question—why did this betrayal happen to me—that leads us to feel that vast range and realm of emotions that we experience.

- "Why was I not good enough? What did she have that I didn't?"

- "I thought I was doing all the right things. Why would they let me go?"

- "I can't understand how or why this could happen. I trusted him more than anyone."

- "I try to make sense out of it, but I can't. I feel more and more depressed, and I start to blame myself. Why can't I figure this out?"

During this state of confusion, we tend to self-blame or, at the very least, we self-doubt. Along with this and our inability to find answers to our questions, we find ourselves experiencing a range of emotions and behaviors:

- Periods of sadness or moodiness

- Bouts of depression

- Sleeplessness / oversleeping

- Fatigue / loss of energy

- Anxiousness and anxiety—a general sense of panic

- Resorting to compulsive or excessive behaviors (eating, drinking, shopping) to cope

- Resorting to unhealthy, inappropriate, or uncommon behaviors to gain back favor of the betrayer or to try to re-secure our truth

Several years ago, a middle-aged woman came in to my office. Her marriage of over thirty years disintegrated before her very eyes; years of solid investment turned into rubble. Her husband announced that he was having an affair, he was in love with the other woman, and he was leaving the marriage. To top of the toxins of betrayal, he blamed my client for ruining the relationship. In moments, my client's life was shredded and her truths shattered. For the past several weeks, she had been resorting to behaviors that she desperately thought would rescue her relationship.

> "I call him fifteen to twenty times a day! He either hangs up on me or we get into the same argument over and over again, and he keeps telling me it's my fault!! I can't sleep at night so I drink a few glasses of wine to help me cope. Last week, he agreed to meet me in a public place to exchange some paper work. I started crying in the restaurant, begging him to come back. He darted out the door and I chased after him! I was screaming and yelling at him in the parking lot and he just took off!! I chased him down the street like a crazy person! I can't believe he doesn't care!! I can't believe I don't matter anymore! I don't understand why... why would he do this?"

My client was and is an intelligent, articulate, caring, and giving woman. She was not and is not a crazy person. She is desperate, desperate for answers that she cannot and will not get. She struggles in a state of confusion, a state we all know so well. We want to find the reason for our wreckage so we can fix it? We want to make sense out of it. If we could understand it, maybe we could move on with our lives? Ironically, what is so difficult and what is so painful about betrayal is that *we cannot make sense out of something that does not make sense.*

- How do we make sense out of an uncle molesting his nephew?

- How do we make sense out of being cheated, swindled, or lied to?

- How do we make sense out of having our years of hard work and loyalty rewarded with demotion or dismissal?

- How do we make sense out of tragedy that shortens our lives, steals our loved ones, and swallows up our sources of security?

I am not suggesting that you dismiss your feelings of confusion. As with each state of being, it is important that you feel what you need to feel and understand why you are feeling it. However, the longer we try to make sense out of the betrayal, the longer we will experience the symptoms of confusion: depression, anxiety, anger, and so on. And sadly, it has been my experience that clients who get stuck in this state of confusion resort to more desperate and destructive behaviors.

About five years ago, a young couple came into see me regarding premarital counseling. Throughout the sessions, the young man disclosed deeply embedded private turmoil—he was sexually abused as a boy by several older men in his neighborhood. This strong, determined young man had learned to cope amazingly well, given that he had not sought out any previous counseling or help. I encouraged him to consider recovery work in this area of pain, but he declined.

> "I am fine. I don't want to go back and relive any of that horrifying experience! I can't do it!! I want to move forward with my life—not backwards. The only thing I need to do is figure out why those monsters would hurt me and why my mom did not protect me from them!! I need to find out why anyone could hurt an innocent child. And, I can do that by myself!"

As a therapist specializing in sexual abuse recovery, I knew that my client was not ready to do the difficult work that lay ahead, and I respected his decision. I offered my help whenever he was ready. The couple continued on with their premarital counseling and shortly after, they married.

Several years passed. Sadly, one day the wife of this young man called my office to schedule a session. She was deeply troubled by her husband's changing behaviors.

> "His anger has escalated and he has been exploding for no reason. He used to leave the house for a few minutes or for a couple of hours to cool off. Now, he is gone for most of the day and has even stayed away all night! Usually, he is so conscientious and never misses work. Recently, he has been fired from two jobs for not showing up, not even calling in to let his bosses know!! I'm afraid to say anything to him because he is filled with rage. And, he gets so depressed! I don't know what is happening or how to help!"

As I listened to and watched this young wife and mother wilt away with worry about what was to come next, I could not help but reflect upon her husband's words: "The only thing I need to do is figure out why…and I can do that myself…"

Working with sexual abuse survivors, I know that the recovery work is typically a lengthy and involved process. It takes months to navigate through tender territory, to sort and sift through the fragmented and fractured pieces of one's spirit and soul, and to gently mend and heal one's inner being. However, knowing that the longer this young man was held hostage to his unanswered questions meant knowing that he would remain in bondage to his state of confusion, and tragically, his previous coping mechanisms would no longer work for him. He would need to resort to more drastic measures to sedate the raging roar of confusion.

In our state of confusion, we live in a lifeless limbo. We navigate through uncertainty as we cling on to meaningless memories. And through it all, we ache while our souls mourn and our spirits erode. We need a rest from the chaos within. We desperately need explanations or justifications; we would accept even a ration of thought, anything to contain the confusion and calm our inner calamity.

- You deserve an answer; you deserve more than you are getting; and you deserve as much time as you need to feel all that you are feeling.

- Remember that you are not alone.

- Confusion and all its many faces are a natural and normal response to betrayal.

- Even though we cannot make sense out of betrayal and we cannot make sense out of something that does not make sense, we can make peace with our pain.

- Confusion is a state, not a trait or a lifetime label. What we thought was true was not so. But there is hope and there is healing. We can rebuild our lives based on new truths. Let us begin with this one.

> **"We don't have to find the answers; we don't have to make our betrayal make sense—not anymore."**

Repeat that phrase again, and again. Let your mind absorb it; take it in. Let your spirit relax in its truth.

> **"We don't have to find the answers; we don't have to make our betrayal make sense—not anymore."**

Before we move on to the next state of being, I would like you to reflect back to chapter one and the activities at the end of the chapter. Look over your notations on betrayal and choose one of your most difficult experiences. For now, write that experience down on a separate piece of paper in your notebook or journal. Next to it, write down a few of the questions you repeatedly asked of yourself and/or of others. What haunted you, gnawed at you, tortured you? Write the questions down. Then, put a check next to the questions that you did not get answers to. If you did get an answer to the question, write the answer and put a check next to the answer if it did *not* help you feel better.

And then, take a few deep breaths. Relax and put your pen/pencil down. We will return to this in the "Activity Section" at the end of the chapter.

2. State of Worthlessness

As we move into our discussion on the next state of being—worthlessness—remember that there can and will be overlapping of states. However, it is typically after we have been catapulted into our state of confusion, and as we are drifting through the fog that has blinded us, that we are also jolted by the wreckage of our newly found reality. Our truth has evaporated. The drought in our lives suffocates us as we gasp for air and grasp onto lifeless lines. Betrayal is the intruder; it has invaded our lives and has derailed our course. We are robbed of what we had; we are redefined from what we were; and we are relinquished to a lesser place than what we knew.

It is during this wounded state of worthlessness that we experience some of the most piercing pain, both emotionally and physically. It is a frightening and fragile state. It is a dark state. We feel vulnerable, violated, and victimized as we come face to face with the trauma and turmoil in our lives.

We probably find ourselves feeling or experiencing some of the following symptoms or manifestations:

- Increased depression, feelings of isolation and withdrawal
- Increased anxiety and anxiousness
- Elevation of moods
- Onset of physical ailments or increase in disturbance of current illness(es)
- Escalation of inappropriate, unhealthy, or destructive behaviors to cope
- Increase in or absence of routine behaviors
- Escalation of anger/periods of rage
- Periods of disbelief and denial
- Rehearsing and rehashing the 'what if's" and "should have's"
- Increase in obsessive thoughts and compulsive behaviors
- Extreme guilt, self-doubt, and/or self-blame
- Feelings of hopelessness/helplessness
- Uncertain of role, identity, or purpose

These feelings/symptoms are expected during this state of worthlessness. Sadly, they are all too common and they are all too familiar. As you read through them and reflect, take some time to soothe your emotions. Be gentle with yourself. If you need to, relax, take in a few deep breaths and slowly release them. Perhaps, take a break from your reading for a short time. Pick the book up again when you are ready. We do not need to re-traumatize ourselves; we want to normalize our experiences. And, we want to take care of ourselves in the process.

Last summer, a former client called to schedule a session. The middle-aged man had spent years in an unhealthy marriage. His wife was an alcoholic and a compulsive gambler. During the later years of the marriage, this gentleman worked diligently on his own recovery: attending Al-Anon meetings (for people in relationships with addicts), setting boundaries, and reclaiming control of his life. Prior to his call, this reluctant but faithful husband separated from his wife. Her destructive behaviors had escalated and were depleting him—personally, professionally, and financially. Shortly after the separation, his wife, who promised to seek help, overdosed on pills and alcohol.

My client's core was crushed, and then crumbled. Betrayal was the wrecking ball. His worth devalued in a moment and his meaning lost in seconds. His years of investment, dedication, and commitment were met with his most lethal adversary—the loss of his loved one. His words reeked with emotional carnage:

> "I can't sleep. I can't eat. I can't work. I can barely put one foot in front of the other… I can't believe she is gone…Even though I had moved out, I was checking on her every day. I was making sure she had what she needed. She was doing better; at least I thought she was. Why didn't she call me?"

He paused as he tried to contain the emotional hemorrhaging, but could not…

> "I don't know who I am any more. I don't know what to do with myself— where I belong, if I belong. I feel empty. I feel invisible."

Although this broken man carried with him tremendous grief and self-blame for the loss of his wife, he was ripped apart by the loss of who he was to her. Most of us can relate to what he was feeling. At the very root of our worth is the belief that who we were, what we represented, what connected us to this person or thing, was of value. We carried around a sense of significance, of importance, of meaning. We were secure in our truths because our perceptions reinforced those beliefs. What we did not expect, what we did not think twice about, what we could not have predicted, is that what we held to be true was not so for the betrayer.

We lose when we are betrayed. And, each and every loss is devastating. When we enter into the state of worthlessness, we are not prepared. We are not trained to come into the ring with the foreign fighter—the one who abolishes our absolutes; the one who rearranges our realities; the one who tosses out our truths.

- How are we to know that we are not as important or valuable as we believed?
- How are we to know that we are not as important or valuable as the other person, thing, opportunity, desire, or need?
- How are we to know that we are not worth anything at all to our betrayer?
- How are we to know who we are when our role, purpose, or identity has been stripped away from us by the betrayer?

Commonly, our first instinct is to reject these thoughts for they are too poisonous to process. A second reaction is to rationalize them or to intellectualize them. We have to make it ok and we have to be ok. After all, we have our history together; we have our investment and commitment at stake; we have our beliefs, promises, and truths; we have our integrity as humans to honor.

Sadly, those defense mechanisms work for a very short time. When we raise our veils and reveal our vulnerability, we let in the thief of our truths. Tragically, it is this immeasurable loss of worth that plunges us into the depths of despair and we experience indescribable pain. We fall prey to the trappings of trauma and into the riptides of turmoil.

It is during this state where I see clients needing the most support, validation, and at times, medical/therapeutic attention and/or intervention. During the state of worthlessness, we frequently feel like being alone, isolating and insulating ourselves from the rubbish of our realities. Depression is our constant companion while anxiety and anxiousness pull us in all directions. Additionally, we are weighted down with anchors of pain, shame, and blame. Our new reality has relegated us to a foreign theatre. We don't know how to act; we don't even know what play we are in. We desperately struggle to resist a role we didn't ask for, a role we don't want, a role bestowed upon us by our betrayer.

A couple of years ago, I was working with a vibrant, intelligent, articulate middle-aged woman. Enjoying the rewards of being at the peak of her career, she was highly respected in a business largely dominated by men. This amazing woman worked most of her adult life to achieve her current level of success. Her years of loyalty, dedication, and commitment to her employer had brought her personal as well as professional satisfaction. Our time in therapy was spent on balancing healthy life skills and strategies, nothing pressing or stressful.

Surprisingly, one day she received a call from a family member. A close relative was experiencing a severe mental health crisis. My client was asked to help with the situation. It meant she would need to take some time off from work. She would be out of town for several weeks to help with the situation. Because my diligent client had never asked for any time off, her boss gave his blessings and wished her well during the time away.

During my client's leave, she maintained contact with her office, checking in on projects and following through with matters that needed attention. When the family crises resolved to a level of moderate stability, this dynamic woman returned to her position, re-energized by work-related thoughts of planning, preparing, and producing. Her comfort zone was beckoning her and she was eager to heed its call.

As my client sat across from me, I didn't recognize the vibrant being I had come to know. This fierce but fragile hummingbird was silenced, her wings clipped, and her movement stilled. In a barely audible whisper, she detailed her emotional amputation.

> "Yesterday, I returned to work. As I walked down the hallway towards my office, it was eerily quiet. When no one made eye contact with me, I knew something was terribly wrong. Entering my office, I was greeted by a brown box, a sterile box filled with my professional and personal belongings. My 'welcome back' came in the form of a hand-scribbled note —See me in my office as soon as possible (signed by the vice-president).

On the soft, white sofa across from me, this injured hummingbird fluttered a bit, changed positions, and tried to maintain her balance. She struggled on.

> "I was told I wasn't needed any more. My job title and position were dissolved; the duties and responsibilities delegated elsewhere. I was told that during my absence, it became abundantly clear that the company could function

just as practically and efficiently without me. I served no purpose.

I was told to finish clearing out my things and to leave the office by noon. My last check would be mailed to me. I asked for a brief meeting with the president. My request was denied, my presence was dismissed, and my worth was demolished."

My client disappeared in front of me. What she was and who she was were ripped from her. Ferocious winds of words left irreparable damage. Her professional and personal identities were brutally stripped from her, leaving her naked without passion and without purpose.

"I have always worked. I've never been fired or let go. I thought I mattered. I believed in the vision and direction of the company, and I thought the company believed in me. I don't know where to go or what to do. I don't know who I am; I feel completely lost."

My client was lost. The betrayal bandit stole her position and her person. She was left valueless and meaningless, and to her, nameless. The hummingbird was no more.

Many of us know exactly how this client felt. During this state of worthlessness, we feel victimized. We are very vulnerable and fragile, and we have every right to be. We desperately need affirmation and validation, but because we are in a weakened state, many of us are re-injured by our own survival instincts or by additional reactive behaviors from the betrayer. Many of us succumb to the newly imposed stressors on our lives and are held hostage by physical, emotional, and psychological maladies. Please know that you are not alone in these feelings. Please know that seeking out professional medical/therapeutic help is often needed and necessary.

In our state of worthlessness, we feel alone because all we believed in, trusted in, and held on to as truth, is no more. We desperately need the emptiness washed away; we need our worth restored and our identity reclaimed. Somehow, some way, we need to trust again or to believe in someone/something again. We, too, need to be believed and to be believed in.

- Feeling worthless and living through all its damaging effects are a common and normal response to betrayal. It takes time to sort and sift through the rubble, to find yourself and rediscover your worth.

- You deserve as much time as you need to feel what you are feeling and experiencing.

- You deserve more. Whatever was taken, robbed, or stripped from you, you didn't deserve it, you didn't ask for it, and you weren't to blame for it.

- You are not alone; others feel what you feel.

- Even though we don't feel valuable or important, and we may not know who we are right *now,* we can replenish our spirits and renew our souls.

Worthlessness is a state, not a trait nor a timeless title. What we believed in, what we trusted in, what we held true about ourselves and others was not so for the betrayers. But we have hope and we have relief in our grasp. We can reclaim our value based on new truths. Let us add this one:

> **"We don't need to have our worth determined by our betrayer, nor who we are defined by the betrayal—not anymore."**

Say the phrase again, and again. Say it aloud. Say it loudly. Let your mind hear it. Listen to it and let it in. Allow your entire being to take comfort it its truth.

> **"We don't need to have our worth determined by our betrayer, nor who we are defined by the betrayal—not anymore."**

Before we move on to our next state of being, I would like you to look at your notes from the 'State of Confusion' section of this chapter. Again, I would like you to write down one of your most painful encounters with betrayal (perhaps it is the same one from the previous section—that is fine). Next to the notation of the experience, write down all the ways in which you believed you held value or significance to your betrayer. Then, put a check next to those that proved untrue because of the betrayal. Lastly, write down some descriptions of how you felt when your role, your purpose, your identity was stolen from you by your betrayer. Put a check next to those feelings which meant little or nothing to the betrayer.

I know that this is difficult. When you are ready, put your materials down. Take a moment to rest. Close your eyes and breathe deeply. We will return to this in the "Activity Section" at the end of the chapter.

3. A State of Powerlessness

As we continue our conversation on our final state of being—powerlessness—I want you to take comfort in knowing that there is no timetable for experiencing each state. And, although the three states of being generally present in the order of our discussion, there is frequent overlap and blending of feelings associated with each state. However, I typically find that is after we have climbed away from the calamity of confusion, and as we are surfacing from the well of worthlessness, we enter into the prison walls of powerlessness. This state can be crazy-making. We often find ourselves fluctuating from one of two extremes—one that binds us and one that keeps us spinning.

In this state of powerlessness, we are confronted with our lack of control over what happened to us. At times, we feel drained and depleted; we feel hopeless and helpless. We are without energy and emotion. We are stuck in our circumstances; circumstances we did not create. Our voice is gone. It serves only to remind us that we are bound by the ties of betrayal, pulled so tightly that we are paralyzed. We are frightened because we are without the resources we thought we had, and we are without the reinforcements we thought were available to us. We are vulnerable; we are at the mercy of the wrongful warrior; and we are left unarmed.

It is also in this state of powerlessness that we can vacillate from vulnerability to volatility. We are angered, even enraged, because we cannot control the betrayer or change the betrayal. We find ourselves resorting to behaviors that are foreign to us, with the sole purpose of reinstating our reality. We are frustrated and frantic because we can't find the reigns to lead us forward. When we grab hold of hope, it slips through our fingers. In our ineffectiveness to reclaim what we had, or what we thought was ours, we often escalate our attempts at restoration. We are usually met with re-injury and further rejection, and once again, the betrayal ball bounces. We are volleyed to the other side of the court, cornered and bound by our lack of control.

This constant mental struggle with our two opponents—feeling controlled by our betrayal and trying to control our betrayer—is inescapable. At one end, life is unsafe; at the other, life is unstoppable. It is a time where we feel a wide range of emotions and, thus, a myriad of symptoms and manifestations.

Some of those feelings, behaviors, and/or symptoms include the following:

- Depression
- Anxiety and anxiousness
- Extreme frustration / feeling frantic
- Increased anger and/or rage
- Hopelessness and helplessness
- Resorting to inappropriate or unhealthy behaviors to regain a sense of control or to release yourself from feeling controlled
- Increase in use of substances or other self-soothing behaviors
- Frightened and/or fearful
- Victimized or re-victimized
- Vulnerable and fragile
- Unusually withdrawn or aggressive
- Self–blame, guilt, or shame
- Extreme resentment, bitterness, or hatred
- Loss of worth and loss of esteem

These feelings/symptoms go hand in hand with our state of powerlessness. They are all too common and, sadly, many of us feel like we are going crazy. Most of us are already in a weakened state at this point in our betrayal. The one hope we held on to was that our imposed sentence was not permanent; we would get a reprieve or we would be released and the pain would stop. We believed that there was a chance, or an opening, or perhaps a means to change or at least rearrange our circumstances. If we had an opportunity, we could convince our betrayer to change; we could reverse the betrayal; or we could delay or derail further damage. At the very least, maybe we could right our capsized souls. And yet, how can we when we continue to take on water?

About ten years ago, a young man came in to see me. I will never forget him or his pain. He was in his late twenties, separated from his wife and two small children. He was HIV positive—a hemophiliac who had been given the virus through a blood transfusion many years previous to our visit. What struck me about this client was how over-whelmed and over-wrought he was. His power had been whittled away by the betrayals he had suffered and his attempts at survival continually short-changed. He was in the process of losing his wife and family. Legal battles had drained him personally and financially. His job was at stake, missing work from obligations had eaten up his sick leave and vacation time. His body, too, was now betraying him; the medications becoming resistant to his illness. He was depleted, devastated, and diminished by the lack of control in his life.

> "I have never been a quitter. I have fought hard all my life to overcome obstacles. But, everywhere I turn, I come face to face with failure. I feel like my life is disappearing before my very eyes, and there is nothing I can do to make it reappear. I'm not one to sit back and give up, but right now I don't have the strength to keep going. In fact, why keep going? Nothing is going to change. I know I have no control over anything!"

This young man's demeanor moved into depression and despair. He felt imprisoned by his circumstances; he was held captive by his powerless position. We know this feeling and it is frightening and paralyzing. When our repeated attempts to revive our lives, restore the remnants of the relationship, and/or recover a morsel of self-worth, are deferred or discarded, we are left lifeless. What we did not and could not anticipate, or even think possible, is that in the eyes of the betrayal beast our reason, our role, and our reality were meaningless and pointless. While we fight with every fiber of our being to resuscitate ourselves and resurrect the relationship, we cannot imagine that none of this matters to the betrayer; there is no impact and there is no power to change or control what is.

It is normal and human to feel these feelings of deep disillusionment. It is not our nature to accept what is not acceptable, to tolerate what is not tolerable, or to give in or give up when we deserve to be heard. Most of us navigate through life with a healthy sense of respect for others and for ourselves. Most of us expect to be received with a responsible level of regard and consideration for our gifts, talents, and insights. Most of us give that in return. Most of us invest into people and things trusting what we bring to it. Most of us do this willingly. When we enter into the state of powerlessness, those beliefs are tested.

- How are we to know that whatever control or power we perceived we had is non-existent?

- How are we to know that there is nothing we can do or say to change or control our betrayer or the betrayal?

- How are we to know that who we are, what we need, what we want, what we say, is irrelevant?

When we can muster up enough strength to lift up the betrayal blanket and catch our breaths, most of us experience a sense of panic. Some of us retreat immediately to our place of brokenness; others rebound and enter the ring for another round with the betrayer. This can cause extreme injury and damage. We can find ourselves caught in the vicious tug of war over power that we do not have, and control that we cannot get.

Many years ago, a striking woman in her mid-sixties came in to see me. I had heard her name in the community in which we both lived. Her family was prominent; they were well-respected and admired for their professional as well as personal contributions to the area. The family was generous with their success and, thus, they were known for their philanthropy. This articulate lovely lady sat across from me. She attempted to maintain her composure but she was splitting apart; her life, as she knew it, was in shreds. Her husband, who was having an affair, was leaving her. He asked for a divorce so he could marry the other woman, who was a non-blood relation. The large extended family was fractured and fragmented, embarrassed and humiliated. Sides were taken, mostly in favor of my client. Business and financial portfolios were at stake. Children and grandchildren's future holdings were in question. Understandably, emotions were running rampant while grand gestures to get control of the situation were underway. My client released her desperation.

> "As a family, we have tried everything. My sons have met with my husband, and they tried to talk some sense into him. He wouldn't listen. We planned and carried out a family intervention but my husband walked out! Our family lawyer and friend went over to see my husband and my husband threw them out! We have had our friends intervene, called upon our pastor, but we can't seem to get through to him! We don't know what else to do; there is so much at stake! Our family is sickened by his selfish actions; he won't even return our calls. It is driving us all crazy!! He has disowned us all! What can we do now? How can we make him see that he is making a terrible mistake? How can we make him come back?"

This pillar in the community crumbled before me. She and her family were desperately trying to salvage their reality. They utilized some healthy means and resources, and that is important to do so. They were committed to keeping the family as safe and intact as they could; that too is needed and necessary. However, when this matriarch came to my office, it had been over a year since the betrayal. The family was still spinning. They were searching for signs of change, defending their case, chasing down possible hope, all to no avail. Frantic feelings took over rational reasoning while additional damaging effects were beginning to infiltrate the already injured family bonds.

It is said that desperate times call for desperate measures, and to some extent, I do not disagree with that. At the same time, what I have witnessed and experienced is how much or to what degree we succumb to our powerless instincts or to what length we resist them can determine our length of stay in our bondage of betrayal. As with the other two states—confusion and worthlessness—I encourage you to feel what you need to. Do not dismiss or disregard any of what you are experiencing. At the same time, keep a pulse on how it is affecting and infecting you. It may be taking more of a toll on you than you think.

In our state of powerlessness, what we need, we cannot have or get. What credentials we brought with us are of no value to the betrayer; thus, we have no leverage. This concept is painful because it cuts at our core. We feel raw, we feel vulnerable, and we feel naked.

We are an easy target; yet, out of fear, we are quick to strike back thirsting for an ounce of control. We fluctuate from defense to offense, wanting neither. We need a neutral zone; we need to find our voice and fill our spirits. We need a safe place to do both.

- Feelings of powerless, with all its waves of emotion and reaction, are human and to be expected.

- You are not alone. I feel with you and for you.

- You deserve to be empowered again. Being stripped of your rightful position, being silenced by the stealer of truths, being sentenced to obscurity was the work of the betrayal beast. It had nothing to do with what you did or didn't do.

- Even though we don't feel free right now from the bonds of betrayal, nor do we feel relief from the futility of trying to control the betrayer, we can embrace and embody a new and better sense of freedom.

Feeling powerless is a state, not a trait nor a permanent placement. It takes time, and sometimes the help of professionals, to re-secure your sense of self, to restore your rightful place, and to renew the well-earned privilege within each. It can be done.

One of the saddest elements about betrayal is that the longer we hold on to it, the longer it holds on to us. And as long as we hold on to the betrayal, it will erode our spirits and rob us of our potential. If we let go for just a moment, if we take that chance, we can begin again. We have a change within our grasp. We have a new truth to welcome. Let us try it out:

> **"We no longer need to be changed or controlled by the betrayal; we no longer need to control or to change our betrayer—not any more."**

Read it again, say it again. Say it strongly; shout it if you want to! Let your voice reflect your new found freedom. Allow your spirit to soak it in and your soul to bask in its freshness. Let your being succumb to its truth.

> **"We no longer need to be changed or controlled by the betrayal; we no longer need to control or to change our betrayer—not any more".**

As we conclude with our last state of being, I again ask you to recall one of your experiences with betrayal (perhaps the one you have chosen previously). Write it down in your journal or notebook. Below the experience, make two columns:

Betrayal Experience:	
Ways I was controlled by my betrayal	**Ways I tried to control my betrayer**
:	:
.	.

For each column entry, list as many feelings associated with each behavior (controlled or controlling) as you can. Take your time; write freely and openly. When you are done, go back and put a checkmark next to the feelings and/or behaviors in both columns that did *not* matter or were of *no* significance to the betrayer or the betrayal.

Then, pause and take a few more deep breaths. Relax. We will continue with this exercise in the "Activity Section" of the chapter.

As we conclude this chapter, I am reminded of a client's words that were shared with me over ten years ago. Early into our recovery work, she compared her healing to a cluttered, closed-off closet.

> "It took me years to come to therapy; in fact, I wasn't even sure why I called. All I knew and felt was an unbearable ache that I carried around with me constantly. I know I have much work yet to do, but I feel like I have opened up a door to a closet—one that has been shut and sealed for many years. I've gone inside the closet, acknowledged and named my emotional clutter, and learned how and why it got there. I am no longer afraid of my pain. I feel relieved and re-energized. I feel ready to sort and to sift through the clutter, clean it out, and rearrange my closet."

Although the past two chapters have been difficult, we have completed some of our most important work. We have opened up our bag of betrayal, examined its contents, identified its presence, and empowered ourselves with knowledge and understanding of how and why it takes residence within us. Strengthened through our self-discovery and awareness, we, too, are embracing our healing journey with validation and hope.

Exercises — Chapter 2

If you have not already completed the exercises within chapter two, complete them now. The instructions are as follows:

1. For the *state of confusion*, recall a betrayal experience. Then, write down the questions you asked of yourself and of others. Put a check next to the questions that you did *not* get answers to. If you did get an answer to the question, write the answer and put a check next to the answer if it did *not* help you to feel better.

2. For the *state of worthlessness* (using your same betrayal experience), write down all the ways in which you believed you held value or significance to your betrayer. Then, put a check next to those that proved untrue because of the betrayal. Lastly, write down some descriptions of how you felt when your role, your purpose, your identity was stolen from you by your betrayer. Put a check next to those feelings which meant little or nothing to the betrayer.

3. For the *state of powerlessness* (using your same betrayal experience), make two columns:

Ways I was controlled by my betrayal	Ways I tried to control my betrayer
:	:
.	.

For each column entry, list as many feelings associated with each behavior (controlled or controlling) as you can. When you are done, go back and put a check next to the feelings and/or behaviors in both columns that did *not* matter, or were of *no* significance to the betrayer or betrayal.

Activities – Chapter 2

Choose one of the following:

1. Look over your writings from the chapter exercises on the three *states of being*. These notations are a reflection of your old truths—what you believed of yourself and of others at the time. We have embraced three new truths. Write each of them down (leaving several lines free after each one).

   We don't need to find answers; we don't need to make our betrayal make sense—not any more.

   We don't need to have our worth determined by our betrayer, nor who we are defined by the betrayal—not any more.

   We no longer need to be changed or controlled by the betrayal; we no longer need to control or to change our betrayer—not any more.

   After each new truth, write freely and openly on how you feel and what these truths mean to you. Take your time and don't hold anything back. Let your voice be heard.

2. Look over and reflect upon your writings from the chapter exercises. Then, recall how you felt before you read chapter two. Write freely and openly about how you were feeling (based on your old truths) and compare that to how you are feeling now. Describe the ways in which your three new truths have impacted your feelings, emotions, and behaviors.

Take as much time as you need. This is your time to heal.

3 To What Degree and How Long Will I Feel this Way?

"You can close our eyes to the things you do not want to see, but you cannot close your heart to the things you do not want to feel."

Author Unknown

The Anatomy of Betrayal

Once we understand what our pain is and why we have it, most of us want answers to more questions. As with most debilitating issues, we want to know what we can expect regarding the severity and the duration of our discomfort. These are reasonable concerns and they deserve to be addressed.

- "When will the pain stop?"
- "Will I get some relief—soon?"
- "Does everyone hurt this deeply?"
- "I just think I am feeling better, and then I have a setback, why?"

These questions, and others similar to them, are relevant to our discussion on betrayal. We all want relief; we all need the pain to lessen. As with most injuries, whether physiological or psychological, there are no quick and easy answers. However, it has been my observation in working with clients, as well as my personal experience, that in examining the anatomy of betrayal, we will discover some relevant structures that will enable us to understand our levels of pain and to anticipate their duration.

An Underlying Principle

In chapter one, we learned what betrayal is. Our discussion was centered on three definitions/explanations:

- An investment that is met with rejection or abandonment
- A belief that is shattered / A truth that becomes a lie
- A profound trust which is profoundly violated

We know that inherent in each of these three explanations are a myriad of experiences. Each and every encounter with betrayal has its own unique and distinctive characteristics as well as damaging effects. Every person has his/her individual threshold for and tolerance of pain. Everyone has his/her inner strength as well as support systems. However, given these and other differing features and factors, I have observed a critical common denominator of betrayal, a consistent and constant underlying principle, that is a reliable indicator of the duration and severity of symptoms.

> **The degree to which we invest, believe, or trust in someone or something is directly proportional to our degree of injury from betrayal.**

Read it aloud, and think about it as you are saying it. Listen to your words.

> **The degree to which we invest, believe, or trust in someone or something is directly proportional to our degree of injury from betrayal.**

With great investment comes enormous loss; with strong belief comes shattered truth; with profound trust comes unspeakable violation. The *degree* to which we are subject to each of these will determine our level and duration of injury. Let's take a closer look at the word *degree* and its meanings as it relates to the first part of the underlying principle—*the degree to which we invest, believe, or trust in someone or something*. Its varying interpretations and applications will help us to understand its implications and impact on our own experiences with betrayal.

Degree as a "length of time"

As I reflect upon clients who experienced unimaginable devastation and destructtion from their betrayal, they were usually individuals who had invested, believed, or trusted in someone/something over a long period of time. In many cases, it was the duration of the relationship that armed them with the strength to fight for what was theirs. It was their history with the person or thing that gave them reason to stay and to reinvest.

Often times, I heard clients crying out and trying to figure out how the time invested meant little or nothing to the betrayer.

- "We had over thirty years of marriage together. How could that not count?"
- "We've been friends since childhood. Gosh, we've know each other forever. Didn't that matter?"
- "I was with the same company for over fifteen years. I guess my loyalty meant nothing."
- "Our relationship lasted just over two years. I thought we were going to make it."

It is only natural that the more time we put into someone or something, the more time we spend with a person or thing, and/or the longer we perceive someone or something to be a certain way, the more difficult it is to accept its lack of value to the betrayer. If our past has served us well, or at least, if time-endured experiences justify our perceptions, we have every right to feel completely depleted. We trusted in *time*, and it too, failed us.

At the same time as we are discussing the premise that longer investment is indicative of lengthy and more severe injury, I do not want to discount short term investment and its implications. Brief relationships can be intense with much risk, significant resources and reputation often at stake. Great loss is frequently the consequence of brief encounters or investment; and tragically, that loss is compounded with issues of self-blame. We question our judgment. Decisions were made on impulse, on emotion, or out of desperation. Our self-doubt can turn into a sense of self-betrayal, regretting our choices and wishing we could have done things differently. These short-term experiences bring with them deep despair and dark days and the span of pain can far surpass the initial time of investment.

As we assess the level of impact the betrayal has brought to our lives, we can use time as a reliable indicator. Although there are some exceptions, typically, with more time comes a greater sense of betrayal. Instead of being held hostage by the spent time, or beating ourselves up for time lost, we can embrace those days, months, and years. For now, I would like you to take your notebook or journal and write down one or more of your betrayal experiences. Next to each, notate how much time you invested, trusted, or believed in this person or thing. That is all for now; we will return to this in the "Activity Section" of the chapter.

Degree as "what we gave / what was taken from us"

When we discuss *degree* in connection to our examination of injury, we must take into account what we gave of ourselves or what was taken from us. On one hand, we can spend a great deal of time with someone or something, but not feel any loss over a betrayal incident. At times, we are relieved to be away from or out of a certain situation or relationship. Although there are many reasons for this, one important consideration is that we have not given too much of ourselves or our resources away, or at least not without knowledge of its lack of importance. However, when we are deeply wounded, or when we feel blindsided by the betrayal beast, we usually have depleted our emotional, physical, and financial banks. In addition, what we have freely given was disregarded, discounted, or destroyed. We are spent and there is nothing much left to fall back on. My client's piercing and poignant words reflect this degree of damage.

- "I raised the kids; kept an immaculate house; managed a career; and had his meals on the table when he got home. I did nothing for myself and I have nothing to show for it."

- "I spent my whole life trying to make her happy—working harder, making more money, buying bigger houses, taking more trips. Now that she is gone, I don't know who I am anymore."

- "Being let go from my job has left me nameless, penniless, and soon to be—homeless. I gave them endless hours of my life; they gave me nothing in return."

- "I trusted someone I loved. He stole everything from me—my innocence and my inner being. Who am I?"

Most of us desire a relationship where we can give. Most of us thrive in a relationship that is reciprocal. Tragically, most of us cave in when we have given so much of ourselves, with so little, if any, return. Others of us collapse when we are faced with the realization that our cherished investment, our child-like trust, and/or our grounding beliefs meant absolutely nothing to our betrayer and never would. And sadly, as with the element of time, many of us hurt ourselves more deeply by piling on layers of self-blame and regret. We get caught up rehearsing the "should haves" and "would haves and "if onlys". And, it changes nothing.

As we assess the degree of consequence that the betrayal perpetrated on us, we must take a pulse on our output. *How much did we give and/or how much was taken from us?* We can rely on the understanding that the more we give of ourselves without return, without regard, or without respect, the more fragile and fragmented will we feel. As with the degree of time, we can stay bound to our brokenness, or we can break the bondage of shame, blame, anger, and other emotional restraints. Using your same experience(s) that you chose for the degree of time, and next to the notations on time spent, write down what you gave of yourself or what was taken from you with regards to each. I know that this can be a painful process, so take your time. For now, just briefly list them. We will return to this in the "Activity Section" of the chapter.

Degree as "what was lost"

At first glance, this next segment on *degree* may appear to be similar to the previous one—what we gave of ourselves/ what was taken from us. However, there are some significant implications that need our attention.

Most of us have had the experience of loss in our lives. Unfortunately, at some time or other, we have grieved or mourned over someone or something. Whether we are aware of it or not, there are several variables that have enabled us to move through the grieving process in different ways with varying degrees of severity and duration. In our conversation on betrayal, I believe it is important to examine these variables of loss and how they may impact our injury.

Loss as "personal, relational, and/or material"

In anticipating and assessing our level of impact from betrayal, we must look at the kind or type of loss. Because different relationships and things mean something unique to every person, this section is meant to offer some guidelines, but certainly not absolutes. For most of us, I think that personal/relational loss can be more devastating than material loss. At times, the two are intertwined and that can be even more painful. However, when who we are as individuals, who we are in relation to others, who we are in our roles in life are taken from us through betrayal, the loss is incomprehensible. Many clients come to mind whose wounds reflect this bottomless pit of despair.

- "My innocence was stolen from me! I was just a child! How could he do that to me?"

- "Our only daughter was taken from us so cruelly and so viciously. We will never see her again. We will never have another family birthday, holiday, or vacation together...We are no longer a family..."

- "After my wife died of cancer, I didn't know what to do with myself, or who I was. She was my angel. The disease stole her from me."

- "I managed through the tough times—the lies, the manipulation, the political games—and for what? When it came time for the promotion, they completely overlooked me and went with a younger man. What does that say of me?"

Personal and relational losses encompass many aspects of our lives. Whether we lose a piece of ourselves, another person, and/or a purpose or passion, life is forever changed. Betrayal has re-coded our emotional/psychological DNA and robbed us of life's defining moments. The last thing we need to do is compound our loss with additional self-regret and self-blame, but most of us do. This is understandable. At the same time, as we move through the grieving process, we want to shed betrayal's shroud, and wrap ourselves in a new robe—one of safety and comfort.

Before we leave this piece of loss, I do not want to discount material loss. To have a home, a business, a life-savings, financial support, or other material items of physical and/or sentimental value stolen or taken from us is devastating as well. Lives are ravaged and destroyed by betrayals of this kind; we see it every day. People are left literally picking up the pieces of their lives as injustice strikes in one form or another. It sometimes takes years to regroup, rebuild, or just find a way to get some relief. At times, it never does come, and we are forced into a way of life that we never thought possible.

As we assess our degree of injury, we must acknowledge what was lost. Was it material, personal and/or relational, or perhaps a combination of all three? With any of these losses, we can anticipate intense, lingering, piercing pangs of betrayal. We can choose to lessen the grip of the pain and to let go of it a little at a time. We can place it where we can manage it. For now, next to your other notes, write down the person, relationship, and/or things that you have lost or that was taken from you. Please, take as much time as you need. This is an extremely difficult and important process. Give yourself a rest or pause when needed. Continue when you are ready. We will complete with this activity at the end of the chapter.

Loss as "inner-personal"

Related, and yet uniquely different from the segment on personal, relational, or material loss, is the impact of injury on our inner-personal qualities, character, and being. Because of their nature, facets of our personas that are more private, we often times do not credit them with the attention and time that they so deserve. We are embarrassed or ashamed that we aren't dealing with them very well. Frequently, when our inner-personal pieces are violated and when we have the courage to talk about it, we are dismissed or disregarded altogether. Others frown upon us and our weakness. In their eyes, we should be stronger or we should be able to hold it together; worse things can happen to us. And so, we plod along, wading through our pool of pain and wondering why we can't move through it more quickly, doubting our own level of discomfort.

These losses from betrayal are real and they are common. Very few of us have been exempt from their poisonous sting and lingering infection. Although there are numerous examples, the following are just some of the types of inner-personal loss.

- Loss of privacy
- Loss of identity
- Loss of reputation or title
- Loss of manhood / womanhood
- Loss of status or position
- Loss of safety or security
- Loss of innocence
- Loss of self-esteem, self-worth, self-respect
- Loss of human dignity or human rights
- Loss of faith

When betrayal violates us on such a deeply personal and private level, we must expect that the injury will invade our spirits and souls. We must understand that this *is* its nature. We must anticipate a lengthy duration and give ourselves permission to work through the stay. It is important for us to begin by acknowledging any loss in this arena. Along with your other notes for this chapter, if you have experienced loss of an inner-personal nature, please notate it. If the loss comes from a different act of betrayal than previously mentioned, write down that experience first and then the loss you endured. Do not second guess yourself or dismiss any feelings. Now is the time. Get it out and write it down. Take a break when you are done. We will return to this at the end of the chapter.

As we conclude this section of chapter three, we can rest in the knowledge and understanding that varying factors of our betrayal experience will impact our injury. The *degree* —how much time we invested, believed, or trusted in someone or something; how much we gave or how much was taken from us; what kind of loss we endured—affects the severity and duration of our pain. There is comfort in knowing that we are not alone; there is healing in understanding that what we are feeling and yet to feel is expected. And, there is hope that as we continue to empower ourselves with awareness and knowledge, we affirm and validate what we have been feeling and begin to free ourselves from betrayal's bondage.

Occurrence = *Degree* of injury

As we continue our conversation on "how long and to what degree will I feel this way," we will examine another critical feature of betrayal's anatomy. As I think about many clients and their respective experiences with betrayal, as well as my own, I believe that their severity and duration of injury was related to the occurrence(s) of betrayal. It is common sense that the more frequently we are exposed to a dangerous substance, the more we subject ourselves to its harmful effects. The same holds true for betrayal and/or the betrayer; the more contact with the poisonous thorns, the more the infectious toxins will seep into our souls and invade our spirits.

We will take a look at the types of occurrences and how they may impact our degree of injury. In doing so, we will concern ourselves with two applications: the number of times we were betrayed as well as the frequency of exposure to the betrayer and/or the betrayal environment. As with other features of betrayal, each person has his/her unique experiences and thus, there can and will be exceptions to the explanations. And, it is crucial to remember that the degree of investment, belief, or trust in someone or something should always remain paramount in our assessment of injury. However, drawing attention to the types of occurrences can serve us well as additional guidelines for understanding our level and span of pain.

Occurrence: acute or short term

As I think about clients who were able to move through their betrayal without the long term damaging effects, two factors were in play. One, the degree of initial investment, trust, or belief was not significant. Secondly, either the act of betrayal was short term in nature and/or additional exposure to the betrayer or betrayal environment was infrequent or non-existent. Let's take a look at a couple of samples of clients' experiences with this kind of acute or short term betrayal.

A middle aged single man was overlooked for a significant promotion and year-end bonus. Shortly after he questioned the move by his employer, he was let go. Although he was deeply wounded by the lies and manipulation that led to his dismissal, he was able to take some much-needed time off for himself. A few months later, he moved to a different city and secured another position. As we moved through termination, he credited his healthier state of mind to two factors: one was that the duration of the act of betrayal was fairly quick, and secondly, he was subjected to the betrayer and the betrayal environment for a minimal period of time.

In another, more complex, situation, the client was also able to move through the betrayal with less injury than anticipated. A young wife was told by her husband of about ten years that he was having an affair and no longer loved her. He moved out of the house the following day. A brief time later, the affair ended, but her husband filed for divorce and moved to another country. Although this young mother of two felt unimaginable abandonment, she also disclosed later in one of our sessions that having her ex-husband "out of sight" also kept him "out of mind". In picking up the pieces of her broken life, she commented that she felt free, free from the trappings of betrayal and free from the constant lies and free from the manipulation she had endured.

In both these cases, as is true for most people, there are individual factors to also consider. Each of us has our inner strength; we have our support systems; we have various resources at our disposal; and we have our emotional and physical well-being. If these arenas in our lives are lacking or non-existent, the duration and severity of our injury from betrayal can be intense and severe, even if the initial occurrence is short term and/or the exposure is infrequent.

Occurrence: chronic or ongoing

In contrast to acute or short-term, there is chronic or ongoing occurrence of betrayal. Betrayal, under these conditions, can be the most devastating and the most debilitating. Because there is very little, if any, reprieve from the acts of betrayal and/or exposure to the betrayal environment, we are held hostage to its damaging effects. Injury compounds injury, and we are left holding onto the tight-rope of life waiting for it to snap at any moment.

Although there are many scenarios that illustrate this kind of unimaginable damage, I often recall the many women who I worked with during my year of internship at a Battered Women's Center in Northern California. Every weekend, for a year, I manned the crises phone lines, did the intakes for clients who had come to the shelter, and counseled numerous clients either in one-on-one sessions or in group settings.

Almost without exception, women from all ethnicities and levels of socioeconomic status had experienced chronic or on-going battering. After each battering incident, promises were made and a honeymoon period ensued, only to be followed by a time of tension build-up and another betrayal—another battering incident. Because so many of these women had very little, if any, respite from the betrayer and/or the betrayal environment, their emotional and physical scars were deeply embedded. Most functioned at a level of fear that paralyzed and immobilized them. At times, it was months, and even years, away from and out of their respective destructive environments that enabled them to secure a sense of self and safety.

Watching the evening news, I am amazed at how many people are exposed to chronic or on-going betrayal: survivors living for years in uninhabitable conditions after environmental catastrophes; injured and maimed patients not receiving appropriate medical attention and benefits; victims of crime who are continually subjected to the intricacies of the judicial system with delays, postponements, deals, and so forth—waiting for justice to prevail or to just show up.

As with these examples and numerous others, we need to prepare ourselves emotionally and physically for a possible lengthy stay where we experience injury from being betrayed. We need to give ourselves permission to feel what we need to feel and to navigate our way through it. At the same time, we need to know that there is hope—hope of relief from the betrayal and hope of rising above the circumstances that work against us.

Occurrence: recurrent or episodic

A related, but yet different, kind of occurrence is that of recurrent or episodic betrayal. This can be a tricky as well as insidious type of betrayal because just when we think we are on more solid ground, our foundation is once again rattled. Just when we feel we have a handle on our feelings, emotions, and thoughts, we are thrown into a whirlwind of confusion, worthlessness, and powerlessness, again. As is true for the other kinds of occurrence, with recurrent or episodic betrayal, the depth and length of our pain is also connected to our degree of investment, trust, and belief in someone or something. In addition, because there has been a period of reprieve from one betrayal incident to the next, there is often time for healing and recovery to better prepare us for the next onslaught. With other cases, the level of healing is not sufficient to withstand the new injury, and the severity and duration of pain is debilitating. A couple of examples come to mind.

Often in my practice, I worked with clients who had a partner, or a child, or a friend, who was an addict. One couple I worked with spent years of their lives dealing with their daughter's addiction. There would be months, or often a year or two, when their daughter would stay clean and sober. They and she would pick up the pieces, again, and life would return to some level of normalcy. Then, their daughter would not call or she would disappear for days or weeks. The parents' trust was shattered; their truth became a lie, again. Betrayal reared its ugly head once more. Their hopes were diminished and their healing was derailed.

The other example, one that was sadly quite common, involved couples who had separated and/or divorced and who were dealing with issues around their children. Because there was a need to have some level of contact between the former spouses, these opportunities could lend themselves to recurrent or episodic brushes with betrayal. I found that many times one partner in the couple was willing and wanting to move forward in a healthy fashion, but the other was still in a hurting and blame-filled place. Other times, there were disagreements over the rearing of children and one partner lashed out at the other. There were numerous scenarios related to this dynamic, but the common thread was that a period of calm and of stability was periodically rattled by another tidal wave of emotion and by another crushing blow from betrayal.

We need to understand that with recurrent or episodic betrayal, the length and duration of injury can feel more like an unwanted shadow, lingering behind us as we wait for the next reoccurrence. We feel like we can't shake it and even if we do, it will return to rattle us. This is understandable. However, we do not want to get stuck in this place and lengthen our stay even further. We can move ahead and we can rid ourselves of the shadow. It will take work, but we can do it.

Occurrence: multiple betrayals

One of the most devastating occurrences of betrayal involves multiple betrayals. There is some cross over with chronic or ongoing occurrences, but yet there is an important distinction—more than one betrayal is being experienced, either at the same time or around the same period of time. In other words, the betrayals are compounded. One is heaped upon the other leaving the individual barely able to come up for air. Because of the nature of multiple betrayals, the duration and severity of injury can be long-lasting, debilitating, and depleting. Again, it is crucial to take into account the degree of initial investment, belief, and/or trust into someone or something. It is also important to consider each person's support systems, resources, and inner strength and well-being. Ironically, with multiple betrayals, it is often the support systems and/or resources that play a role in the acts of multiple betrayals.

Working with sexual abuse survivors, I witnessed clients experience multiple betrayals on a frequent basis. Not only was their abuse the initial betrayal, but disclosing it to a trusted parent or another loved one, who didn't believe or support them, compounded the betrayal. In many cases, if the abuse was believed, the survivor was blamed for the abuse and charged with disrupting the family, thus leaving the survivor re-victimized and betrayed again. Some clients chose to pursue legal action; again some were disbelieved, ridiculed, and dismissed. Others were cast out from their families for causing problems and drawing public attention to private matters.

Another case involved a middle-aged man who had invested years building a business from the ground up. When he was not able to make it a success, family members turned against him. He was charged and found guilty by his closest relatives. His investors turned against him and trusted friends, from years of working together, blamed him solely for the failure. When this man turned to his church for comfort and support, he was received with judgment and disdain. Other close friends cut their ties and looked down upon him. Once a pillar in his community, when he had no more to give, others no longer needed him. As his betrayal mounted, he diminished in spirit and in being until there was almost nothing left.

With multiple betrayals, we can anticipate that the stay and level of injury are to be significant. We can rest in that knowledge and we know what to expect. And at the same time, we can find hope in knowing that multiple betrayals do not equate to a life-time sentence of pain. We can move through it and beyond it. We must do so.

Occurrence: re-injury—from self

The last area of occurrence from betrayal is a tender area of discussion, but one that needs our attention—re-injury from our own doing. This means that whether we are conscious of it or not, whether we do this purposefully or not, we often times engage in unhealthy thinking and/or behavioral patterns that lengthen and/or intensify our stay in the betrayal injury.

I realize that many, if not most, of us do this because we don't know what else to do with our pain. We are hurting deeply, and we will do almost anything to make it lessen or stop. We are responding out of reactive emotion often times creating more injury to ourselves and ironically, providing the betrayer with additional ammunition for the next onslaught.

I also know that even after we become aware and knowledgeable of our betrayal and its impact in our lives, we can still stumble and fall. During the recovery process, we can and will feel vulnerable or re-injured, and we can find ourselves resorting to unhealthy behaviors. Part of recovery is relapse—regression into or repetition of maladaptive thoughts and/or behaviors that we have, in the past, utilized as our only means of coping. This is understandable and it is a common occurrence as we try to come to terms with our injury.

In an earlier chapter, I referred to a female client who had a very damaged history as a child, adolescent, and teen. Abuse, abandonment, and rejection ran rampant throughout her formative years. Years later, when she was faced with her husband's recurrent infidelity, she entered therapy. Because of her lifetime of betrayal, her triggers for re-injury were easily ignited. She would work her recovery program focusing on taking care of herself when another betrayal blast from her spouse would send her into an emotional whirlwind. Resorting to drastic and humiliating measures, this desperate woman deeply wounded herself further by participating in a betrayal tug-of-war fighting to reinstate her lost worth but losing herself even more in the struggle.

At this point in our discussion, it is important to be aware that we can intensify our pain and lengthen our stay in the bonds of betrayal through self-induced re-injury. None of us intentionally dreams of doing this or wants it. Recognizing and understanding that this is real and does happen will help us identify the tools we need to embrace recovery and to work through the process of healing.

In conclusion, we need to remember that what is most important in anticipating our level and duration of pain is largely based on the degree of initial investment, trust, or belief placed in someone or something. However, the kinds of degree—length of time; what we gave of ourselves/what was taken from us; what was lost (material, personal, relational, and/or inner-personal)—also impact and influence our depth and stay in the pain field. Lastly, the types of occurrence—acute or short term, chronic or on-going, recurrent or episodic, multiple betrayals, and/or re-injury from self—also play an important role when assessing and anticipating how long and to what degree we will feel our injury.

No matter what the varying degrees or types of betrayal, we can rest in the knowledge that hope and healing remain within our grasp. With hard work and specific tools, we can lessen our pain and shorten our stay in the bondages of betrayal.

Activities – Chapter 3

Choose either #1 or #2 and then do #3.

1. If you have not already made your notations throughout Chapter Three, please do so now. Reflecting upon your betrayal experience recorded in earlier chapters (or selecting another one), write down the experience. Next to it, write down the following kinds of degree of investment, trust, or belief:

    *   length of time
    *   what we gave of ourselves/what was taken from us
    *   what was lost (material, personal, relational, and/or inner-personal)

    After each kind of degree, write freely about how each one impacted you or what each one meant to you. Take your time. Give this your full attention. When you are finished, go on to Activity #2.

2. After you have finished Activity #1, or if you have already completed your notations while reading Chapter Three, complete the following exercise. For each notation that you wrote (for the above kinds of degree), spend a few moments writing *why* each one was/is important to *you*. Give each one as much time and space as needed; dig deep and get your truths out. They were not respected by the betrayer or the betrayal experience, but you can honor them now. It is time to cherish your investment, belief, or trust.

3. For our work in the Recovering Section, please make a notation now of the kinds of occurrence/s you have experienced with your betrayer and/or the betrayal environment. Write down your betrayal experience/s and then next to it, notate the occurrence/s.

    *   Acute or short term
    *   Chronic or on-going
    *   Recurrent or episodic
    *   Multiple betrayals
    *   Re-injury from self

    It would also be beneficial to write a brief description of *why* the type of reoccurrence you chose best applies to you. There may be more than one, and there may be overlapping of occurrences. Again, write freely and thoroughly. Don't hold anything back; release it now. Affirm and validate what you know to be true for you and what you endured. No one can take that from you. When you are done, relax and take in several deep breaths.

Section II:
Other Recovery Considerations

4   **Betrayal and Codependency**

"Caring about people and giving are good, desirable qualities—something we need to do ... but [we] many codependents continue giving long after it hurts, usually until we are doubled over in pain."

—Melody Beattie

As we move towards Chapter Six: Recovering, it is important at this point in our discussion to take a look at two recovery relationships—Codependency and Grief. Chapter Four is intended to highlight an underlying connection between betrayal injury and codependency as well as its relationship to their respective recoveries. At the same time, Chapter Four is not intended to address recovery work for Codependency itself. There are excellent resources available on this topic. Some references are suggested at the end of the chapter.

In Chapter One, we defined/explained betrayal in the following ways:

- An investment into someone or something met with abandonment and/or rejection

- A profound trust in someone or something which is profoundly violated

- A truth that becomes a lie / a belief that is shattered

Then, in Chapter Three, we learned that "the degree to which we invest, believe, or trust in someone or something is directly proportional to our degree of injury from betrayal". Understanding what betrayal is, validating what we feel and why, and anticipating to what degree we will feel pain—all help us to come to terms with our injury and to move forward in our recovery. When I think about clients who were unceasingly held captive to the bonds of betrayal (confusion, worthlessness, and powerlessness), who remained smothered by the remnants of their relationships, and who continually resorted to unhealthy behaviors / thinking patterns in a desperate attempt to reinstate their roles/positions, many of these clients were also dealing with issues of codependency.

Although there are many reliable and sound explanations for codependency, for our discussion, I have summarized its meaning as follows:

Codependency is an issue of "overinvestment" into someone or something.

It is a relationship in which we stay too long while giving away too much of ourselves and our resources all in an attempt to control, rescue, or change someone or something.

The end result of codependent behavior is two-fold:

- The one who is overinvesting is depleted and drained.
- The one receiving the investment is unchanged and unscathed.

Because codependents overinvest, it makes sense that their injury from betrayal would take on a unique dimension of intensity and severity, and thus, add another component to the recovery process.

One of the most heart-wrenching cases I worked with involved a very successful businesswoman in her late thirties. She came in to see me as she was considering leaving her marriage of over twenty years. She and her husband had married young, raised children, and struggled for many years at their relationship. For the past few years, my client had been the financial supporter of the family. Her spouse was an alcoholic, repeatedly out of work, and frequently verbally and physically abused her. The relationship was turning extremely volatile and unsafe. Eventually, my client moved out, separated, and filed for divorce. However, even after two years of being divorced, she continually rescued her ex-husband financially, emotionally, and physically, and she continued to deplete herself in the process. With time, my client remained committed to her recovery and worked tirelessly on her issues of codependency. Although she was in a much healthier place when we concluded our time together, her tendency to over-invest into new relationships continued to make her susceptible to significant re-injury from betrayal experiences.

Many other examples come to mind from clients who were dealing with issues of addiction involving a spouse, child, friend, or a loved one. However, codependency can encompass many other maladaptive behaviors. Remember, the key to identifying with this issue involves our sense of over-responsibility for someone else's behavior and therefore requiring an overinvestment on our part. Tragically, we are often betraying ourselves by continuing to re-invest into someone or something that offers us only pain in return.

If you are uncertain as to whether you might also struggle with this issue, you might find yourself saying/thinking some of these thought patterns:

- "If I just help her a little longer, I know she will change."
- "This time it will be different. I know he is going to change. I just have to give a little more: give him more room, more space, more time to find his way."
- "I know I shouldn't but I'm going to lend her the money, again. She said she would not use it for drugs. I know I probably shouldn't trust her but I have to."
- "Every time I return to the relationship, I think it is going to be different. But it isn't; in fact, it is worse. I feel like I'm obsessed with the situation and the drama in it. I feel like I've lost myself along the way."
- "I know I can make it better. Just watch me."

Codependency on the surface appears to be a compassionate, care-taking attribute of one's character and personality. And, kept in check or in balance, it can be that. But for most of us, who struggle with its consequences and its aftermath, it is an endless and pointless journey of rescuing and resuscitating someone because of his/her lack of responsibility for him/herself. When we are busy rescuing, we feel needed and worthy. But as soon as our efforts fall short, or are discarded, we become angry and resentful. After we beat ourselves up for a while, we move back into our role of over-investing again; we then can feel good about ourselves, at least for a short time. This cycle of behavior becomes who we are and it takes on a life of its own.

For the purpose of our conversation on betrayal and its relationship to codependency, not only is it important to understand that both share in the underlying principle of investment into someone or something, but that neither should be disregarded in lieu of the other in the recovery process. Both need to be addressed. When I think about my own codependency issues as well as those of a myriad of clients, most, if not all, seem to be rooted in some kind of betrayal experience from our past and/or from our formative years. And although I realize there can and will be exceptions to this premise, it is my suggestion that we begin our initial healing by addressing the issues of how we were betrayed. However, if our codependent behaviors/thinking patters are sabotaging, negating, or preventing our recovery work, we may need to attend to those first. And at times, we may need to work on both concurrently because the codependency and betrayal may be significantly intertwined.

Remember, whether our betrayal injury is inflicted from a one time, long term, and/or continual re-investment or overinvestment, we do not want to negate its significance or impact on us. Each of us is the only one who can truly know the degree to which we have invested into the betrayer, and thus, the degree of pain we feel. Also remember, as we acknowledge the betrayal and its relative degree of injury, we affirm ourselves in the process.

In conclusion, if you feel as though you may struggle with the issue of codependency, please do not feel overwhelmed or overwrought. I believe that most of us have some level of codependent behavior in us! Also, there are many valuable resources and support networks available to you. In addition to their individual therapy, many of my clients also attended Al-Anon (for those who have a loved one living with addiction issues) and/or CODA (for those working through codependency issues) groups. These twelve-step groups offer much-needed support and affirmation as well as tools needed to live a more healthy and balanced life.

Activities – Chapter 4

Reflect upon your betrayal experience/s. Given our explanation of codependency, do you think there is a pattern of "overinvestment" connected to your betrayal injury? Whether you answer yes or no, write freely about your thoughts. Better understanding of ourselves leads to better acceptance, and thus, a healthier state of being.

Suggested Readings

Beattie, M. (2011). *Codependent no more*. Center City, MN: Hazelden.

Beattie, M. (1989). *Beyond codependency: And getting better all the time*. New York: Harper & Row.

5   Betrayal and Grief

"Death is not the greatest loss in life. The greatest loss is what dies inside us while we live."

—Norman Cousins

Just as we examined a relationship between betrayal and codependency, we are also going to take a look at another recovery consideration—grief. As was true for Chapter Four, Chapter Five is not intended to address grief recovery. Again, there are many valuable resources available for you and several are suggested at the end of the chapter. However, we do want to acknowledge a connecting piece between betrayal injury and grief and how that may be integrated into our recovery work with betrayal.

In Chapter One, we learned what betrayal is—an investment, a trust, a truth/ belief in someone or something. When these relational gifts are destroyed, dispelled, or disproved, we experience loss. In Chapters Two and Three, we expanded our knowledge and awareness of how and to what degree this loss infects and affects us. We've come to know that *"our degree of investment, truth/ belief, or trust is directly proportional to our degree of injury from betrayal"*. We have come to understand that with betrayal, there are different kinds of loss: time, material, relational, personal, and inner-personal; some of which we gave freely, others which were cruelly ripped from us.

Without question, with betrayal there is loss—loss of self, loss of loved ones, loss of integrity, loss of esteem, loss of possessions. The list goes on and on. The connection with grief is obvious—the element of loss. However, it has been my experience as well as time spent with clients that I have observed distinct and separate features which differentiate their respective recoveries.

The most important difference between grief and betrayal is in their anatomical manifestations—what we are thinking, what we are feeling, and how we act on those emotions. With betrayal, we experience the three states of being (as discussed in Chapter Two)—confusion, worthlessness, and powerlessness. We learned that although there is often overlapping of the three states, we usually navigate through them in the order presented. The states are not just emotions that describe what we are feeling or experiencing. We learned that we have called them *states* because this is who and what we are in that time and in that moment. *Confusion, worthlessness*, and *powerlessness* engulf us, and bind us to the bondage of betrayal, and then, redefine us.

However, when we are confronted with grief, we embrace a very different but real embodiment. Well-documented and researched, most of us are familiar with the five stages of grief introduced by Elisabeth Kübler-Ross in her 1969 book *On Death and Dying*: Denial, Anger, Bargaining, Depression, and Acceptance. In her works, Kübler-Ross has noted that these steps do not necessarily come in the order noted, nor are all steps experienced by all patients. She has also stated that the stages can reoccur many times as part of an individual's specific grief process. Other grief experts understand the grief process as taking place in seven stages, including: shock or disbelief, denial, bargaining, guilt, anger, depression, and acceptance/hope (MedicineNet.com).

Understanding that both betrayal and grief may share in the physical, emotional, and psychological symptoms or representations, it may be difficult or even confusing to navigate our way into and through recovery. We find ourselves feeling distraught, not solely by our loss, but also by the way in which our loss was incurred. I am suggesting that we carefully consider both grief and betrayal recovery when dealing with a loss issue.

One of my most tragic cases of betrayal and grief involved a client who had a very tumultuous marriage. After years of dealing with multiple betrayals—financial uncertainties, gambling, alcoholism, and marital infidelity—this broken but determined woman separated from her husband of over thirty years. After a period of time, her spouse entered individual therapy (with another therapist) and began to work on his recovery. Over time, he embraced a wide network of supportive resources, as did my client. Just when it appeared that there might be a turn for the better, my client discovered that her husband had taken his own life. In an instant, my client's world imploded. Her core was shaken; her hopes were shattered; and her dreams of wellness together were vaporized.

Of course, this was a grief issue. My client had lost her husband, the father of their children, the grandfather to their grandchildren, the friend to so many, and the only man she had ever loved. Her loss was insurmountable; her grief paralleled its depth. At the same time, this grief-stricken woman felt immense betrayal. The years of investment and re-investment, of rebuilding trust time and time again, of choosing to believe a new truth, one more time, all took on the mask of deception. All became betrayers.

As represented in this case, if we experience betrayal in conjunction with our loss, we need to address both in our recovery. We need to understand our states of being—confusion, worthlessness, and powerlessness—and to utilize effective strategies/tools to work through them. We will, most likely, also need to work a grief recovery program. Most importantly, we need to keep a pulse on what we are feeling. We need to be honest with ourselves so that we can communicate those feelings to others and attend to our recovery work. As was the case in the tragedy of my client, I have observed that when we experience the loss of a personal nature, of a loved one, there is frequently a reluctance to express the feelings of betrayal. We feel tremendous guilt in the acknowledgment and disclosure of these feelings: rejection, abandonment, shattered truths, dispelled beliefs, and violations of trust. We must understand that these feelings of betrayal are an uncomfortable but expected response to the traumatic loss we have incurred and endured.

We must give ourselves permission to work through these emotions and we must embrace a safe supportive venue to do this.

As we move through our discussion on betrayal and grief, it is important to mention another differing characteristic. Although it has been rare in my personal experience and of many clients, I believe that we can experience grief without betrayal. If this were to be the case, one of two premises would apply. First, either there was not significant or meaningful investment, trust, or belief/truth placed into the person or thing. Or perhaps, the loss was previously reconciled as a natural occurrence in the events/cycle of life. I often witnessed this as I worked with clients experiencing transitional phases in their lives: retirement, changing careers or positions, moving to different places, addressing health issues, the passing of an elderly parent or terminally ill loved one. These examples of loss are by no means less important; each one carries with it individual experiences, memories, and attachment. If grief recovery is in order, it should be addressed tenderly and compassionately.

At the same time, there may or may not be the additional component of betrayal, and we need to keep that consideration in mind. The betrayal bandit often lurks in the furthermost shadows of our being and if left unattended, it robs us of our full potential towards wellness. So many times over the years, I had clients come in to therapy, ready to address a situation that had brought a significant level of loss into their lives. As we moved through our sessions, and as is often the case, many clients discovered underlying, unfinished business that needed attention. Time and time again, the word *betrayal* would surface. The masks of confusion, worthlessness, and powerlessness were removed for a short time and allowed to breathe. The pain intensified as the guilt, embarrassment, shame, and regret became too much to acknowledge and too much to bear. The masks were quickly adorned and the betrayal was buried, or at least quieted for a moment. Remember, you are the one who lives with the betrayal bandit. You are the one who is stolen from and robbed by its existence. You are the one who can put an end to its residence and reclaim your rightful peace. Listen to the voice inside you. Trust your truth. Move forward with confidence.

In concluding our discussion on betrayal and grief, most of us are aware of the years of excellent research and resources that have become available to us, concerning grief recovery. Many of my clients, whom I worked with in individual therapy, also joined support grief groups, read books, attended seminars, and became active participants in their respective recovery programs. Over time, grief and grief work have become an honored process by the community and by us. It is time we do the same for betrayal and for ourselves. By becoming acquainted with our betrayal, by understanding and working through our unique experiences, we too honor where we've been, heal our injuries, and embrace a hope-filled life.

Activities – Chapter 5

Reflect upon the loss issue(s) in your life. Write down the loss(es) that you still struggle with or that remain unsettled and uncomfortable. Although this may be difficult, listen to the nudging inside of you and pay attention to the anchor weighing you down.

- Are the masks of confusion, worthlessness, and powerlessness hiding in the recesses of your spirit?
- Are you having trouble making sense out of the loss?
- Are you feeling less than or blaming yourself for not doing enough?
- Do you feel stripped of your position and/or place—robbed of future holdings?
- Pause, think, and feel—do you feel betrayed?

If so, take a few minutes and write about those feelings. Take a few deep breaths. Pace yourself. Get them out. Unveil the masks and release the bandit's hold on you. It is time.

Suggested Readings

Kübler-Ross, E. (1969). *On death and dying.* New York: Macmillan.

Kübler-Ross, E., & Kessler, D. (2005). *On grief and grieving: Finding the meaning of grief through the five stages of loss.* New York: Scribner.

Section III: Recovering

6 Recovering: Breaking Through the Bonds of Betrayal... and Beyond

"Character cannot be developed in ease and quiet. Only through experience of trial and suffering can the soul be strengthened, vision cleared, ambition inspired, and success achieved."

—Helen Keller

As we move into our section on *Recovering: Breaking through the Bonds of Betrayal... and Beyond,* I want to talk to you about the process, just briefly. There are several important pieces of recovery that I would like you to keep in mind.

First, if you look at the title of this chapter, you will notice that I started with the word *recovering*—not *recovery*. I chose this form of the word for a specific reason; it is a verb and thus it implies *action*. Too often, we speak of our healing process as a thing—'recovery'—which implies it is a state we get to, pass through, and then leave. If you have read this far and if you have completed the exercises within and at the conclusion of each chapter, you have already chosen to take action on your healing. You have begun your recovering. The next section will also invite you to be an active participant in your process by providing you with tools, strategies, and exercises to work on healing from betrayal. I cannot stress enough that the more you put into this, the more you will get from it. Do not just read the lines; instead, get your notebook, grab a pencil or pen, or even your computer if that feels comfortable, and get ready to continue the work.

Secondly, the five parts of *Recovering: Breaking through the Bonds of Betrayal... and Beyond* are based on a continuum. It is important to implement the sequence of activities for each part in the order that they are presented. Of course, there may be need for individual tailoring within the activities as well as working at your own pace. At the beginning of each part, you will be asked to take stock of your current healing reality regarding the elements within that section and to indicate that placement on the numbered continuum provided. The continuum is as follows:

Part One Right Yourself	Part Two Readiness and Rigor	Part Three Revive and Restore: Mind. Body, and Spirit
1 2 3 4 5 6 7 8 9 10	1 2 3 4 5 6 7 8 9 10	1 2 3 4 5 6 7 8 9 10

Part Four Release and Renew	Part Five Reframe and Refine
1 2 3 4 5 6 7 8 9 10	1 2 3 4 5 6 7 8 9 10

Fig. 6-1: Map of the five parts of the recovery process

At the end of each part and/or selected sub-sections, you will reassess your level of healing in that particular area and to determine if you are ready to move on. It is not our intent to achieve perfection in each arena but to reach a level of healing proficiency, one that will strengthen and fortify you as you move towards the next goal. If, at any time, you feel you need to step back and rework a previous area of healing, of course, do so. This is a natural and expected part of recovering. In fact, not taking the time to rework or revisit previous steps in recovering that need attention most likely will hinder you in reaching your desired state of wellness.

Recovering looks like a large extended staircase (see Fig. 6-2 on p. 63):

Often times, it is during those periods of stepping back, reassessing, and restarting that we learn what is working for us and what is not. It is not only a time of reflection but it is also an opportunity to become reenergized and refocused on the goals at hand. So, be prepared to do the following:

- Be brutally honest when assessing your current level of healing.

- Do the work ahead of you—one step at a time.

- Implement and practice the activities within each part.

- Reassess your level of healing, confidence, and proficiency at the end of each part and/or sub-section.

- Remain open and willing to rework areas of need before moving on to the next part.

- If needed, at any time during the recovering continuum, go back and strengthen any previous parts of the continuum and/or any subsections.

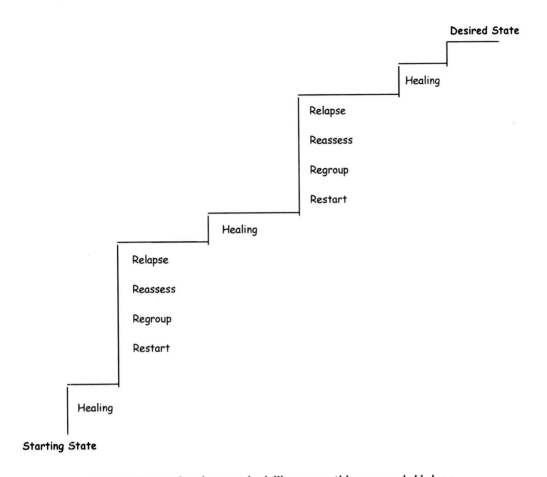

Fig. 6-2: Recovering does not look like a smoothly groomed ski slope

Remember, working towards our desired state is a dynamic process—one that requires change. Giving ourselves honest feedback allows us to see if that change is taking place.

Thirdly, the exercises and activities that I have included and will continue to include are geared primarily towards your thought processes. Because I am a therapist who works mainly with a Cognitive Behavioral therapeutic approach, I have and will continue to ask you to examine your thoughts and work on changing those thought patterns. Yes, I have talked about your feelings and will continue to do so, but our feelings are closely connected to our thoughts. In fact, those of us who embrace this approach to recovering believe it is our thoughts that determine our feelings, not the reverse. Remember, this does not mean that your thoughts are not true or valid; it simply implies that we must restructure those thoughts in a positive, nurturing way to form new truths that will in turn enable us to feel relief. As our feelings heal, we are then better equipped to make healthy changes in our lives and to live (act) differently. Thus, we blend in the Behavioral part of our Cognitive Behavioral approach. Because we are doing our work together through a written format, I will continue to ask you to write much of your work down. I encourage you to read over what you write, several times, and to read it aloud, listening to your voice and your heart as you do so. You will be amazed at what you hear.

Lastly, because we are all so different and our experiences are unique, I cannot emphasize enough how important it is that each of you keep a pulse on your state of being. As with the first part of the book, I frequently provided time for a pause or a rest as you did your reading and your work. However, you are the best judge of when you need time, you know when your triggers are touched, and you know when you need to be still and quiet. To put it simply, pace yourself. Recovering will not take place the faster you read through this or the more quickly you do all the exercises. Racing through will not get you to the finish line. There is no finish line; the tools you learn will need to become part of your lifestyle and of a different way of choosing to be, each and every day.

Let's continue our recovering.

7 Recovering Part One: Right Yourself

"All blame is a waste of time. No matter how much fault you find with another and regardless of how much you blame him, it will not change you."

—Dr. Wayne Dyer

As we begin *Part One: Right Yourself*, assess where you are on the healing continuum. Shade in the number that currently most describes your reality. Then, read on.

0	1	2	3	4	5	6	7	8	9	10

Score	How Do I Feel Right Now?
0-3	My betrayer owes me. He/she/them/it needs to make it right. I was the one who was victimized. I was wronged and I need to convince my betrayer, and others, how badly I was hurt. No one really understands what I have been through.
4-7	I understand that my betrayal is real and that what I am feeling is real. I am confused, I feel worthless, and I am powerless to do anything to change it. I know that others have felt this way too. I am beginning to understand and accept that it is my responsibility to feel better; no one else can do that for me. I have stopped blaming others, but at times, I start to blame myself. I wonder how to move forward.
8-10	I am taking responsibility for righting myself and for healing my betrayal injury. It is my work and mine alone; no one can make it right for me. I know more about betrayal and I understand my experience better. I know what is true and real. I am feeling strengthened, fortified, and validated. I am ready to move on.

Fig. 7-1: Right Yourself—Healing Continuum

The work belongs to the betrayed—only the betrayed

As we continue our conversation on betrayal and move along with the process of recovering from our injuries, I am reminded of an experience that I encountered about thirty-eight years ago. I will never forget it or its impact on me.

I was a sophomore attending the University of California at Santa Barbara (UCSB). Because my family was part owner of a sailboat, I had the wonderful opportunity of being exposed to sailing. I was eager to learn more about this amazing craft and attending UCSB offered me the chance. I needed to fulfill a physical education requirement which I could meet by taking sailing lessons. During the autumn term, I signed up for *Beginning Sailing 101*. The first few classes, which were held out at the Santa Barbara Harbor, consisted of acclimating ourselves to the sport: learning the required knots, familiarizing ourselves with the parts of the skiff (a rudder, two oars, a small mainsail, and the lines), as well as learning sailing terminology and safety procedures. For the first two sessions in the water, the instructor had us practice within the shelter of the harbor waters where the winds were calm, and the area was small and protected. For our third exercise in the water, we were instructed to venture out beyond the safety of the harbor into the open ocean waters. Each skiff had two people; my partner and I were a little nervous, but we knew we had each other, or so I thought.

As we made our way further out, the winds began to pick up. The instructor motored about in his teacher's boat yelling directives to us with his bullhorn. My partner and I seemed to be doing fine when all of a sudden, out of nowhere, a huge gust swept across the waters. Unprepared for a sudden blast of wind, our little skiff was tossed slightly up in the air, throwing us both out. And then it flipped, not just on its side but all the way over. When I came up for air, I searched for my partner and for our capsized refuge. As I continued to tread water, the instructor's words rang through my head, "If you run into trouble, remember these two rules: Don't leave your partner. Don't leave your boat." I spotted my partner swimming to another boat!! Yelling at him to come back, I was frantically making my way through the icy waters to our skiff.

The instructor quickly motored over towards me. "Good", I thought, "he is coming over to help me. I'm too weak, too scared, and too cold to do this by myself." He stopped about five feet away and began blurting out his commands through his over-used bullhorn!

"Holli, pull yourself up on top of your boat. Get a hold of the side, give yourself some quick strong kicks, and hoist yourself up there! Hurry up, we don't have all day!"

For a moment, I was in a daze—shaking, numb, and confused. Wasn't he supposed to help me? Couldn't he see that this was not my fault, that my partner had abandoned me, and that I was in no shape to do this alone?

"What are you waiting for? The winds are picking up and we need to get back to port. Get going!"

With every fiber in my being, I refocused and reenergized myself. Out of the corner of my eye, I saw the entire class staring at me from their safe little skiffs waiting to see what I would do. I reached up, grabbed hold of the bottom of the boat, and with a few strong kicks, I thrust myself up and over the skiff. Laying across the metal hull like a seal sunbathing on a rock, I drew in a few deep breaths still awaiting my rescue and hoping for help.

"Ok—Holli. Well done!" yelled the commandant. "Now, reach down and under the boat and bring down the mainsail. If you can't make it, you may have to get back in the water again. Give it a try! Hurry up!"

"This can't be happening! Is he nuts?" I thought to myself. I looked up and around. There were eleven sets of eyes upon me; one set from the coward who swam away. Slithering over to the starboard side of the skiff, I was able to reach down, feel for the tie to the mainsail and unhook it. I pulled it in and secured the rope in my hand. I returned to my beached position on top of the boat and then rested myself in the warmth of the momentary calm. I knew what lay ahead. The captain spoke.

"Ok, Holli! Get going; there's no time to waste! Right that boat!"

As I lay there, hearing his words, it all seemed surreal. I set out to take this class for fun, to learn, to better myself. I trusted in the rules of the game; I felt secure in the structure promised and in the safety provided. I had no idea that I would be alone, on top of a little skiff out in the ocean, shivering and quaking from the cold and from the wet clothes that stuck to my skin. I had no inkling that when things went wrong, I, alone, would have to make it right. The admiral gave another charge.

"Come on, Holli!! What's keeping you? Right that boat!!"

Mustering up every bit of energy and strength, I repositioned myself according to the captain's commands. With my fingers clenched to the starboard side of the boat, my feet on the hull, and my body crouched in a ball, I began to stretch upward while gingerly stepping backward to the port side. The boat started to turn, slowly. My arms shook with pain and I could barely hold on. My legs felt like soggy noodles giving way underneath the cold, the strain, and the weight.

"Right that boat!" A chant came from the eleven mouths.

Suddenly, the boat flipped! The mast, once again, was pointing to the heavens! It happened so fast that I was thrown back into the water again. When I surfaced, the rope to the mainsail was still in my hand. I was tethered to it so I pulled it over to me. The little boat bobbled as I gave one last kick to hoist myself into the comfort of its hull.

As I lay at the bottom of the boat, staring into the skies, I heard a noise in the distance, applause from my classmates. I felt the tears well up and the warm soothing drops run down my face. I, too, applauded myself. I had done something that I never thought possible. After all, I hadn't planned for it, nor had I anticipated it. And although, in the moment, I would have preferred that someone else do the work and that someone else make it right, it would not have served me well. It would not have served me at all.

Betrayal is like that. When our bodies, minds, and spirits are capsized, when they are turned upside down by a cyclone that blows us off course, and buries us, we have just one choice—to right ourselves. No one can do this for us; we must do this by ourselves and we must do this for ourselves. Understandably, it is our first inclination to think or feel that the betrayer owes us and that he/she/it will have to make it right for us. After all, it was they who wronged us! The more time we spend in this mind set, the longer we will delay our recovering. Think about the following implications of waiting for our betrayer to make it right for us.

First, recall for a moment what you felt or experienced if you asked and/or received what you needed from the person or thing that betrayed you. Although, there may be exceptions, it has been my experience as well as my clients' that one of several consequences takes place. When you ask for something, you risk additional rejection, denial, or dismissal. Remember, the betrayer does not see your perspective and/or value your position. Thus, we experience re-injury and/or prolonging the process of our recovery. Also, if you have been fortunate enough to get what was asked for, what work have you done on yourself? What changes did you make to avoid re-injury? What growth and healing came from the quick fix? Also, if you settle for less than you deserve or need, or what is healthy for you, what have you taught yourself and others about you? What we accept from others teaches others to treat us as such. Is this the message you really want to send?

Secondly, when we wait upon the actions of others or when we wait for our betrayer to right us, we hold ourselves hostage to their choices, to their time-lines, and to their lives. The time we have spent feeling betrayed has already stolen so much of ourselves. Why would we want to give away more of us? Part of getting through and beyond betrayal injury is having you make the choices, you determining the time-line, you making your life what you want it to be. Tethering yourself to uncertainty or to the whims of others will not allow you to move forward; it will not allow you to grow and to heal from betrayal.

This is your challenge right now—you must right yourself. You must be willing to do so. If your mind is saying, "But he did...but she needs to... but they owe....", say it one last time, and stop. It has not gotten you anywhere and it won't. It has not changed anything and it won't. If you need to, get your journal and write it down one final time. Finish with it.

Now, take your notebook, if you do not have it already. Write down these two phrases:

The work belongs to the betrayed—only the betrayed.

The work belongs to me—only to me.

Say it again. Say it aloud.

The work belongs to the betrayed—only the betrayed.

The work belongs to me—only to me.

Now, pause for a few minutes and relish in its truth. It is yours for the claiming. As I shared with you, righting that little boat by myself off the Santa Barbara coast on a gusty cold day was not what I thought was fair, or just, or worthy of its toll on me, but, looking back, I wouldn't have had it any other way. Being willing to right myself gave me the freedom to reclaim and redirect my course in life. It gave me the opportunity to grow while doing so. You can claim it too. Right yourself, and I will be right here alongside you bellowing your process from the recovering bullhorn!

Armed with knowledge

Another important piece of righting ourselves is the knowledge that we are right about what we know. Part of what I mean by this was covered in Chapter One – What Is Betrayal? However, I want to take what we learned about betrayal and put it into the context of our recovering process.

In Chapter One, we learned what betrayal is. We clearly defined and explained it:

1. An investment into someone or something met with rejection and/or abandonment

2. A profound trust in someone or something which is profoundly violated

3. A truth that becomes a lie / A belief that is shattered

We learned about how and when betrayal can happen. We looked at who and what can be involved. We came face to face with the different emotional, psychological, and physical symptoms that can manifest. We read stories and accounts of people whose lives had been ravaged by the destructive forces of betrayal. We were touched by their experiences because we could relate to them.

In our process of healing, it seems to be our nature to want to tell our stories and to find someone who would just listen or someone who would understand or at least be moved by our experience. We reach out to others because we are so hurt and vulnerable. Unfortunately, most of us do not get what we need because others do not know how to help. And, as we are learning, it is not their responsibility to do so. As we continue to repeat and revisit our stories, we push others away as their empathy turns to frustration. Their inability to give us what we need proves them as unworthy as we feel about ourselves. Loved ones begin to pull away and we begin to isolate. The cycle continues and we delay our recovering even longer.

In a previous chapter, I talked about a client who, after thirty years of marriage, was discarded by her husband to be with another woman who could finally meet his needs. My client's devastation was malignant, spreading throughout her body, mind, and spirit. She had an enormous need to tell and retell her story to anyone who would listen, and especially to her close family members. Although she was extremely loved and supported by her family, eventually they began to pull away from her. Even her grown children could no longer shoulder their mother's burden, and they too, distanced themselves from her, not just for their sanity but because their listening and consoling did not promote their mom's healing. Tragically, my client was additionally wounded by her children's withdrawal from her. She found herself alone and she found herself exhausted, wasting away her truth and her knowledge on to those who could not make it right for her.

Another trap that we seem to fall into is feeling that the more we can explain or justify our betrayal injury, the more we can right our position. This is futile; it wastes times and changes nothing. In the beginning of the book, I mentioned that your perception is your truth; however, it may not be someone else's truth. If you think that you can right yourself by trying to convince someone else of your truth (the way you perceived your betrayal experience) let alone expect him/her to understand the depth of injury, you will set yourself up for disappointment and lingering pain. The more we attempt to explain what we are feeling and why, the more we dilute our position and deplete our place of being. And over time, when we do not get the validation we need, we become more victimized.

Again, I remember the same client who continued to retell her story also moved into this phase of her injury especially when others tired of the place she was in. Time and time again, in her desperation to have others validate her perspective (her truth), she stated her case. Whether or not she received the response she needed, my client continued to argue her position which angered others and pushed them further away from her. Her grown children, who were supportive, were also hurting because they still loved their father. They began to distance themselves even more so. They were struggling to make things right for themselves and experienced firsthand that they could do nothing to make it right for their mom. For many sessions, my client sat across from me, broken from the betrayal and shattered from the silence of others. Although she continued to struggle, over time, she realized that her healing belonged to her. She was the only one who could make it right, and she was the only one who could affirm herself in the process.

Your betrayal experience belongs to you. You know your story. You have put a name and a face to your betrayal. You no longer need to tell and retell your story to make it truer. You know that what you feel is real. You no longer need to expend your inner resources explaining, defending, or justifying your pain. It is your truth and your knowledge. You, and you alone, must right yourself.

Right now, take a look back at Chapter One and the activities on p. 16. If you have not completed one of the activities, please do so now. If you have or after you have done so, on a new piece of paper, write down your betrayal experience and the definition/explanation that it falls under. If more than one applies, write down all that apply. When completed, write down the following statements:

My betrayal is real.

My betrayal is true.

I am right about what I know.

I am armed with knowledge.

Read it over again. Say it aloud. Say it loudly.

My betrayal is real.

My betrayal is true.

I am right about what I know.

I am armed with knowledge.

As you write, read, and absorb these new truths, you are continuing the righting process. Your capsized spirit is starting to turn. Hold on tightly as we continue the work.

Fortified with understanding

In addition to doing our own work and arming ourselves with knowledge, another piece of righting ourselves comes from fortifying ourselves with understanding. In Chapter Two – What We Are Feeling and Why, and in Chapter Three – How Long and To What Degree Will I Feel This Way and Why, we learned more about betrayal and its anatomy.

As we did with the previous section, we will take what we learned in those two chapters and apply it to our righting process.

When I was composing Chapter Two and explaining the states of being—confusion, worthless, and powerlessness—I recalled many clients who were buried beneath the rubble of those destructive emotions. In disclosing some of their stories, I was pulled back in time to a personal experience that relates to the purpose of our discussion—fortifying ourselves with understanding. It seems fitting to share it with you now.

For most of my teenage and young adult life, I struggled with frequent bouts of anxiety, irritability, and depression. It wasn't until my late twenties, after having married and giving birth to my daughter, that the occurrences seemed to escalate and intensify. Because there were days and sometimes weeks of normalcy, I believed I was simply losing my mind. I was going crazy. After a divorce and continued bouts of hysteria, my future husband became the recipient of my out-of-control behaviors. Anger turned to rage; depression turned to complete hopelessness /helplessness; and anxiety turned into irrationality. My supportive fiancé continued to encourage me to seek out help, to find out what was wrong, and to get some relief from the turmoil within. I was reluctant because I was afraid no one would know what was wrong and no one would understand.

In the fall of 1985, I was teaching at a middle school. Through a series of conversations with a dear teacher friend about her daughter's health issues (which paralleled mine), I felt safe enough to share what was happening with me. My friend immediately gave me the name and number of a respected and progressive Ob-Gyn in our town. With some hesitation, I made the call to the doctor's office. Because he was heavily booked, I agreed to meet with his Physician's Assistant—Mary—who was experienced and knowledgeable.

A few days later, I sat in the examination room waiting for Mary. I felt alone. I felt cold. I felt frightened. Doubtful thoughts raced through my mind. What if she doesn't know what is wrong? What if I am crazy? What if she cannot help me?

When Mary entered the room, she smiled and introduced herself. She sat down and began taking a long history: background, symptoms (duration, frequency, severity) diet, exercise, sleep patterns, stressors, medications; in other words, an overall health and lifestyle assessment. We talked for over an hour. Mary asked questions and described what she thought I might be feeling and experiencing. For the first time in years, I began to hope. I no longer felt alone or frightened. Mary could paint a portrait in words of what was etched on my mind, body, and spirit. Mary understood and she proceeded to help me to understand.

"Holli, I believe you have Premenstrual Syndrome (PMS); in fact, I think you have a severe case. I need to do some blood work to rule out other possibilities, but from all that you have shared, I am confident this is the underlying disorder. Dr. Francis and I believe in addressing this with a natural treatment approach requiring you to make some drastic lifestyle changes. It will take hard work and commitment on your part, but we have seen excellent results with this treatment plan.

Mary saw the relief and release on my face. Tears were streaming down my cheeks. She continued, "Holli, you are not crazy, although I know you felt like you were. This disorder is crazy-making! There is hope and healing and with time and consistent work, you will feel better and better."

As Mary continued to map out my lifestyle regimen for the next three months, I listened and I learned. Leaving the office that day with all my instructions, reading materials, and other recovery to do's, I knew I had a great deal of work ahead of me. I knew I had to make this right. Most importantly, I understood my pain and someone else understood it. And because of that, I felt fortified.

Because so many of us have carried around our betrayal injuries for extended periods of time and because their devastating effects have wreaked havoc in our lives for so long, it is human nature to feel that no one else understands. This is simply not true. Nor is it true that if our betrayal injury is from a recent experience then we must endure this alone and that no one else can relate to and normalize what we feel. Recall for a moment what we came to know in Chapters Two and Three. (At this point, I want to encourage you, if you have not done so already, to complete the activities in Chapters Two and Three. And, if you have, briefly look back at your notes for both chapters and the activities.)

In Chapter Two, we learned about the states of being—confusion, worthlessness, and powerlessness. We know how difficult those states can be, how we often get stuck in them, how debilitating the presenting symptoms are, and how we must claim new truths in order to begin our recovering. In Chapter Three, we also learned that the degree of injury from betrayal is directly proportional to the degree of investment, trust, or belief in someone and/or something. We know that the degree of injury is also connected to our degree of exposure to the betrayer/ betrayal environment. Most importantly, through the vignettes of clients, we know that many others have thought, felt, and behaved in the same ways that we have. Others understand what we have been through, what we have endured, ways we have tried to cope, and how alone we have felt in the process.

However, just as it was with the illness that ravaged my life, it is your responsibility to embrace what you now know and use it to move yourself forward. It is your work to claim that understanding and to continue to right yourself.

Grab your notebook or journal. Write down the following truths.

Understanding betrayal injury normalizes my experience.

Understanding betrayal injury comforts my spirit.

I am fortified with understanding.

When finished, read over these truths again. Say them aloud.

Understanding betrayal injury normalizes my experience.

Understanding betrayal injury comforts my spirit.

I am fortified with understanding.

Avoid allowing old thought patterns to rob you of this opportunity, to cause doubt or disbelief. Replace them now, fortify yourself now, and continue to bring that capsized spirit to its rightful position.

Validated with truth

As we conclude our discussion on righting ourselves, we will add one last but crucial piece—validated with truth. We know that our work belongs to us and only us, we know that we are armed with knowledge, we know that we are fortified with understanding; now, we must act upon that. We must do so in two important ways.

First, in choosing to do the recovering work, we are not just saying that we are changing our lives, we *are* changing our lives. It doesn't matter how much we talk about it or even think about it, if we don't act upon it, our greatest intent means nothing. How many people do you know who have said things such as:

"I just read about a great diet! I may try it out."

"I'm thinking about joining the gym. Maybe I can get back into shape!"

"I've been attending that support group for several weeks. It is interesting, but I don't think it applies to me. I'll give it a few more times and see if it does."

"Oh, I've tried that and it doesn't work. Maybe you will have better luck!"

Although there could be some exceptions, when I hear these words, I believe people are not taking responsibility for their lives, invalidating the place that they are in and thus, remaining stuck in their respective issues. And in many cases, when little or no change takes places, people become bitter, resentful, and cynical. They start blaming others and embracing the role of eternal victims.

On the other hand, when we take action we send ourselves a message of reinforcement. As we work our recovering step by step, as we pace ourselves and manage our changes, and as we begin to feel the healing take place, we are stronger and intrinsically refueled to continue our work. Because we are doing the work, we are validated. And because we are attending to our betrayal injury, we are honoring our truth. In short, our actions speak louder than our words. Our actions speak for us, through us, and in us.

Secondly, by acting on our recovering (by validating our truth), we strengthen ourselves against some real and possible forces: external and internal pressures. No matter how hard or how much we are working on our recovering, relapse can and does happen. A part of any credible recovery program includes relapse prevention where we learn strategies to assist each of us from falling back into unhealthy thinking and/or behavioral patterns. Although I will address relapse prevention throughout the recovering chapters, for now, it is important to talk about it with reference to where we are in our recovering process.

When we first begin our recovering work, we are most susceptible to relapse. Perhaps others doubt us. They doubt that we can and will change. Sadly, some people relish in the fact that we are stuck and we are not able to fully enjoy our lives. Thus, we lack in the healthy support that we need. Still, others challenge what we are doing. Negative comments and attacks are thrown our way. Disbelief and dismay at our new-found hope are tossed in our direction. These external forces are difficult to manage.

The PMS diagnosis that I received in the mid 1980s exemplifies my point. During this time period, not only was PMS basically categorized as a joke for almost everyone at the time (something females made up to excuse or justify angry or moody behavior), but it was frequently misdiagnosed and undertreated. Even after my diagnosis, recovering work, and publishing of a book on the issue, still I was told that I was suffering from a myriad of disorders including bipolar. One person even told me I was demon-possessed!

What I did was hold on to my truth, continue my recovering work, and remain validated by it. Yes, I experienced relapses but each one was less lengthy and less severe than the previous one. Each time, I picked myself up and continued my work. Each time, I embraced what I knew, refocused and re-energized myself, and thus reinforced the righting of myself.

In addition to the external pressures, sometimes we succumb to our internal negative tapes or thought patterns. We doubt ourselves. We doubt what we are doing or aren't doing. The recovering is hard and it is not producing the drastic changes we thought. There are days where we feel much relief; others where there is less. We think it would be easier to just go back and do what we were doing before. When we begin to believe that lie, we start to negate our truth and we start to position ourselves for relapse.

I know this place all too well. Because I had suffered so long with PMS, the negative internal dialogue was intense. No one else needed to beat me up; I did an excellent job of it. Many times, I used this destructive self-talk to justify giving up. And at times, I did just that, only to rediscover that the pain of the disorder was more difficult to bear than the challenge of the healing myself.

Again, we will address internal sabotaging more thoroughly throughout our recovering chapters, but for now, be aware of it. For now, know that when you are least likely to feel like acting upon recovering is when you must persevere. Know that you just need to take one day at a time, one step at a time. Know that each time you take even one small action and you press on, you are taking responsibility for righting yourself.

Let's continue to validate our truth and to take action. Let's do that now. Grab your notebook or journal, and write down the following statements:

Read each aloud as you copy it.

I choose to take action on my recovering.

I am refueled by my actions.

I am validated with truth.

Read it again. Say it slowly and steadily.

I choose to take action on my recovering

I am refueled by my actions.

I am validated with truth.

Claim it now. It is yours! Invest every bit of strength and stamina to right your-self. As you do, the internal mast of wellness will surface and point towards the heavens. You are on your way.

Activities – Chapter 7

Activity #1 is optional but strongly recommended.
Do either #2 or #3.
Do #4.

1. We have learned that telling and retelling our betrayal story to others does not right us and, over time, it pushes others away from us. In previous chapters, we have written about our betrayal experiences, but we have done so piece-by-piece in order to understand it better. If you feel you want or need to revisit your experience in its entirety, please do so now. Write your story out one last time. Do this for yourself, for no one else. Write as much or as little as you want, but write what you need to, and in the way that you need to. Take as much time as you need and let all emotions flow freely. Do not hold back anything. When you are done, put the story away in a safe, comfortable place. Or, if you prefer, dispose of it in a way that is healing and healthy.

2. Throughout *Part One: Right Yourself*, we were introduced to and embraced four righting statements:

   - The work belongs to me—only to me.
   - I am armed with knowledge.
   - I am fortified with understanding.
   - I am validated with truth.

Write down each of these righting statements again. Below each one, write freely what each one means to you and how it is helping you to right yourself.

Take your time. Read and reread what you have written.

3. After reading *Part One: Right Yourself*, we acknowledged and claimed four righting statements:

   - The work belongs to me—only to me.
   - I am armed with knowledge.
   - I am fortified with understanding.
   - I am validated with truth.

In one paragraph, write freely about how you thought, felt, and what you did in your past to right your betrayal injury. In a second paragraph, write freely about what these four righting statements have taught you and how they have changed you. Take your time. Read and reread what you have written when you are done.

4. After reflecting upon the contents of this chapter, commit to at least two righting actions (thinking and/or behavior patterns) for each righting statement. Jot them down in your notebook or journal and start working on them today. Do not delay!

Example:

- Righting statement: Armed with knowledge.
- Action: I commit to keeping my betrayal story private.
- Action: I commit to honoring my truth each day (not expecting others to do so).

End of Chapter – Healing Continuum

After completing the reading of *Part One: Right Yourself* and completing the activities, reassess your current reality on the healing continuum on p. 65. Then pace yourself accordingly:

0	1	2	3	4	5	6	7	8	9	10

Score	Next Actions for You
0–3	Reread Chapters One through Three and rework the exercises within and at the end of each chapter. Then, reassess your levels before moving on.
4 - 7	Reread Part One again. Rework the exercises. Then reassess your levels before moving on.
8 - 10	Move on to Part Two!

Fig. 7-2: Right Yourself—Next Actions after Reassessment

8 Recovering Part Two: Readiness and Rigor

"Courage consists of the power of self-recovery."

—Ralph Waldo Emerson

Part One Right Yourself	Part Two Readiness and Rigor
1 2 3 4 5 6 7 **8 9** 10	1 2 3 4 5 6 7 8 9 10

Before we begin *Part Two: Readiness and Rigor*, assess where you are on the healing continuum. Shade in the numbered box that best describes your current reality. Then, read on.

0	1	2	3	4	5	6	7	8	9	10

Score	How Do I Feel Right Now?
0-3	I am not functioning well on a daily basis and I probably need to see my doctor and/or a therapist. Friends and family have expressed their concern for me; others are worried about me as well. I feel depressed and angry. I don't have anyone who can really deal with what I am going through or anyone who is there to fully support me in what I am feeling. I want to get past this, but I don't have the motivation to do so.
4-7	Although I am still deeply wounded from my betrayal, I am taking steps to take care of myself. I am eating better and exercising again, and I am returning to some of my every day activities. I am learning how to trust in a few close friends and I am staying away from unhealthy people and places. I want to feel better and I am working my healing plan. I want to do more, but I am not sure how to proceed.

| 8-10 | Although I have good days and bad days, the good outweigh the bad. I take each day, one day at a time. I am committed to working my recovering plan. I have a small support system and I am learning to trust more fully. I am ready to call on a professional if I need further support. Each day, I feel stronger, more confident, and better equipped to tackle the work ahead of me. |

Fig. 8-1: Readiness and Rigor—Healing Continuum

Keeping a pulse on your place and position

As we continue our conversation about our recovering, I want to spend some time discussing your readiness and your rigor. Doing so will play an important part in caring for and pacing yourself throughout the recovering process. I can't stress enough how important it is that you are brutally honest with yourself, and if needed, you consider seeking an objective perspective from a professional. Of course, we want to move along in our recovering. We want to experience the relief and release that we are longing for; however, we do not want to overlook our overall mental and physical well-being in the process. Part of what I have to say may or may not apply to each of you, and/or part of what I have to say may apply to you at different times throughout our recovering. Whatever the level of impact may be, it is important to implement the practice of keeping a pulse on your place and position in order to ensure the best recovering experience possible.

Keeping a pulse on your place means a number of things:

- How are you feeling emotionally right now?
- How are you feeling physically?
- How are you responding to people and things?
- Are your coping mechanisms unhealthy or destructive?
- Are you able to maintain a consistent level of stability in your daily life?
- Have people who care about you expressed a concern for your well-being?

Many of my clients, who were struggling with betrayal injury, were having difficulty functioning in their daily lives. Some clients came in to therapy presenting with some of the following disorders:

- Depression and other Mood Disorders
- Anxiety Disorders (Post Traumatic Stress Disorder; Compulsive Disorders)
- Substance-Related Disorders: abuse and dependence
- Eating Disorders
- Chronic illnesses

A number of clients who come to mind were reeling from a Major Depressive Episode when they entered therapy. Although their betrayal experience appeared to precipitate the onset, it was imperative to assess, intervene, and address the depression first. Other clients presented with Dysthymic Disorder, a low-level, long-standing form of depression. Their betrayal injury worsened and/or intensified their level of depression and thus interfered with their ability to function. This, too, needed to be addressed first. A number of clients who struggled with issues of addiction and/or other compulsive disorders found themselves re-engaging in unhealthy behaviors after their betrayal injury. These disorders, as well, needed tending to before and during their recovering process.

Earlier in the book, I referred to a client who had experienced tremendous betrayal throughout her entire life. When she came in to therapy to work through her marital issues, she informed me that she suffered with Bulimia. She had been through therapy for the Bulimia and worked consistently on this issue. As we worked together, we both kept a pulse on her level of ego strength and stamina. The triggers, which often ignited Bulimic episodes, were quite sensitive and needed tending to. At times, we would need to lessen the intensity of our work; other times, we were able to move through more difficult territory. My client kept a pulse on her place and we moved along accordingly.

I am asking you to do the same. You are the one who truly knows what you are feeling and how you are feeling. If you or others are concerned about your daily level of functioning, I must recommend that you seek out professional support. Or, while we are doing the recovering work, at any time if you feel that you do not have the emotional or physical well-being to do the work, you must seek out professional help. There is no shame in doing so; there is great risk in not doing so.

Many of you who are reading this have continued to function in your daily lives, but you are deeply hurt and wounded. I ask you as well to keep a pulse on your place. Each of you has your own levels of energy, stamina, and strength—emotionally and physically. Each of you is triggered at different times and in unique ways. You know how much you can take in and how much you can give out. The recovering process is hard work. We want to give it our best and we want to be at our best each and every step along the way. If needed, please do not hesitate to seek out professional support and guidance.

Let's take a look at the second part of keeping a pulse on your place and position. Keeping a pulse on your position means a number of things:

- How healthy is the environment in which you live, work, socialize?

- With regards to the betrayer and/or the betrayal environment:

  1. How often and/or to what degree are you in their presence or vicinity?

  2. Is there an ongoing relationship or connection which can or cannot be avoided?

  3. Are there reminders and/or triggers that you are exposed to?

Just as with keeping a pulse on your place, you must also keep a pulse on your position—where you are in reference to or connection with your betrayer and/or your betrayal environment. This is an effective practice no matter where you are in your recovering process. However, it is especially important in the initial stages of our work. We often become more sensitive and reactive to our surroundings. We may find that our tolerance levels are not what they normally are. Maintaining a pulse on your position will help you to implement self–care measures.

As I have mentioned, a large part of my practice was devoted to trauma/abuse recovery (especially sexual abuse recovery). Tragically, many of my clients had to remain in the vicinity of the betrayer and/or the betrayal environment. Part of our work together always encompassed keeping a pulse on their levels of exposure while sensitively attending to their triggers, addressing re-injuries, and maintaining protective measures.

One of my clients, whom I mentioned in a previous chapter, was sexually abused by her older brother. Even after she was a grown woman, married, and a mother of small children, she was forced to come into contact with her betrayer. After being released from prison, her brother would show up, unannounced, at family gatherings. To make matters worse, other family members would excuse his evil behaviors and welcome him back into the family. Clearly, my client's family environment was not safe. Her brother's presence easily and understandably re-triggered her betrayal injury. Keeping a pulse on her position was a critical piece of recovering.

Keeping a pulse on your place and position helps you to move forward at the pace and within the parameters that are healthy for you. To check that pulse, ask yourself these questions:

- How am I feeling?
- What am I feeling?
- Why am I feeling this way?
- Are these feelings affecting my ability to perform on a daily basis? If so, how?
- Do I need professional support?

Respond to these questions now and continue to do so throughout your work.

Whether professional intervention is needed or if it is not, make it a practice to attend to your readiness by implementing the following self-care behaviors:

1. Pace your reading and activities. Do not rush through them.

2. Choose a block of time to do your reading and activities that is free from responsibilities or pressures.

3. Choose a place (bedroom, office, patio, or outdoor area) that is safe and one that is free from the influence of your betrayal experience.

4. Allow enough time after your work for processing and reflection. Practice one or more of these self-soothing behaviors:

   - A quiet walk, yoga, or another form of relaxing exercise, meditation or prayer.
   - A warm bath or shower.
   - A nap or resting in a comfortable chair.
   - A cup of tea or herbal drink.
   - Other healthy behaviors that help to calm your emotions.

Commit to keeping a pulse on your place and position and commit to implementing these self-care tools. Ready yourself and maintain that readiness throughout our recovering work.

Protecting yourself / Building a support network

When we are recovering, it is important to take steps to protect ourselves. At the same time, it is also extremely helpful to develop a support network. By doing so, we are better prepared to embrace the continuing work ahead of us.

When we are injured through betrayal, our emotions remain raw and our spirits are sensitive. We continue to feel quite vulnerable and we are usually easily triggered. And although we know that it is our work to right ourselves, it is additionally injurious when other people do not agree with, understand, and/or support us in our betrayal recovering. Obviously, we can't block out the world around us, but we can take steps to protect ourselves and build a support network.

1. **Keep your circle of confidence small.** You do not need to tell everyone about your recovering work. If you feel like sharing it, carefully select those persons whom you trust and with whom you feel safe.

2. **Carefully consider who is worthy of your trust.** As you think about your family and friends, determine who, if anybody, can be trusted. Although you may be very close to someone, he/she may not be the most trustworthy. During this recovering period, it is important to be able to share your feelings with someone who will keep those confidences private. Spend some time on this; don't rush your decision.

3. **Plan how much information you want or need to share.** Know ahead of time, what you want or need from your confident. I encourage you to share just what you need to. Sometimes, we tend to give away too much of ourselves. Also, tell your trusted person what you need from him/her: to listen, to help you with something, to encourage, and so on.

4. **If there is no family member or friend to whom you can turn, consider the following sources:**

   - A professional counselor or therapist.
   - A leader in a faith position: rabbi, priest, pastor, person on staff.
   - A small group you know well (faith-based, support, recovery, study).
   - A mentor or role model (someone you trust and respect).

5. **Distance yourself from toxic and/or negative people.** We will discuss boundary setting in Part Three; however, for now, it is important to remove yourself as much as you possibly can from unhealthy people (those by whom you feel easily re-injured and/or people who hinder your recovering in any way). If you cannot remove yourself from their presence, at the very least, keep your contact to a minimum.

6. **Take some time for yourself.** Sometimes, we just don't feel like saying much to anyone and that is perfectly ok! When I don't want to commit to someone, be somewhere, or do something because I am in a place of recovering, I simply say,

"I am taking some time for myself."

That is all you need to say. You do not need to explain or justify it. Just say it. Remember, protecting yourself during your recovering is paramount. This is your work and no one can do this for you. It is my hope that there will be someone on the sidelines to cheer you on and to support you. If so, choose wisely and carefully. If not, protect yourself. That, in itself, will provide more support than you know.

Embracing the work ahead of you

If you have read this far and worked on the activities provided, you already have been embracing your recovering. You have been unearthing the layers of betrayal injury: learning about, acknowledging, understanding, and validating your experience. Participating in the cognitive exercises, you have been restructuring your thoughts and healing your feelings which accompany them. This is definitely hard work!

As we continue our conversation on recovering, we will implement more behavioral tools in addition to healing our thought patterns. As we invest more and more of ourselves into our recovering program, we know how important it is to pay attention to our readiness by keeping a pulse on our position and place as well as protecting ourselves and building a support network. It is equally important to maintain a healthy level of strength and stamina to modulate our levels of rigor.

Learning a few strategies to assist you in embracing the work ahead will make your betrayal recovering more manageable.

1. **Know yourself—customize your recovering plan.** You know yourself best. You know your level of energy and your commitments. You know how much you can give out and how much you can take in. Do not compare your recovering plan to anyone else. Customize it to fit your needs.

2. **Set time/s and days to do your reading and exercises.** Build your recovering into your routine. I recommend that you set time/s and days in advance with a goal of working specifically on your recovering exercises at least 3-4 times a week. Space them out over the week.

3. **Review your schedule weekly.** Once a week, look over your schedule for the following week. Do not wait for the week to sneak up on you! Make any adjustments in your recovering schedule as needed.

4. **Maintain a daily motivational journal or chart.** This is a very concise way to check your level of rigor and validate yourself in the process. On a piece of paper, make two columns:

What I worked on today	How I am feeling
:	:
.	.

Write down just a few words at the end of each day. At the end of the week, review your progress. It is common to have good days and not-so-good days! Pride yourself on the good days!

5. **Schedule downtime.** Make sure that you have some days/nights where you have nothing scheduled except some down time. Use this time to relax in healthy ways.

6. **Give yourself permission.** If you have a setback, give yourself permission to let go of it. Don't beat yourself up. It wastes time and it wastes away your strength and stamina.

7. **Heal one day at a time.** You probably have heard this statement before. We use it in recovering because it makes sense and it works. Adopt this mindset. Persevere; don't give up; do so one day at a time. Each day will bring you a new opportunity to embrace the work ahead of you.

Breaking through the bonds of betrayal requires that we accept responsibility for righting ourselves and for maintaining healthy, balanced levels of readiness and rigor. Let's continue to move forward by implementing additional tools that will condition us to be in the best recovering shape possible. Let's continue our work!

Activities – Chapter 8

You are to work on all three activities for at least one week. For each activity, commit to the action steps outlined for you.

Take a new piece of paper and label it "Action Plan".

1. **Keeping a pulse on your position and place.** Look over the six self-care behaviors beginning on p. 81. Make a decision right now about the following:

    * When is a good block of time to do your reading and exercises?
    * Where is a safe place to do your work?
    * Choose at least 2-3 self-soothing behaviors to implement after your work.

    Write down your responses.

2. **Protecting yourself / building a support network.** Look over the six self-care behaviors starting on p. 81. Choose at least four to implement. Do more if you need to.

    Write them down on your action plan.

3. **Embracing the work ahead of you.** Review the seven exercises starting on p. 82. I strongly recommend doing exercises # 1-3. Purchase a small personal calendar, BlackBerry™, or iPhone™.

    Get your recovery schedule set and maintain it. This is extremely important!

    For exercises #4-7, choose at least two that meet your needs and implement them into your schedule. Write these down on your calendar. If you choose exercise #4, write this down in a small private notebook or something that is easily accessible.

End of Chapter—Healing Continuum

After reading *Part Two: Readiness and Rigor* and implementing the activities into your recovering plan which work best for you (for a minimum of one week), reassess your current reality on the healing continuum on p. 77. Then, pace yourself and proceed accordingly:

0	1	2	3	4	5	6	7	8	9	10

Score	Next Actions to Take
0-3	I strongly urge you to strengthen yourself in several ways: • See your medical doctor. There may be need for further evaluation, assessment and/or medication. • See a counselor or a therapist. There may be other issues that need attention and/or intervention. • With either of the above, get a referral for an appropriate support or a Twelve -Step recovery group.
4-7	After selecting your activities on p. 84, implement them into your recovering plan. Work on these strategies for two to three weeks. I strongly encourage you to work on exercise #2—building a support network/ protecting yourself. Also, just to be on the safe side, please consider talking to a professional regarding your level of functioning (how you are feeling and performing on a daily basis). After 2-3 weeks of working your program, reassess your levels before moving on.
8-10	You are in a strong healing place. Move ahead.

Fig. 8-2: Readiness and Rigor—Next Actions after Reassessment

9 Recovering Part Three: Revive and Restore

"Learn to get in touch with the silence within yourself, and know that everything has a purpose."

—Elizabeth Kübler-Ross

Part One	Part Two	Part Three
Right Yourself	Readiness and Rigor	Revive and Restore: Mind. Body, and Spirit
1 2 3 4 5 6 7 8 9 10	1 2 3 4 5 6 7 8 9 10	1 2 3 4 5 6 7 8 9 10

Now that you have embraced the concept of righting yourself and you have attended to your levels of readiness and rigor, we can implement additional recovering tools and strategies. Because we are each unique in our betrayal experiences, there will be some interventions that may be more relevant and beneficial for you than others. Although I have arranged the sequence of healing activities in the order that I feel is most effective, you may need to tailor it to accommodate your individual needs. As you read through each subsection, be selective. Choose one or two tools at a time that apply to your injury and blend those into your daily recovering program. Once you feel confident in the healing of a particular area of injury, add another recovering strategy. Implementing too many tools at once will overwhelm you.

As we begin this section of recovering, I am reminded of a tragedy that my sister and her family faced many years ago. My sister along with her husband, son, daughter, and thousands of other fans, was getting ready to enjoy a baseball game in San Francisco when suddenly they felt the thunderous rolling and shaking of the stadium. It was 5:04 PM, October 17th, 1989, and an earthquake struck in the Santa Cruz Mountains. The epicenter was Loma Prieta, just ten miles from my sister's house. Everyone was evacuated. My sister and her family slowly and gingerly made their way home. There were tiresome hours of detours, roadblocks, and careful navigation around the remnants of structures. Finally, well after mid-night, they arrived home, or what was left of it. Their magnificent mountain refuge had been shaken off its foundation, raised up fifteen inches, pivoted eighteen degrees, and dropped. Its stunning multi-level decks, staircases, and windows lay entangled together in a massive web. With the car's headlights shining on their monument of memories, the family sat in shock and dismay, and then, drove away.

When my sister and her family were able to return and retrieve what they could, and when it was safe to do so, they were amazed at what they saw. In the center of their maze-like home stood a large marble fireplace soaring at least seventeen feet in height. Amidst the ruination and rubble, this tower of strength remained—a testament to its tenacity and its endurance. Although further geological assessments had to be done, my sister and her husband decided they would rebuild with whatever improvements, fortifications, and supports were needed; this would remain their home.

Amidst the brokenness of your betrayal, your core—your inner statue of strength—has brought you this far. In this section of our recovering, we will continue our rebuilding: cleansing and cultivating our internal and external spaces, bracing ourselves with supportive structures, and fortifying our inner towers. Let's forge on as we unearth the internal layers and excavate the external layers of betrayal injury to revive and to restore mind, body, and spirit.

Because *Part Three: Revive and Restore—Mind, Body, and Spirit* is a lengthy recovering chapter, you will assess where you are on the healing continuum in three different sub-sections: *Cleansing and Cultivation of Internal and External Spaces*; *Boundary Work, Bracing Yourself with Supportive Structures*; and *Fortifying Your Inner Tower*. Let's begin by assessing your levels of internal and external wellness. Shade in the space that best describes your current reality. Then, move on.

Subsection One: Cleansing and Cultivation of Internal and External Spaces

0	1	2	3	4	5	6	7	8	9	10

Score	How Do I Feel Right Now?
0-3	I don't respect myself at all, and my words and actions reflect that low level of respect. I say and do things that continue to reinjure me and I regret it later. My betrayal is still defining me. I feel that what I have to say doesn't matter. I still feel like I don't matter. I talk about my betrayal too much and to anyone who will listen. At times, I feel like a loose cannon. I feel immobilized by my surroundings. There are so many memories and reminders of my betrayer and/or betrayal environment. I don't know where to start or what to do.
4-7	I am doing better by reclaiming my self-respect a little at a time. I am implementing self-respecting behaviors. I also have stopped blabbing so much about my betrayal. I am learning whom to trust and I don't feel like I am burdening others with what I have to say. I've started to do some cleaning out of external reminders/triggers of my betrayal. At times, I get stuck and don't know what to do. Then, there are unexpected triggers that really set me off. I get frightened, scared, and even a little depressed. But, I continue to make progress.
8-10	I am feeling a level of respect that is freeing and restoring. My thoughts and actions reflect a healthy level of self-respect. When, and if, I speak of my betrayal experience, I do so with dignity and grace. I also value my position, perspective, and truth by implementing healthy guidelines and boundaries. I am taking care of myself externally by cleaning out reminders/triggers of my betrayal. Those items which remain nurture and comfort me. Items which I cannot change or control, I am learning to deal with in healthy ways.

Fig. 9-1: Subsection One—Healing Continuum

Cleansing and Cultivation of Internal Spaces

Respecting yourself and your choices

Our inner core is our center. It holds us together, much like the marble fireplace in my sister's home. When we are injured from betrayal, our internal tower is disrespected, and thus, it is weakened. In order to revive and restore our spirit to its rightful place, we must treat it with great care; we must cherish it and tend to its condition. In order to accomplish that, our first internal restoration requires that we give respect back to ourselves. What does that mean? How will you know if you are practicing this? Ask yourself these questions:

- Do you treat yourself with respect (emotionally, spiritually, physically)? If so, how? If not, describe that as well.

- Do your actions/behaviors reflect a healthy level of self-respect? If so, how? If not, describe what is going on.

No matter what we currently are or are not doing in this area of cleansing and cultivation, there is always room for growth and for work. Let's take a look at some specific strategies which will enable us to tend to our inner core, our foundational spirit and being. Some of you may be attending to these practices already. Others may need to start implementing them or to brush up on them.

1. Respect your recovering work

Make your recovering work a priority. Continue with your recovering calendar, schedule, and plan. Make changes and adjustments as needed.

Consider complementing your recovering plan by engaging in additional support venues. Many of my clients also attended various recovery and support groups. Witnessing others working through similar issues, my clients felt validated and affirmed in their own work.

2. Respect your spiritual work

Make sure you are attending to your spiritual needs. Many of us tend to fall away from the practices that bring us comfort when we have been betrayed. Many of us feel our higher power has not heard us or been there for us. Reassess your position and place in this arena and consider moving back towards the process that speaks to you.

One of my clients stepped away from singing in the choir, a favorite pastime that ministered to him in many areas of his life. He felt he needed some space and time for healing. When he returned, he realized how much he missed his church family and fellowship.

3. Respect your emotional needs

Although there may be trust issues that need addressing, take care of emotional needs that feel safe for you. Consider reengaging in activities that you enjoy and/or with people whom you can be comfortable.

One of my clients who had experienced tremendous betrayals all throughout her life found great solace in the sport of rock climbing. Although she was hesitant to return to her team after a lengthy time away, she felt reenergized and renewed by reconnecting with a sport that not only met her needs for solitude but one that also challenged her to re-engage with a small trusting group of friends.

4. Respect your physical well-being

How well we treat and take care of our bodies is a direct reflection of how little or how much we respect ourselves. We have discussed how easy it is to resort to unhealthy behaviors in order to soothe the wounds of betrayal. Continue to keep your pulse on this and continue to take steps towards wellness in the arenas that challenge you.

5. Respect your choices

Carefully guard against seeking out multiple sources of external input and/or validation of your choices. This can be confusing and disorienting. It is important that once you make your decisions, or your choices regarding your well-being, that you take the mindset of respecting your position. It doesn't mean that you are always right; it means that you are willing to believe in yourself and in your journey.

When my sister and her husband decided to rebuild on the same land, where they had lost their home, many people discouraged them; others were supportive but wary. My sister and her family moved ahead with their plans, trusting in their informed decision and believing in their process.

We must take charge of cleansing and replenishing our inner space. Each time we give respect to ourselves, we break down the betrayal bond of disrespect imposed upon us by our betrayer. Each time we practice self-respect, we reinstate our worth and value, and we actively take charge of our own restoration. To further our internal cleansing and cultivation, we also want our voice to serve us well by representing our healthy, balanced, and respected core. Let's take the next step. Let's find our voice, dust it off, and display its polished presence.

Finding our voice

Our voice represents who we are. It is a mirror that reflects our inner-core: our emotions, thoughts, feelings, dreams, beliefs, purposes. Each and every persona we take on is displayed once we voice the words that accompany that role. It is much like the smoke released from a fireplace. Its color gives away its content; its formation gives away its character.

For some of us, injury from betrayal dampens our voice and our spirits are weakened from the devastation. For others our voice is silenced; our spirits are demolished amidst foreign repositioning. We must resurrect that voice, and we must revive and restore its content and character. Doing so will not only heal our inner spirit, but it will mirror to the world the reflection of a strong, valuable, and worthy being.

In tackling this second internal cleansing and cultivation—finding your voice—you want to accomplish two goals:

- Continue to honor and value your betrayal experience with dignity and grace.
- Continue to honor and value your position, perspective, and truth with healthy guidelines and boundaries.

Let's take a look at the first goal.

- **Continue to honor and value your betrayal experience with dignity and grace.**

How, when, where, and to what degree we speak of our betrayal experience is a reflection of our inner well-being. Reviving and restoring our voice will mean that we learn new ways to validate our feelings while disclosing our experience in healthy ways.

Read over the following exercises and choose one or more to complete.

1.   **Write a letter to yourself.** This letter must contain the response, answer, solution, reflection, etc. that you wish you had received from your betrayer and/or betrayal environment. What are the words that you so desperately long to hear from him/her/it/them? Include any and all emotions that you want to have expressed to you. Throughout and at the conclusion of the letter, affirm and validate your voice. Tell yourself that what you have to say matters. Tell yourself that you matter. Speak to you injured spirit, and let it hear its value and importance. Do not write this letter in anger or in resentment. Write this with a gentle, consoling, and empathic tone. Allow your outer voice to heal your inner voice. Take your time and make sure you say everything you need to say.

     When you are done, read over your letter. Read it aloud. Reread it as many times as you need to, whenever you need to. Reread this until you feel and know that your voice did and does matter. Give it time. Let yourself believe its truth.

2.   **Make a tape for yourself.** Follow the same instructions as for exercise #1. However, for this exercise, speak what you need to hear. Record in on a tape. As with the letter, it is important that you are not feeling angry or bitter during the exercise. Make sure you are in a calm, nurturing state when you do this.

     When you are finished with the tape, go back and listen to your voice. Listen to your tape as many times as you need to, whenever you need to. Allow time for your mind and spirit to take in what you need to hear and what you deserve to hear. Each time you listen, claim the value and importance of your voice.

3.   **Make a set of cards to honor your voice.** Buy or make yourself five to ten 3x5" cards. On each card, write a healing and valuing statement about your voice,

your words, and your spirit. For example:

- My words matter—I matter.
- What I have to say is important—I am important.
- My voice is valued—I am valued.
- I value my opinion, my perspective, and my truth. I value myself.
- I choose to honor my spirit and the words reflected by it. I honor myself.

When you have completed the cards, take one card and place it where you will see it each day (bathroom mirror, desk, etc.). Read it, say it aloud and reflect upon it for several moments. Do this each day for as many days as needed. Do not remove or change the card until you have internalized this truth. You must claim it and you must believe it. Repeat the process until you have finished with all the cards. Take your time; do not rush this. Allow your mind and spirit to soak in what it needs—to be heard and honored.

For all three of these exercises, repeat or revisit them if and when you doubt the importance of your voice. There is no weakness in needing to do so; there is regret in not doing so. When you are ready, move on to your second goal.

Let's take a look back at our second goal.

- **Continue to honor and value your position, perspective, and truth with healthy guidelines and boundaries.**

Many times our voice is lost because we are not as selective and discerning as we need to be in our disclosures. We must value the content of what we have to say. We must respect the way we deliver it and to whom we deliver it. In order to find our voice and reinstate its worth, we must honor our position, perspective, and truth with healthy guidelines and boundaries. Read over the following exercises and choose to implement those which fit into your recovering plan.

1. **Schedule time for your voice.** This type of exercise may sound a little strange at first, but it is quite effective. Schedule a set time during the day (I recommend in the evening) to think about your betrayal. Also, set an amount of time (10-15 minutes). Stop everything else and go to a safe, quiet place. During this set period of time, allow yourself to say whatever you need to say and however you need to say it, about your betrayer/betrayal. Get out every emotion: anger, grief, sadness. Do not hold anything back. Stop at the end of the time period.

   While you are exercising your voice, you can (if you wish) incorporate other therapeutic practices: journaling, praying, meditating, deep breathing. Just remember:
   - Do this alone.
   - Do this for a short period of time.
   - Do this as needed (3-5 times per week).
   - Give yourself time to relax and rest afterwards.

   This exercise gives you the freedom to express yourself in a healthy, contained way while protecting you from further re-injury. If and when you feel tempted during the day to disclose your betrayal to others, remind yourself that you have set aside this time to heal yourself with dignity.

2. **Contain your experience.** In an earlier chapter, we discussed keeping our circle of confidence small by trusting only those who are worthy of your voice. This exercise is similar, but it helps you to contain your experience in a healthy, structured way. Remember, the more people you share your voice with, the higher the risk of re-injury, and the more you give away, the more diluted your voice becomes.

There are two parts to this exercise:

A. On a piece of paper, make two columns:

Worthy of my voice	Unworthy of my voice
:	:
.	.

Take your time and think over people that you know to whom you disclose information. As each person comes to mind, carefully think about how each one typically responds to you and how that response has hurt or helped you. Put his/her name in the appropriate column. Once the list is complete, begin to implement it. If you need to share your voice regarding your betrayal, do so with a person on your worthy list. Adjust or alter your list as needed.

B. Prepare a statement in advance.

For those who are worthy of your voice, you also want to be selective in how much you disclose. By keeping our disclosure concise and contained, we protect ourselves and honor our experience. When we rattle on and on, even those whom we trust tire from our stories and, at times, from us. So that we practice this effectively, it is best to prepare what we want to say in advance. Keep your statement affirming, positive, and brief.

Write down a few statements. Choose one or two and put them to memory. A few examples are as follows:

•   "Yes, my betrayal injury is still a struggle. However, I am working through it and learning from it."

•   "I had to come face to face with my betrayer again. I am continuing to work on myself and to heal my wounds."

•   "I know I have been struggling with this betrayal issue for a long time. Now I know it does not define me or prevent me from being all that I am. It takes a lot of work, but I am committed to feeling better."

Practice this exercise almost like you would a script for a role in a play. Have it ready to implement and to test out when the cue is given! You will be surprised at how much better you feel when your voice shines in you and through you.

3. **Anticipate and rehearse.** When you think you are going to be in the presence of your betrayer and/or your betrayal environment, or if you come across unanticipated triggers, it is critical to have a rehearsed plan for your voice. Prepare the following in advance:

   ▪ Know what you will say and have your statements ready. These statements may be the same as for exercise #2, or you may need to alter them somewhat.

   ▪ Practice how you will say it. Remember, you can say your statement to yourself (you do not need to say it aloud or to anyone else).

   ▪ Know under what conditions you would say your statement aloud to someone else, especially your betrayer. Would you do this alone, with others around, a friend with you?

   ▪ Think about why you will say it. Check your motive and risk factor.

   ▪ Have an exit strategy in place (redirect your attention to someone or something else, walk away, leave the room, or leave the place).

One of my clients struggled tremendously when she had to talk with or see her betrayer. Her circumstances were such that she remained in contact with him for some time. Because the betrayer would deliberately try to re-injure my client, her rehearsed statements reflected her situation:

"We are done discussing what we need to. This conversation is over."

She would then hang up the phone, walk away, drive off, etc. This short but reliable exercise was effective. Her voice protected her. She valued and honored her voice.

Finding your voice takes practice. Each time you embrace the strategies and feel them working, you will sense your content and character return. You will revive and restore your voice. Your voice, in return, will represent and serve you well. Give it time; it will happen.

At this point, I want you to pause for a moment. First, make sure that you have selected and that you are implementing as many of the self-respecting practices that apply to you and your recovering (respecting your recovering work, respecting your spiritual work, respecting your emotional needs, respecting your physical needs, and respecting your choices). Secondly, check to see that you are practicing at least one exercise for each of our goals in finding your voice. Make sure that the exercises are working and that you have spent the time needed on each one. If you have not chosen to take action yet on cleansing and cultivating these internal spaces, do so now.

When you are ready, move ahead to our second area of cleansing and cultivation.

Cleansing and Cultivation of External Spaces

After my sister and her family made the decision to rebuild their home and they secured their resources to do so, they faced another daunting task—what to do with the rubble and the remains of their home. Over the next several weeks, they found themselves (with the aid of a geological inspector) climbing through the broken, entangled structure, sorting and sifting through years of memories. Once they salvaged what they could, my sister, her husband, and her two children faced one more poignant question posed to them by the contractor:

"Do you want me to haul away the debris or do you want me to bury it?"

After weighing the costs, both financially and emotionally, the family decided to bury their beloved refuge in a gully where it still remains on their twenty acres of property. After watching a ball and crane smash and crush the remainder of their house, my sister and her family ceremoniously detached themselves from it and then began to make room for a new place to call home.

Not only do we need to make internal improvements, but we must also assess and address our external debris and make improvements. As difficult as this is, when we tend to the material triggers of our betrayal, we experience a level of healing and closure. By cleaning out the old and detaching from the past, we make room for fresh experiences and new memories.

As we begin to take inventory of the reminders and remnants of our betrayal experiences, we are confronted with some challenging questions:

1. When do we clean out?

2. What do we clean out?

3. How do we clean out and where do we put things?

Because each of our betrayal experiences and environments is so individual and varied, your decisions need to be tailored to your situation. Some of the exercises may apply to you and others may not. Some may apply at different times during your recovering process as your circumstances change. Also, because each of us is triggered at different times, and in different ways, the degree of external cleansing will vary from person to person, as will the timing or pacing of your work.

Let's proceed with a two-part exercise.

One client of mine needed to complete her external inventory at a very slow pace. After forty-five years of marriage, there was a tremendous amount of work to do. As she moved her way through her list, she realized that her grown children wanted some of the items. Checking in with them and discussing their distribution was a long and painful process. In addition, so many decorations in her home were gifts from the betrayer, some of which she cherished greatly. It took weeks, and sometimes months, to make the decision how to deal with these items. As her healing progressed, her decisions became clearer.

Another client moved very quickly. Shortly after his betrayal, he sold his house and most of the items that were triggers for him. The remainder of the items was given to charity or to his grown children. Eventually, he moved to another city where he felt he could best continue his recovering.

Set aside some quiet alone time. Carefully take an inventory of your environment, not just your immediate surroundings but in any location that is connected to or with your betrayer/betrayal. Write down anything that triggers injury. Put each trigger into one of two columns:

Can be changed/removed	Cannot be changed/removed
:	:
.	.

1. **Things that can be changed/removed.** For the list of items that can be removed from your environment, make three different categories:

    - Items to store away.
    - Items to give away.
    - Items to throw away.

    Slowly and thoughtfully sort and sift through your list placing each item into the section that best brings healing for you and to you. This cleansing process varies greatly from person to person so do not rush it or compare yourself to anyone else. Keep a pulse on your position and place as you do this.

    There will be items you choose to store away and/or to keep in your presence. You are in charge. You know what you need to nurture your spirit and you know what is harmful. As your healing progresses, act upon it accordingly. For many clients, the act of discarding items brought a significant level of relief, a sort of cathartic emotion. One client went out into the middle of the desert, dug a deep hole, and buried the toxic reminders of her betrayal. Another client held a mini-bonfire in his backyard, burning the memorabilia and releasing the burdens along with them. Whatever your method, make sure it is safe and make time to tap into the emotional cleansing during the process.

    Where it is needed and where it is possible to do so, clean out other environments that contain triggers: place of work, car, purse/wallet, locker, etc. There may be other unique circumstances that apply to you. Attend to those as well.

    Remember, there is no timeline for this process; however, I encourage you to move forward doing as much as you can, when you can. Also, if you need the support or assistance of a trusted person, allow him/her to be there for you.

2. **Things that cannot be changed/removed—Rehearsed cleansing.** Obviously we cannot always remove all outward reminders from our presence. We go to places and we do things; we live life. In doing so, we often come face-to-face with the forces of our betrayal. However, we can practice and implement a

four-step exercise that will help us to navigate through these occurrences with a cleansed perspective.

Stop–Whenever you are confronted with an external trigger that you cannot change or remove, stop yourself. Take a moment to realize what is taking place and check your thinking.

Calm–Calm yourself. Take in a few deep breaths and breathe out slowly. Listen to your breath. Sit or rest for a moment.

Cleansing Thought–Think a cleansing thought to replace the triggered thought. Examples include:

- I am safe from him/her/it.
- I am protecting myself from him/her/it.
- I am free from further re-injury. I am strong.

Note—other options include using a visual replacement (imagining yourself in a safe and peaceful place); saying or repeating a short prayer, scripture verse, poem, or even a line or two from a song.

Proceed when ready—Choose one of the following:

- Remove yourself from the trigger, if possible (even if it is just for a moment).
- Redirect your attention or direction.
- Detach and move towards a safe person, place, or thing.

This exercise works so well. Whether you are confronted with a smell, a sound, a visual, a word, or anything in your environment that triggers injury or additional betrayal, you have this tool at your fingertips. Utilize it and feel it work.

Because of their living situations, most of my clients remained in their home environments. One of my clients worked with her betrayer in a large successful company; she was the co-owner of the business. Even after she left, she was continually confronted with customers, business dealings, and places of travel that were still an important part of her life. At times, just driving down a certain street in her neighborhood was a painful trigger. She practiced this exercise daily, sometimes moment to moment. When she needed to replace her triggered thought (step 3 and 4), she would put a favorite CD into her car stereo to detach and divert her thoughts/ feelings. This worked wonders for her.

This exercise does take practice. So, plan it out and rehearse it ahead of time. Imagine a situation that you might encounter and mentally rehearse it. Then, utilize it whenever and wherever you need to. Because you have it at your finger tips, you need not fear re-injury, reaction, or relapse. We can cleanse ourselves even when we cannot control our external surroundings, and we can safely navigate through difficult territory, protecting what we think and how we feel.

Remember, as you make improvements, both internally and externally, you are cleaning out the old and you are securing room for the new. Each time you release the betrayal bonds of the past and let go of their hold on you, you revive and restore another part of you.

At this point, I again want you to pause and take some time to select and implement the external cleansing and cultivation exercises that apply to you and that will blend into your recovering plan. If needed, schedule time on your recovering calendar to begin with the cleansing of items that can be removed. Allow as much time as you need to, but commit to certain dates to start the process. With people/things which cannot be removed, make sure that the rehearsed cleansing exercise is practiced to the point that it is second nature to you. Make sure your spirit feels cultivated and confident.

End of Subsection One: Cleansing and Cultivation of Internal and External Spaces—Healing Continuum

After reading this sub-section of *Revive and Restore—Mind, Body, and Spirit,* and implementing the activities/exercises into your recovering plan which apply to you, reassess your current reality on the healing continuum on p. 89.

Then, pace yourself and proceed accordingly.

0	1	2	3	4	5	6	7	8	9	10

Score	Next Actions to Take
0-3	For one week, do the following: • Choose one self-respecting exercise and practice it. • Choose one find your voice exercise and practice it. • Work on your external inventory. Enlist the help of a trusted individual, if needed. List one or two items; then, deal with them (store away, give away, throw away). Do not add more to your list until you have dealt with the items on the list. • Memorize the rehearsed cleansing exercise and practice it (stop, calm, cleansing thought, proceed when ready). • Reward yourself at the end of the week. Reassess your levels. Repeat the process until you are scoring at least an 8—10. Then, move on.
4-7	For two weeks, do the following: • Choose two self-respecting exercises and practice them. • Choose two finding-your-voice exercises and practice them. • Work on your external cleansing inventory. The first week, set a day and a time to do this; do not procrastinate. The second week, set another day and time to work on the actual cleaning (give yourself a set period of time). Do not give up!! • Practice the rehearsed cleansing exercise (stop, calm, cleansing thought, proceed when ready). Memorize it. • Reward yourself when accomplishing your goals. Reassess your levels before moving on. Repeat the process if needed.
8-10	Continue to practice and implement the exercises which cleanse and cultivate your internal and external spaces (respecting your choices and finding your voice). Continue your cleansing exercises as you heal and detach from external triggers/reminders of your betrayal. Move ahead.

Fig. 9-2: Subsection Two—Next Actions after Reassessment

Subsection Two: Boundary Work—Bracing Yourself with Supportive Structures

When my sister and her husband were ready to rebuild their home, they knew they were safe to do so. The soil and ground passed the needed tests; new earthquake codes were in place; and they secured a contractor who was well-respected and experienced in meeting the highest of building standards. And although living in California means knowing that more earthquakes are inevitable, my sister and her family proceeded, bracing their home with the most supportive structures available and moving ahead in hope and in trust and with excitement.

As we continue to revive and restore mind, body, and spirit, we too want to embrace our journeys with a renewed anticipation and fresh spirit. In order to do that, we too must equip ourselves with the best structures possible. We must put into place some support devices that will serve us better as we embrace new experiences and that will help to protect us against further re-injury from betrayal. And, if we do experience another betrayal quake, the support systems we have in place will help us to weather the aftershocks more effectively and allow us to heal and to hope more confidently than before.

In this sub-section, we will address three facets of boundary work:

1. Maintaining an awareness of your betrayal barometer (Fig. 9-4)

2. Boundary-based decision making

3. Betrayal-proofing your relationships

Let's begin by assessing your levels of healthy boundary awareness, structure, and implementation. Shade in the space that best describes your current reality. Then, read on.

0	1	2	3	4	5	6	7	8	9	10

Score	How Do I Feel Right Now?
0-3	I find myself repeating the same behaviors over and over again and expecting different results; then, I am re-injured. I will set a boundary and immediately ignore it. I still trust too soon and too much. I give myself away to unhealthy people. At times, I feel like I betray myself. I feel stuck.
4-7	I am learning to be aware of my levels of sensitivity and vulnerability, and then making decisions from that understanding. I am learning what it is to set boundaries and how to maintain them. I am in the process of examining my relationships and determining how to invest into them or how not to. This is a challenge for me, but I feel more confident and hopeful than before.
8-10	I am consciously navigating from a comfortable and secure position: staying in tune with my betrayal barometer; utilizing boundary-based decision making; and employing the strategies for betrayal proofing my relationships. I continue to stretch myself by moving out of my comfort zone; and yet, I do so with enthusiasm and excitement.

Fig. 9-3: Subsection Two— Healing Continuum

Let's begin with our first important area of boundary work.

Maintaining an awareness of your betrayal barometer

Once we have experienced a given trauma, illness, and/or injury, we are more sensitized to the causes, manifestations, and outcomes of that particular life event. That awareness will typically pull us into one of two directions: one that paralyzes us with fear and anxiety, and one that empowers us to be proactive in defending and/or protecting ourselves from re-injury. Most often, we navigate between both ends of the spectrum. With betrayal, it is no different. We need and want to move forward in a healthy and confident manner; and yet, we often get stuck fearing that which caused us so much pain in the first place.

We can, and we must, take a proactive approach. We are not going to allow our betrayal to paralyze or define us. Instead, we are going to use our betrayal experience to teach us, to inform us, and to guide us towards making healthier choices. We are our own best source of information and we must tap into it to determine our course of action. Our navigation tool is our "betrayal barometer".

I want you to imagine that residing within you is a barometer that measures your levels of betrayal sensitivity, vulnerability, and/or immunity. The readings on this barometer, of course, can and will vary depending on several factors:

1. Where you are in the recovering process

2. Recent exposure/re-injury from the betrayer or betrayal environment

3. Additional betrayal injury

It is natural to feel differently every day and even throughout the day. What is important is that you develop a deliberate awareness of your betrayal barometer. How will you do this?

It is actually very simple, but you must practice the following exercise. Do so several times a day, every day, until it is second nature to you.

- **Step One:** Visualize your betrayal barometer within you.

- **Step Two:** On a color scale of red, yellow, and green, determine how you are feeling given your current circumstances, conditions, or expected changes.

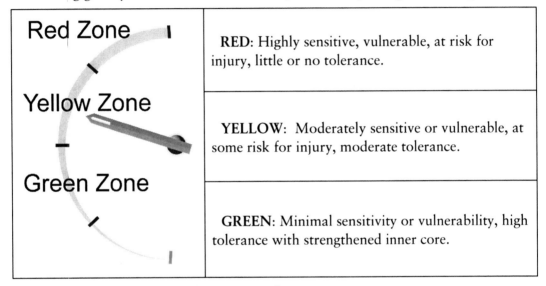

Red Zone	**RED:** Highly sensitive, vulnerable, at risk for injury, little or no tolerance.
Yellow Zone	**YELLOW:** Moderately sensitive or vulnerable, at some risk for injury, moderate tolerance.
Green Zone	**GREEN:** Minimal sensitivity or vulnerability, high tolerance with strengthened inner core.

Fig. 9-4: Betrayal Barometer

- **Step Three:** After you assess where you are on the betrayal barometer, make a mental note of it. Be brutally honest!

This exercise is not a measurement of weakness or of strength; it is a vital indicator of awareness and self-understanding. You are communicating to yourself what boundaries you will need to set, maintain, or shore up as your move ahead in confidence, self-trust, and hope-filled anticipation.

I remember how this exercise helped a particular client who struggled daily in his recovering from a painful divorce. There were multiple betrayals in his life and this recent blow of rejection and violation of trust was extremely damaging. There was shared custody of their young daughter and thus, my client was in frequent contact with his ex-spouse. These exchanges were rarely healthy and productive. Most of the time, their communication was highly emotionally charged and injurious to both parties.

My client began maintaining an awareness of his betrayal barometer. He realized that his levels of sensitivity and vulnerability hovered between the red and yellow zones, especially when he was scheduled to talk to or meet with his ex-wife. By practicing this exercise, he took responsibility for taking care of himself by navigating from a position of self-awareness, understanding, and acceptance. Over time and with continual practice utilizing this informative structure, he moved into a place of empowerment and confidence by implementing healthy boundaries.

Pause for a moment and practice tapping into your betrayal barometer. Do it now. Go through the steps. Where are you on the color scale? What zone are you in? Don't fudge! Be honest!!

There is no right or wrong zone, healthy or unhealthy zone. Just know where you are so that you are informed and you are ready to move to the next step. Know where you are so that you can brace yourself with a critical supportive structure—boundary-based decision making.

Boundary-based decision making

Once we are comfortable tapping into our betrayal barometer and maintaining a deliberate awareness of our current reading, we are ready to move on to implement boundary-based decision making. We will utilize the information we have learned about ourselves to make healthy decisions while addressing three areas of recovering:

- Protecting our current healing reality.
- Challenging and stretching ourselves as we embrace new realities.
- Propelling ourselves towards our desired recovering state with a courageous and confident spirit.

Let's take a look at a couple of client examples which demonstrate the implementation, practice, and effectiveness of boundary-based decision making.

The male client I mentioned previously maintained a fairly structured and set schedule for his daughter's visitations. Therefore, he knew when his contact with his ex-wife would take place. When the scheduled exchanges took place, he assessed his current levels of sensitivity, tolerance, etc. on his betrayal barometer. If he was in the red to yellow range, he would set and adjust his boundaries accordingly. For example, he would implement the following behaviors:

1. Keep the exchange short.
2. Be respectful.
3. Keep the communication focused on their daughter, nothing more.

If, on the other hand, he was in the green zone, he would alter his behaviors just enough to protect himself but also continue to move forward in trust and strength:

1. Continue to be mindful of the time element; do not over-extend.
2. Be respectful.
3. Be open to friendly conversation but limit personal disclosures.

Two important points need to be made concerning both examples. First, although we can plan and set boundaries according to our own betrayal barometers, we can never foresee or control what/whom we may encounter. Therefore, we need to be comfortable with the idea that we may need to adjust our boundaries if unexpected triggers arise and our betrayal barometers fluctuate. Secondly, I have observed that, over a period of time, with consistent experiences under our belts, we will come to know what boundaries to set for ourselves that secure us in a comfortable, and yet courageous place.

For example, let's refer again to the client previously mentioned. As he grew stronger and more healed in his recovering from betrayal, his boundaries remained consistent, navigating from the green zone, even though his ex-spouse would make deliberate attempts at re-injury. This ability to remain consistent and yet mindfully protective of his position further propelled him into a peaceful and enthusiastic place of being.

Let's take a look at another example of healthy, boundary-based decision making. One of my clients who had worked several years on sexual abuse recovery was in an extremely strong and healed place when her extended family invited her to a large family reunion. The family member who had betrayed her, years previously, had since passed away, but my client knew there would be conversations along with old videos and pictures of this sinister man who had disguised himself as a loving family member. After determining that she still wanted to attend the reunion, my client made her boundary-based decisions from a strong (green) barometer reading. Her boundaries were as follows:

1.   Disengage and detach from any conversation concerning the betrayer.

2.   Have a practical exit plan.

3.   Employ her husband as an ally, source of support, and/or person to whom she could redirect her attention and conversation.

4.   Allow time for herself to implement the four-step rehearsed cleansing exercise (explained previously in this chapter).

5.   Prepare in advance "I" statements that were protective of her without disclosing private information (to use if needed with unanticipated or uncomfortable situations).

When my client returned from the reunion, she felt even stronger than before she left. Her boundary-based decisions protected her and also empowered her. She shared an interesting story from the experience, one that challenged her but that also brought her another level of healing. Before she left the reunion, one of her cousins gave her a special gift—a video that had been assembled over the years of the family's history. The video contained footage of all the family members, including her betrayer. My client accepted the video without comment, tucked it away in her suitcase, and disposed of it before she flew home. This amazing young woman disclosed that although having the video in her presence for a short period of time was difficult, removing it from her luggage, smashing it to pieces, and then tossing it into a pile of refuse at an obscure location felt both releasing and reinvigorating! She continued to grow. She continued to revive and restore her mind, body, and spirit.

Another important rule of thumb to remember in boundary-based decision making is that the current betrayal barometer reading is not sufficient to tell you *what* to do—it merely reflects your current state of mind. It does mean that as you make your decision, you *take responsibility* for protecting yourself as well as propelling yourself towards wellness. If healthy boundaries cannot be implemented, either because you are not ready or because of the dynamics of your situation, you must remain honest with yourself and navigate from a position of honoring your place.

For example, even though my previous client decided to attend her family reunion, at first she was very leery to do so. Her betrayal barometer was in a strong place, but she wasn't sure she wanted to deal with all the different variables. She gave herself permission to think through the situation, reflect upon her place of healing, consider the challenges before her, and delineate firm boundaries before she decided to attend.

Because each of our experiences with betrayal is so unique and varied, it would not be possible to tell you what your decisions should be nor would that be beneficial to your recovering, but I can supply you with a set of criteria from which you can guide and base your boundary-based decision making.

Before making a decision, consider and respond to some or all of these questions:

1. What is my current reading on my betrayal barometer? What does that indicate or reflect? What does that mean for me?

2. Should I proceed at this time, or should I wait for more information, more time, or more healing?

3. What did I do the last time I was faced with this situation, or a similar one? What did I learn from it? What do I want to do differently this time? What worked well?

4. If I do proceed, what areas need specific boundary attention?
    -   Time—how long, how much.
    -   Place/s—where and why.
    -   People—who, why, and what.
    -   Things—what and why.
    -   My voice—"I" statements, level of disclosures, levels of containment.
    -   Respect issues—what will you accept from yourself; what will you accept from others? What will you not accept from self or others?

5. What protective devices do you have in place that need shoring up?
    -   An exit plan
    -   Rehearsed cleansing
    -   Support system/s
    -   Other self-care tools or practices

6. What challenges would you like to tackle? What would move you out of your comfort zone and stretch you? What would create a bit of tension and anxiety but also fill you with anticipation and excitement?

Go through each one of these areas. Think about each one carefully as it applies to your situation. Then, set a time and write out a boundary-based decision or decisions that meet with our three goals:

- Protecting our currently healing reality.
- Challenging and stretching ourselves as we embrace new realities.
- Propelling ourselves towards our desired recovering state with a courageous and confident spirit.

Then, implement and practice utilizing your boundary-based decisions. Experiment! See what works and see what doesn't work. Alter, adjust, and move ahead. This process of self-regulation keeps us informed as we learn which boundaries are serving us well and which need revision.

Once we are maintaining an awareness of our betrayal barometer and we are actively engaging in boundary-based decision making, we are ready to move on to our third area of Boundary Work—Betrayal -proofing your relationships We are going to do some fine tuning of our relationships, of our investments into them, and of our expectations of ourselves as well as others within those relationships.

Betrayal-proofing your relationships

Since the San Francisco earthquake and then the Northridge earthquake, many new building codes have been put into place to protect home and business owners from the massive destruction incurred from both those disasters. We call this process earthquake-proofing. And although there are no guarantees of skating through the next quake without injury or harm, having our structures retrofitted with the proper materials and resources and bringing them up to the highest possible standards just makes sense. Why would we rebuild the same way we did before? Why would we deliberately leave ourselves open for experiencing the same consequences when there were supportive devices to put into place?

As we continue with our boundary work, we too, must address how we choose, develop, and maintain our relationships. We can maintain a deliberate awareness of our betrayal barometer, make healthy boundary-based decisions, but if we navigate into and through our relationships with the same faulty or weakened codes (belief structures) as we did previously, we cannot expect different results. We will embrace three steps as we work on this area of boundary work:

1. Reassessing relationships
2. Selective investment
3. Setting and adjusting expectations of self and of others

Step One: Reassessing relationships

I believe that one of the many benefits that have come out of my own experience with betrayal is that I maintain healthier relationships than I did before the experience. It taught me that I have choices in relationships and that I can and must act upon those choices.

Although I have done this exercise at other times in my adult life, shortly after my betrayal injury, I sat down and reassessed my relationships. Simply put, I wrote down two columns on a piece of paper:

Healthy relationships (Balanced; mutual respect; flexible; honoring; affirming; supportive)	Unhealthy relationships (One sided; emotionally charged; rigid; power driven; depleting; negative)
:	:
.	.

I began filling in the columns. It might sound strange coming from a Licensed Therapist, but in assessing my personal relationships, my column of unhealthy people largely outnumbered my column of healthy people. I was surprised!

Once I completed that part, I went back and wrote down why that person/ relationship was healthy or unhealthy. A pattern started to emerge and I was both angry at myself as well as relieved. I was angry because I had chosen to stay in these relationships; I was relieved because I could now choose to make some changes.

Over the years, I have often had clients complete this exercise if it was appropriate for their healing. I remember some of the comments they shared after completing their lists:

- "I realize that most of my relationships are with people who just take from me!! I do all the giving! I feel used and depleted after being with them."

- "I didn't think that I spent so much time around people who are so negative or who blame, play the victim, and are always complaining about something!! It's exhausting."

- "I have always thought I stayed away from drama, but in reality, I see that I surround myself with people who have so many problems and whose lives are in a constant state of theatrical display!! I am tired of it!"

- "I tend to spend too much time with people who are always partying. It's not really what I want to do or where I want to be. Then, I blame them for my behavior."

- "I don't feel I can really be myself around this person; I am always on edge, or walking on egg shells, or trying to please her. It's not me or who I want to be."

This exercise may seem a little harsh, but sometimes honest assessment requires brutal reflection. Also, remember, the degree of your honesty in assessing your relationships will directly impact the next two steps. Set some time aside and complete this exercise. Take your time and think through any and all significant relationships in your life, personal as well as professional. Also, as you move forward and take on new relationships, use this tool as you continue to work on your recovering. Completing this first step will allow you to move to the next—selective investment.

Step Two: Selective investment

After we have completed our relationship assessment, we have three options:

- We can continue the relationship.
- We don't have to continue the relationship.
- In some cases, we must continue the relationship.

However, whether we want to continue the relationship or if we must continue the relationship, we are free to choose how much of ourselves we want to invest into it. No one can make us invest more than we want to. We have that power; we can choose to implement selective investment. How do we do that? What does that look like?

Let's take a look at a client example. After one of my clients completed her assessment of her relationships, she realized that almost every one of her relationships involved people using her by taking advantage of her time, her money, and her resources. She surrounded herself with takers, not givers, including her own family. Although she knew that part of her personality which gave her worth involved being a giver, she was bankrupt from her betrayal experience and was ready to make changes in her investments with people. One of the things she did was discontinue being the "bank" for her grown children. She informed them of the closing date, gave them a last dividend, and held strong against their resistance. She also stopped consistently picking up the tab for dinners out with friends and/or family. And although she loved being a grandmother, she stopped being the free drop-off daycare for any and all babysitting. She started planning time for herself and communicated to her children when she would be available for them.

Another example demonstrates a more subtle manner of selective investment, but nonetheless, one that is extremely important. One of my clients worked for an extremely difficult, demanding, and moody boss. My client excelled at his profession, worked overtime, and produced quality results. However, he was constantly feeling betrayed by the unhealthy leadership behaviors his boss displayed towards him. Because my client had to remain in the relationship, his selective investment took on a more covert manner. My client did several things:

1. Kept his communications with his boss as limited as possible.

2. Kept his focus on his work. He also utilized cognitive thought-stopping and replacement exercises to refrain from obsessive thinking about his boss.

3. Started investing more time, energy, and resources into his own staff that admired and respected him, his position, and his leadership. This, in turn, enabled my client to detach from the importance he was placing on his boss's approval, something he rarely received.

These few approaches to selective investment radically changed how my client felt about himself and about his position. Over a short period of time, he felt empowered, knowing he had a choice between giving away himself to someone who did not honor him or giving himself to those who affirmed and appreciated his being.

There will be some relationships that need to be ended or, at the very least, maintained with minimal contact. There are some relationships where no matter how strong your selective investment approaches are, the personality disorders at play may defeat your strategies and tactics. As hard as it is to make these choices, the relief and release that follows your decision to end or limit these unhealthy relationships will affirm your stance on selective investment.

Again, because each of our betrayal experiences is so varied and unique, I will give you three criteria to consider when implementing selective investment into your relationships:

1. How much do I want to give of myself to this relationship?

    - Physically
    - Emotionally / Psychologically
    - Spiritually
    - Intellectually
    - Intimately

2. How much do I want to give away of my resources to this relationship?

    - Money / material possessions
    - Time
    - Energy
    - Personal talents, attributes, qualities

3. Lastly, after your last encounter in this relationship, ask yourself, what did I learn from this? What worked well for me? What didn't? How do I feel? What would I want to do differently next time?

Selective investment, as is the case with boundary-based decision making, is not a one-time exercise. Yes, I do want you to set aside some time, reflect on your relationships (healthy and unhealthy), and decide how you want to proceed. And, yes, I do want you to delineate some specific criteria (boundaries of selective investment) for those relationships which you want to continue or must continue. Start with a few boundaries. Test them out. Adjust and alter accordingly, but remain true to yourself. Expect resistance and anticipate judgment. Grow and stretch yourself. Most importantly, remain strong in your choices.

As we are reassessing our relationships, and implementing selective investment criteria, we will add a third step to betrayal-proofing our relationships—setting and adjusting expectations of self and of others.

Step Three: Setting and adjusting expectations of self and of others

Even with all the improvements and supportive devices put into place, it would be unrealistic for my sister and her family to expect that there would never be another earth-quake in their area or, if there were, that they would not experience any damage or injury. At the same time, my sister's family was determined to live in faith, hope and confidence and not in fear of the unknown. They had done everything they could do for the time being and their expectations for safety were realistic and sound. They would continue living their lives courageously and openly. When and if circumstances changed or more information was brought to their attention regarding potential danger, their expectations would obviously need attention and adjustment.

We, too, must develop a full awareness of our expectations, not just of ourselves, but of others as well. We can make our internal and external improvements and implement strong boundary structures through tapping into our betrayal barometer and utilizing boundary-based decision making, but if we neglect an honest and realistic approach to setting and adjusting our expectations, we will betray ourselves. We will navigate from a false perception of beliefs which can and will lead us down a path of re-injury.

So many times, clients shared statements such as:

- "I feel so much better. I know everything between us is going to be alright."
- "Now that I am stronger, I know that she will change."
- "I am in a better place. How can they not see it and respect me for it?"

I am not saying that I don't want you to be hope-filled and joy-filled! Of course I do! And I want you to move ahead with courage, strength, and potential for continuing growth. Most importantly, I want you to stretch yourself and challenge yourself, keeping a pulse on the realities in play. Remember, just because we are recovering and growing doesn't mean that others are or that they will respect or even understand our place and position. Your truth, always has been, and always will be yours. And you must be the one to honor it by setting and adjusting your expectations of self and of others.

A friend of mine recently agreed to meet with the person who had betrayed her several years previously. A significant level of healing was in place—her barometer was a strong (green) reading and her boundary structures were in place. There had been minimal contact with the betrayer. My friend discussed ahead of time with her betrayer what would be discussed and what was off limits. Both agreed. When my friend met with her betrayer, her expectations were boldly realistic:

1. He would probably violate the terms of conversation.

2. He would blame and re-injure.

3. He would continue to be the victim.

4. She would keep strong boundaries: not engage, not respond, and not justify or explain herself in any way.

5. She would model the wellness she had achieved.

Although there were some moments of respite, for the most part, my friend's expectations were right on the money. Her betrayer was still residing in his place of blame, bitterness, and belittlement. My client, however, was not re-injured. She was, in fact, encouraged and elated that she moved through the experience with grace and dignity! She walked away stronger and more whole than before, more confident than ever, and more grounded in her truth than she thought possible.

When setting and adjusting expectations of yourself, and of others, navigate from these two premises:

1. Expect yourself to honor your place of recovering: healthier, stronger, more worthy, more knowledgeable, more empowered.

2. Don't expect the other person or thing to be any different.

Define and tailor your specific expectations according to your betrayer and/or betrayal experience and as you continue to work on betrayal-proofing other relationships. Again, this is not a one-time process; it is ongoing. As you learn what works and what doesn't, adjust your expectations accordingly. And as you gather more information, the other parts of the boundary work will reflect that also as you reassess the relationship and employ selective investment. This process takes time. Give yourself permission to experiment, to test the waters, and to dive in! Most importantly, as we have repeatedly discussed, be real, be brutally honest, and remain true to your beliefs.

Pause now for a while, and if you haven't already, select and implement some of the exercises and practices that we have discussed in *Bracing Yourself with Supportive Structures*. Are you easily maintaining and navigating from an awareness of you betrayal barometer? Have you established some set boundaries to use with your betrayal experience and/or betrayer (keeping our six areas of criteria in mind)? And lastly, what steps have you taken to implement the betrayal-proofing strategies (reassessing relationships, selective investment, and setting and adjusting expectations of self and of others)? Give yourself as much time as you need on this, but do not put this off. Start today and schedule time in your recovering calendar to continue with this work. You will be amazed at how differently you feel once these supportive structures are in place. You are now in charge. You are charting your course. Enjoy as you navigate with courage and confidence!

End of Subsection Two: Boundary Work—Bracing Yourself with Supportive Structures—Healing Continuum

After reading *Subsection Two: Boundary Work—Bracing Yourself with Supportive Structures of Revive and Restore: Mind, Body, and Spirit*, implementing the activities/exercises into your recovering plan, and practicing them for several weeks, reassess your current reality on the healing continuum on p 102.

Then, pace yourself and proceed accordingly.

0	1	2	3	4	5	6	7	8	9	10

Score	Next Actions to Take
0-3	For one week, do the following: • Practice maintaining an awareness of your betrayal barometer. Set specific times during the day (morning, noon, and night) to reflect upon your levels of sensitivity, vulnerability, etc. Do this every day without fail. • Choose one relationship that is difficult for you; set a boundary based on any one of the criteria list; and practice this boundary. Adjust or alter it, but don't give up!! • Make a list of your healthy/unhealthy relationships. Choose one relationship you would like to continue and to work on. Look over the selective investment criteria and set one boundary for yourself with regard to your investment into that relationship and set one boundary with regard to an expectation you have of yourself within that relationship. • Reward yourself at the end of the week. Practice this again for one more week. Reassess your levels. Repeat the process until you are scoring at least an 8-10. Then, move on.
4-7	For two weeks, do the following: • Practice maintaining an awareness of betrayal barometer. Set three time periods through the day to do this: morning, noon, and night. Continue to schedule this until it becomes second nature to you. • Work on your boundary-based decision making. The first week, choose a relationship/situation/event that continues to injure you. Reviewing the criteria on p. 106 write down 3-5 boundaries to implement. The second week, or when the situation arises, act upon those boundaries. Alter and adjust accordingly. • Work on betrayal-proofing exercises. The first week, make a list of the healthy/unhealthy people/relationships. The second week, choose one or two relationships you want to continue and to work on. For each of those, write down answers to the selective investment questions with regards to this relationship. Then, set two or more expectations that you have of yourself and of the other person which will enable you to move from a healthier place in the relationship. Implement these boundaries Adjust and alter if necessary. • Reward yourself when accomplishing your goals! Reassess your levels before moving on. Repeat the process if needed.

| 8-10 | Continue to navigate from a conscious awareness of the placement on your betrayal barometer. Continue to implement boundary-based decision making and to practice the strategies for betrayal- proofing your relationships. Continue the hard work and reap the rewards! Move ahead. |

Fig. 9-5: Subsection Two—Next Actions after Reassessment

There is no question. Boundary work is hard, it is ongoing, and it needs re-visitation and revision. However, the rewards of its implementation and maintenance far outweigh the damaging aftershocks of betrayal re-injury. Strap on that boundary belt and utilize the tools within your reach! Then, once you are comfortable bracing ourselves with supportive structures, it is time to move to your last step in your healing sequence of *Revive and Restore—Fortifying Your Inner Tower.*

Subsection Three: Fortifying Your Inner Tower

In the summer of 1991, one and a half years after the reconstruction began on their stunning new home, my sister and her family were ready to move in. All the hard work was complete, the months of living in a cramped trailer on the property were over, and the magnificent masterpiece, which stood before them, awaited its bouquet of fresh memories. The spacious tower passed and surpassed every structural code and inspection; and yet, my sister and her husband knew that their fortifications were not yet quite completed.

In order for this faith-believing family to live in the house, and to live out their lives with a deepened trust and confidence, they would need to fortify their inner towers. My sister and her family chose to do so by planning a formal celebration and declaration, a spirit-filled event which honored their God and His role in their restoration process.

Before moving in, the ceremony took place. I remember sitting on the hearth of the elegant marble fireplace which soared upward to meet the wooden beams twenty-seven feet above. I watched reflectively as close family members and cherished friends mingled while sampling the delicious trays of food and drink; I listened as the soft, heavenly music filled the air, lifting our spirits and preparing the way for the message ahead.

When it was time, we all gathered in the cathedral-like living room. The voices were stilled as my sister and her family, alongside their pastor, revealed the meaning and message behind their prayer-filled dedication:

"Our new home is dedicated to God and turned over to Him for His keeping. Each and every day, our family is committed to breathing life into this home and to serving others with its presence."

As the prayer concluded and the musical pieces sent a spiritual fragrance throughout the room, I could hear the beats of joy-filled hearts and the noise of dancing spirits. The heavy burden of recovering from life's betrayals and of facing whatever lie ahead was lifted and put into the trusting arms of the Almighty. The healing journey of reviving and restoring took an eternal turn, heading down the divine path of fortification.

There is no debating that we are to do our work, we are to stay the course, and we are to finish the race. Doing so empowers us as we break through the bonds of betrayal and move beyond them. However, as we continue to revive and restore mind, body, and spirit, we have the opportunity to tap into in a power greater than ours, to call upon it, to embrace it, and to utilize it for our well-being. We can fortify our inner towers and experience the deepening calm and strength that comes with turning over and trusting our healing and rebuilding to a Higher Power. Each day, we can move ahead confidently and assuredly, committing our recovering to God and relying on Him as we experience our healing within and as we live it outwardly.

Let's first begin by once again assessing your current levels of trust in a Higher Power and your levels of commitment in living out that trust each and every day. Shade in the area that best describes your current reality and then, read on.

0	1	2	3	4	5	6	7	8	9	10

Score	How Do I Feel Right Now?
0-3	Although I am experiencing healing on many different levels, I do not trust what the future holds. I really don't know what it means to trust in a Higher Power; I feel that I can do this on my own. It is a lonely feeling and, at times, I live with uncertainty and even fear. I don't feel that I can ever really break free from the fear, but I think I can learn to manage it.
4-7	I have worked extremely hard on my recovering and I am feeling and experiencing the healing within. Trust is the hardest issue for me. I do trust in a Higher Power, but whenever I feel insecure or afraid, I want to take back the control. I want to live more freely. I want to trust more fully. I want to get to a place where my outward journey reflects an inward sense of peace, calm, and commitment.
8-10	I feel that I am in a strong healing place. Each day I work hard on my recovering program. At the same time, each day I break through bonds of fear and uncertainty by consciously placing myself in the trusting arms of my Higher Power. Every day, I choose to let go of the reigns of control and turn them over to the One more powerful than me. I am learning to live freely and I am finding peace in allowing my newly-found trust to speak for itself, one day at a time.

Fig. 9-6: Subsection Three—Healing Continuum

Breaking Free

As we have talked about, the betrayal bandit has stolen much from us. Reinstating those lost pieces has been the major focus of our recovering. As I worked with clients and as I have experienced personally, learning to trust again is probably the most difficult loss to revive and restore. When we trust, in someone or something, we let go. We let go of a piece of control. We crack open a small opening of the protective shell which keeps us safe. Sadly and ironically, by not trusting, we keep ourselves in bondage to betrayal. We hold back, and we allow that hold to redirect and derail our full potential for living freely. Am I suggesting that you let down your safeguards and protective devices that comfort and secure you? No, that would be unwise and invite premature re-injury. However, I am suggesting that you consider developing a Higher Trust, one that is rooted in faith —not fear. It is a unique kind of trust that involves reaching out to your Higher Power and placing yourself in His safe keeping. It requires that you release a piece of the control, in your own way and in your time, and turn over that control over to One who will cherish your investment.

I remember a pastor who once said, "As long as you hold on so tightly to the reigns of your life, how can you ever freely enjoy the ride?" I am challenging you to release the reigns, a little at a time. I am encouraging you to turn them over and to trust them in the Power of your choice. Each and every time you do this, you will crush the betrayal bandit. He can no longer rob you of the peace and calm that you so desperately desire. He has no power over you. Each and every time you practice developing a Higher Trust, you choose to move ahead in faith and not fear; you choose to break free from betrayal's bondage.

Many of the clients, whom I worked with, were people of faith. Some felt that their betrayal experience was also a betrayal by God. Their words revealed a similar message: "If He really existed, if he really cared, why would He allow this to happen?" I do not want to dismiss this point, but on the other hand, this is not a book about religious doctrine or interpretation of, and I am no expert on either. If you feel betrayed by your God, I do want to suggest the following:

1. Seek out spiritual guidance and direction from a source you respect.

2. Work through your betrayal with God much as you would with any other person or thing.

3. Give yourself time to work through the anger, disappointment, and grief. Return to your core beliefs when you are ready or allow them to alter and change as needed. Healing brings new perspective and fresh opportunity to reinvest.

One last comment regarding this point deserves mentioning. When I was going through a difficult time many years ago, I became very angry at God. I wondered where He was and why He wasn't tending to my needs. In my despair, a close friend comforted me with words that I have never forgotten.

> "God is always there. He doesn't always give us what we want. Whatever you are going through, know that He is preparing you for what lies ahead, protecting you from the unknown, and promising to give you what you need to grow and heal through the pain."

When I think over the past twenty years of embracing this belief, it has always proven true. I may not have received what I wanted, but I got exactly what I needed for that moment and place in time. I made the choice to trust again and to believe in that trust.

You have the same opportunity as I did. It is your decision to break free and to trust. No one can do this for you. This is your work. This is your time. May I suggest the following?

1. Pause for a period of time (a few minutes, a few hours, or even a few days). Allow this concept of trusting in a Higher Power to filter through your mind and your spirit.

2. Think through the benefits as well as the risks of trusting. Think through the

possibilities of not trusting. Weigh both sides.

3. Allow your heart and your spirit to have a voice in your decision. Your mind may say one thing, but what do they need? You may need to spend some additional time of reflection:

   - Journal
   - Pray
   - Meditate
   - Read
   - Talk with a close confidant or friend
   - Consult with a respected advisor or counselor

4. When you are ready and in a manner that is meaningful, safe, and comfortable for you, make the decision to break free and to trust. Say it aloud. Say it over and over again. Believe in what you are saying.

5. Allow for time to absorb this experience fully. Feel the feelings; embrace your truth; breathe in the newly found freedom.

6. When you are ready, share your decision with at least one other person of trust and value.

Just as is true of the other healing practices within our recovering process, fortifying your inner tower by developing a Higher Trust is not a one-time event. It is a practice that you must do each and every day. There will be times when you simply do not feel like you need to turn over your control, or you feel discouraged and disappointed, or you just feel like there is no reason to continue. This is exactly when you need to give up the reigns to your Higher Power. Don't allow the thief of betrayal to rob you of one more moment!

As you break free from the betrayal bandit and revive and store your sense of trust, you will fortify your inner tower. You will strengthen your spirit, calm your fears, and move forward with a more confident and secure presence. In time, you will, with the consistent implementation of the other recovering practices, begin to trust in others. It is most likely that this trust will feel different than before, as it should be. This trust is molded from a healthier, more whole place of being and one that is free from bondage.

Living Free

Once we have the practice of placing our trust in the arms of a Higher Power implemented into our recovering routine, another important piece in fortifying your inner towers is living free. This means that you work your recovering program, and that each and every day you accept responsibility for implementing the tools and strategies that heal, grow, and propel you to levels of wellness. It means that you work hard, harder than you have ever done before to defeat the bandit. Most importantly, it means that if you have a set back or relapse because of re-injury or other dynamics that come into play, each and every day you have the opportunity to begin again.

At the beginning of the Recovering Section, I showed you two line graphs (see p. 63).

Remember, our recovering does not look like the smooth ski slope; it resembles the jagged staircase. Living free means not beating ourselves up when we have a se back or relapse; that is exactly what the betrayal beast wants! It means that we move forward by recommitting ourselves to our recovering program, to ourselves, and to our Higher Calling—the One in whom we have placed our trust.

One of the saddest moments that I witnessed with clients, who experienced re-injury and/or relapse, was watching them beat themselves up with guilt issues after enduring tremendous betrayals and working tirelessly on their recovering. Spending time taking guilt trips only gives the betrayal bandit more time robbing us of potential healing and growth; in fact, I believe we betray ourselves when go down that destructive path. We need not be perfect in our recovering; we need to be committed and to live out that commitment with a free spirit.

Just as my sister and her family did, it is critical to complete our process of reviving and restoring mind, body, and spirit. To fortify your inner towers by breaking free and living free means to develop a Higher Trust and to maintain a Higher Calling and Commitment. The venue in which you choose to practice this is completely individual; however, I will provide you with some guidelines to blend into your recovering program. Tailor them to suit your needs and lifestyles; allow this process to complement your routine.

At least once a day, or as many times as needed:

1. Choose a time during your day or night which is quiet, peaceful, and private.

2. In a manner that is meaningful to you, connect with your Higher Power.

3. In a manner that is comfortable for you, practice letting go of control and of placing trust in a safe place. Feel it and experience it.

4. In a manner that is peaceful for you, practice calling on your Higher Power for strength, courage, commitment, and recommitment. Allow yourself time to absorb and process your feelings.

5. If needed, let go of any self-doubt, negativity, or guilt.

6. Rest in this experience; relax in its meaning.

This practice may seem awkward or uncomfortable at first. Give it time. Dedicate yourself to its implementation into your recovering regime, just as you have with the many other facets of *Revive and Restore – Mind, Body, and Spirit*. As your internal tower is fortified, you will break free from the bonds of betrayal, and you will live free, knowing your investment, truth/belief, or trust is in a Higher Place of Keeping.

End of Subsection Three—Fortifying Your Inner Tower- Healing Continuum

After reading this subsection of *Revive and Restore—Mind, Body, and Spirit*, and implementing the recovering practice explained above (for at least a period of two weeks), reassess your current reality using the Subsection Three healing continuum on p. 116.

Then, pace yourself and proceed accordingly.

Score	Next Actions to Take
0-3	It is extremely hard to move from a position of fear and uncertainty to trust and faith. It is hard to let go of control and the things we feel protect us. Do the following: 1. Write down all the recovering steps that you are implementing into your life and how they are helping you. 2. Write down the changes you have made and how you feel. 3. Write down the things that you do have control of. 4. Write down the things you do not have control of. Each day, read over these notes and add things as they come to mind. Spend time reflecting on all the progress you have made. Then, take one thing that you do not have control of and practice the break free/live free exercises. Do only one each day. Repeat the process until you have gone through all the items on the list of things you do not have control over. Also, as you go through your day, stop any self-doubting or fearful thoughts that come to mind. Immediately replace them with reminders of your successes! Practice for two weeks; reassess your levels before moving on. Repeat the process if necessary.
4-7	Make certain that you are implementing your breaking free and living free practices every day. Also, take a piece of paper and write down what is hard about letting go of control. Next, write down what (insert some auxiliary like 'is' or 'may be') the worst thing that could happen if you let go of that control. Then, write the best thing that could happen if you could let go and trust. Read and reread this every time you start to doubt yourself. As you go through your day, check your negative thinking. Replace those self-doubting thoughts with positive statements/affirmations of letting go. Do both of these exercises for two weeks. Then, reassess.

| 8-10 | Continue to move ahead from a position of trusting into your Higher Power and of maintaining a Higher Calling and Commitment. Continue to break free and live free! |

Fig. 9-7: Subsection Three—Next Actions after Reassessment

End of Part Three

As we conclude *Part Three: Revive and Restore—Mind, Body, and Spirit,* we want to acknowledge that a great deal of rebuilding and restructuring has been put into place. The mounds of rubble that dwelled within have been excavated; our internal and external spaces have been cleansed and cultivated for new growth and healing. We restored and reinforced our structures by bracing ourselves with supportive devices: maintaining an awareness of our betrayal barometer; implementing boundary-based decision making; and betrayal-proofing our relationships. And lastly, but just as importantly, we fortified our inner towers: navigating from a position of Higher Trust and Commitment.

The earthquake that destroyed my sister and her family's home did not destroy them. It gave them an opportunity to grow and flourish, in ways they never thought possible or imagined. We, too, have endured the betrayal quake, and we have embraced the restoration process. Our betrayal experiences did not bind us; we broke free from them. And in the process, we grew and we blossomed, stronger and more brilliant than before.

Let's continue our journey of healing and hope!

10   Recovering Part Four: Release and Renew

"Peace is always beautiful."

—Walt Whitman

Part One Right Yourself	Part Two Readiness and Rigor	Part Three Revive and Restore: Mind. Body, and Spirit
1 2 3 4 5 6 7 8 9 10	1 2 3 4 5 6 7 8 9 10	1 2 3 4 5 6 7 8 9 10

Part Four Release and Renew
1 2 3 4 5 6 7 8 9 10

When I started writing this book, I was in a place where I felt that it was not necessary to forgive one's betrayer and/or acts of betrayal in order to work towards full wellness. That might sound odd coming from a therapist, and one who understands the trappings of betrayal bondage. However, at the time, I felt indifferent towards my betrayer, and I thought indifference was a neutral and safe place to be. Unfortunately, that proved not to be the case. Over time, the resurgence of painful triggers coupled with fresh knowledge and insight caused me to revisit my perspective.

When I was ready to absorb it, I realized that keeping someone or something in a place of indifference took work. I kept my betrayal compartmentalized; much like a small box tied up with string and placed in the recesses of my mind. I got to a point where its presence was faint, and I thought I was rid of the anger and resentment. Then, because of a trigger, a life circumstance, or even an innocent comment, the ties unraveled and out-poured the toxic emotions. Indifference took a back seat to momentary but monumental disgust and disdain for my betrayer; I quickly shoved it back into the indifference coffin. The ties were bound, stronger than before, reassuring me that I could keep this safely contained. It was not to happen, and I began to resent myself for the wasted time, energy, and resources that I was putting into this futile effort. I found myself saying one thing, "I must be rid of this; I need to be released from it; I don't want to keep repeating this cycle."

As we continue our discussion on betrayal recovering by breaking through lingering layers of bitterness, anger, blame, and resentment, I will give you a sequence of strategies to release any residual betrayal bonds and to renew yourself. We will take a look at the concept of forgiveness, reframe its meaning to apply to our betrayal experiences, and implement a healing approach that is comforting and safe. As was the case with the other recovering sections, you will be the one to determine your timeline. You will decide when you are ready, and when you need to give yourself more time. However, I strongly encourage you not to disregard this chapter, especially if you are thinking, "I don't need this. Why on earth would I ever want to forgive? I am the one who should be asked for forgiveness!" Please, read on. The seeds of release and renewal are ours for the taking. It is up to us to implant them into our beings and allow them to take hold. No one can release us; we, once again, must do the work.

Before we begin our discussion, you will once again assess your levels of healing in the areas of release and renewal. Shade in the space that best describes your current reality. Then, read on.

0	1	2	3	4	5	6	7	8	9	10

Score	How Do I Feel Right Now?
0-3	I feel so much bitterness, hatred, and disgust towards my betrayer. However, there is no way that I will ever forgive that person and what happened to me! If anything, he (she, it, or they) needs to ask for my forgiveness! Sometimes, it is the anger inside me that keeps me going; other times, I feel depleted and robbed even further by the resentment that dwells inside of me. I guess I just have to live with it.
4-7	Most of the time, I do not think about my betrayer or what happened. If and when I do, I feel angry and resentful. I try to just push it out of my mind. Sometimes, I will be upset for a day or two, but then it goes away again. I don't feel like I can ever forgive my betrayer, but I am learning ways to let go of lingering pain more quickly than before. I still would like to break through this bond in a healthier way and feel more of a release from it.
8-10	I choose to release myself from my betrayer/ betrayal experience and from the bonds of anger, resentment, bitterness, and disdain. It is something that I practice whenever I need to; I have the tools and the mindset to do so. Instead of regret or remorse over lost energy spent on my betrayer, I feel renewed and reenergized. I feel free.

Fig. 10-1: Release and Renew—Healing Continuum

In order to break through the bonds of anger, bitterness, resentment, and disgust towards our betrayers and/or our betrayal experiences, we need to be willing to do so. This is our choice. We can hold on to it as long as we want, or we can let it go. The irony in holding on to it is that we hurt no one but ourselves. Our betrayers go free. We remain imprisoned by our emotions. Every second we spend hating, or cursing, or mentally punishing our betrayer, we give away more of ourselves to them! Let's not waste away any more time or any more of us. Let's put our skills and our wills together and let's take action!

Forgiveness/Releasing

Forgiveness is a powerful word. It triggers in all of us different meanings, emotions, and feelings. For our discussion, I would like to reframe it so that its implementation is tailored to our recovering from betrayal. When most of us think of forgiving someone or something, we feel as though we are letting that person or thing off the hook. After all, aren't we are giving our permission for the betrayer to be excused from the responsibility or accountability of the wrong doing?

I remember a client who suddenly lost her husband due to medical complications from a routine surgery. Although she worked through her betrayal recovering and grief issues, she continued to be filled with anger and bitterness towards her doctors. When I suggested she work on forgiving them, she said, "Why should I give them the privilege of being set free from causing my husband's death. I will never see him again; I will never feel free again," Sadly, this wounded woman was right about one thing—she would never feel free again, or at least not until she was able to release her betrayer.

When we think of forgiveness, we want to think of it as "releasing". When we forgive someone or something, we let go of it. We stop holding on, we stop obsessing, we stop rehearsing bitter exchanges; we cut the final rope of bondage between the betrayer and us. The betrayer does not gain a thing; we do!

Forgiveness is a choice. When you choose to release, you are the one who is healing; you are the one who is repositioning your mental outlook and stance; you are the one who is controlling the emotions which feed and fuel you. You are the one taking charge of how you invest your energy, time, and resources. You benefit, not the betrayer.

I know that when I was able to let go of my betrayer, I felt like a different person. I felt lighter; I felt reenergized; I felt like a cool wind blew through my body and cleansed out the festering fumes that filled my lungs. Over time, and with continued release and renewal, life looked more inviting; life felt more invigorating.

Are you ready to let go? Are you willing to sever this bond and free yourself? Let's take a look at the process and a sequence of exercises to implement your releasing.

Get acquainted with the mindset of forgiveness that we have adopted. You release the betrayer and/or the betrayal. Reflect upon it.

Think about the beliefs you have of forgiveness. Take some time to write them down. Write down the reframed concept of forgiveness and how it is different or similar to your beliefs. Allow time to feel comfortable with its meaning to you.

Think about how you might benefit from this reframed meaning? How would you feel if you were able to let go? What changes in yourself would you see? Again, write about your reflections and insights.

Practice releasing

Practice releasing by visualizing it. Choose something that is meaningful to you and visualize the release. One client chose holding on to a balloon; then letting it go. Another chose placing an old bottle at the mouth of a stream and watching it drift away.

Other clients have chosen their faith practices to incorporate into this process. Many chose to pray, visualizing themselves letting go in ways that were meaningful, safe, and comfortable to their respective beliefs and rituals.

Rehearse your visualization until it feels comfortable and natural.

Incorporate your lingering feelings about your betrayer and/or betrayal experience into your releasing visualization.

When you have practiced your releasing visualization, and it is second nature to you, blend in your painful feelings, emotions, and thoughts. For example, visualize putting all your anger and resentment into an old bottle, placing it into the stream, releasing it slowly, and watching it drift away—further and further away from you.

Sometimes, it helps to choose a favorite place of solace or refuge. Because the ocean was a close distance from where we lived, many clients would often go to the beautiful beaches near us for vacation, retreats, and much needed renewal. Some of them chose to visualize themselves at their favorite locations on the beach, releasing their betrayers in ways that brought them peace and calm. Because their images were innately meaningful to them, their visualizations were easily incorporated into their mindsets.

Choose to do this, practice this, until you can recall your image easily and readily.

This may seem unnecessary, but remember, we think, say, and feel what is natural or what we are used to. We are creatures of habit, and we need to change those old patterns. Set specific times during the day when you will commit to practicing this exercise. Don't rush it; give it time, and allow its meaning to take hold.

Thought, stop, and replace

Once you have your visualization releasing comfortably in place (so that you can call it up at any time), incorporate one last part into the process. As you navigate throughout your day or night, anytime you think about your betrayer and/or betrayal experience and it and/or they bring the unwanted negative emotions, do two things immediately: tell yourself to stop the thought; then replace it with your releasing visualization. We cannot think two opposing thoughts at the same time; the releasing image will wash away the toxic fumes.

If the negative thoughts return, continue the thought-stop, replace practice. Spend several moments reflecting or meditating on your releasing visualization before moving on. Allow time for the process to take hold.

Utilize this practice whenever you are triggered.

Whether it is an anticipated or unanticipated trigger that brings on emotional wreckage from your betrayer and/or betrayal experience, you have this tool of release at your command. You are in control; you have the power to release. It is your choice. Take time to relish the feelings of renewal.

With consistent implementation of your releasing, you will experience levels of renewal. Because we are so accustomed to the bonds of betrayal, give yourself permission to relish the freedom from them. Set some time aside to journal, meditate, pray, or other healing rituals where you connect with your release. Relax and enjoy the process.

Although I believe strongly in reaping the intrinsic rewards of our work, I also think it is important to validate ourselves in extrinsic ways as well. When you feel that your work in this area has improved significantly and you are experiencing new levels of release, reward yourself with a favorite, healthy pastime or treat. Again, take in the feelings that accompany your growth in this area.

When I think of clients who came full circle in their respective recovering from betrayal, I think of those who came to a place of forgiveness or release. I will never forget a young couple who came to me, both broken and bitter from their intertwined betrayals. The young woman led a secret life of promiscuity. Once it was known, more lies were told, more secrets were kept, and more betrayals were layered on her angry diminished spouse. Through therapy, the young wife disclosed the multitude of betrayals in her own life: an alcoholic abusive father, a mother who was completely absent and totally self-absorbed in furthering her own career; childhood abandonment coupled with childhood sexual trauma. This amazing couple worked tirelessly through their betrayals and other presenting issues: they never missed a session, they did their homework (and called for more!); they practiced every exercise and created more that worked for them; they made their recovering a priority and held themselves accountable for their work. When we moved into forgiveness/ releasing, both these young people had every reason to blame their betrayers and to sink into the pool of bitterness. But, they chose not to. With a significant level of insight, healing, and growth behind them, they both chose to release their betrayals; they chose to let them go. They needed the freedom to move forward, with themselves as individuals and together as a couple. The rewards of renewal awaited their embrace; they grabbed hold and didn't look back.

Releasing and renewal are very individual processes and they are on-going. Don't be discouraged if you have good days and not-so-good days. Give yourself permission to be human and to experience a range of emotions. However, don't give in to the betrayal bandit! Keep your recovering tools sharpened and ready to implement at a moment's notice. Keep your focus on your releasing path; keep your mind and spirit open to renewal! Prepare yourself to embrace the rewards.

Before we conclude this section, I want to remind you that part of working through betrayal issues may also involve resolving grief issues (as we discussed in Chapter Five). If you are working through the stages of grief, you will experience anger, as well as other emotions. It is important to allow those feelings to surface and not to repress them or block them. Use the above tools to help free you from emotional bandage from betrayal, but not necessarily from the grieving process which is instrumental in your healing. If needed, consult with a counseling professional to assist in differentiating between your grief and your betrayal emotions, and in addressing them accordingly.

End of Part Four: Release and Renew—Healing Continuum

After incorporating the mindset and practicing the strategies of release for at least two weeks, reassess your current reality on the healing continuum on p. 143. Then, pace yourself and proceed accordingly.

Score	Next Actions to Take
0-3	Go back and spend at least two weeks on #1 of the releasing process. I would also suggest that you spend some time talking with a trusted friend, person of faith, or professional about your feelings of releasing. Sometimes, having another person listen and connect with your feelings helps in the process of letting go. Also, perhaps there is more unfinished business going on that may need some attention. Incorporate #2 in the process at the end of two weeks, or sooner, if possible. Allow yourself as much time as needed to become safe and comfortable with this part of the process. Allow yourself to feel the sense of renewal that comes with letting go. Choose to do this, even if you do not want to. Don't allow the bonds of bitterness, hatred, disgust, and disdain hold you back one more moment. Break free; do it now. Slowly implement #s 3–7 of the releasing process. If you start to fall back into old thinking patterns and to reinvest time and energy into your betrayer and/or betrayal experience, go back to steps 1 and 2. Begin again. Do not waste any time; choose to release, one step at a time and one day at a time. After several weeks of consistent releasing practice, reassess your levels on the healing continuum and move forward accordingly. Repeat the process if necessary.
4-7	Make certain that you have fully embraced the concept of releasing. Go back and spend at least one week on #1 on the process of releasing. Give yourself permission to fully absorb this new meaning. Talk about it with a trusted friend or professional. Then, when you feel more comfortable with the concept, move onto #2. Again, spend at least a week practicing a safe visualization. Do this every day; several times a day. Choose to do this, even if you don't feel like it! Move forward and implement #s 3–7. Choose it; don't give in to old thought patterns and negative pulls. Break through this bond. Be bold! Do this until it is comfortable and you feel this release. Reassess before moving on.
8-10	Releasing has become an easy and comfortable part of my recovering routine. I spend very little time or energy dwelling on my betrayer or betrayal experiences. If and when I do, I quickly practice my releasing exercise and move forward. I feel free from the bondage of bitterness, anger, and resentment. I feel renewed and re-energized! I am excited to move ahead!

Fig. 10-2: Release and Renew—Next Actions after Reassessment

As we conclude *Part Four: Release and Renew*, we again want to take a moment to ponder where we have been and where we are. We have come a long way on this journey of betrayal recovering; we have broken through layers of bondage; and we have worked hard to get to this place. Sometimes, in the midst of our healing, we don't take time to relish how far we have come. I remember a story from a client who took his recovering seriously and diligently, but who was always demanding more of himself, never feeling quite satisfied with his performance. He came into session one day, after returning from a well-deserved vacation, and shared his adventure of ice-climbing in the mountains of Washington.

"I was following my teammates, exhausted but exhilarated by the climb. I was cold to the bone, but with every methodical move, I slowly made my way up the mountain. After hours of climbing, I looked up to the peak, which seemed as far away as it had that morning. I didn't know if I could make it, or if I wanted to. With the wind cutting across my eyes, I turned to look away and to look back. When I did, I was stunned; I was elated. To my surprise, I could barely see the camp ground where we had begun our journey. I had come a long way; in my effort to reach the top, I forgot where I had been. I forgot how far I had come. I felt a sense of pride and accomplishment. I felt reenergized as I worked to catch up with my teammates. "

As I listened to this insightful amazing man, he continued.

"I now see my recovering that way. I am always feeling that I haven't come far enough. I need to look back and see where I've been to appreciate where I am. For the first time, in a long time, I feel good about myself; I feel hope; I feel joy."

As we move toward our last section—*Part Five: Reframe and Refine*, I want you take a moment and look back. Renew yourself as you think about the work you have done, in the progress you have made, and in the being you have become. Take stock in how the rubble and ruins of betrayal have been transformed into a tower of purpose, worth, and strength. Take pride in how you have chosen to make that happen.

Let's continue our healing journey.

11 Recovering Part Five: Reframe and Refine

"Life can only be understood backwards, but it must be lived forward."
—Søren Kierkegaard

Part One	Part Two	Part Three
Right Yourself	Readiness and Rigor	Revive and Restore: Mind. Body, and Spirit
1 2 3 4 5 6 7 8 9 10	1 2 3 4 5 6 7 8 9 10	1 2 3 4 5 6 7 8 9 10

Part Four	Part Five
Release and Renew	Reframe and Refine
1 2 3 4 5 6 7 8 9 10	1 2 3 4 5 6 7 8 9 10

Congratulations! You have taken an incredible journey with me! And, here we are; we have reached our final recovering phase—*Reframe and Refine*. Together, we have come a long way from where we started. Our work thus far has brought us to a renewed and refreshed level of being. We can move ahead with confidence knowing that we have a healing experience under our belts, and we have tools and strategies in place and at our disposal. Additionally, we now know and understand betrayal, with all its intricacies and trappings, and we now have a deep insight into what we experienced and why. Most importantly, we know we are responsible for taking control of our recovering, and that we can challenge ourselves to do even more.

In my years as a therapist, I have embraced the idea that recovering means moving a client or clients into a place of healing, of growth, and of purpose. During my formative years in practice, I would often encourage my clients by using the phrase, "You are not a victim; you are a survivor", or "It is one of our goals to move you into a place of survival and out of victimization". I still embrace this idea of survival and am always touched by those who attain this level of wellness. I am continually moved by survivors who openly share their courageous testimonies and who desire to reach out to others by sharing their experiences. However, I have moved into a place where being a survivor is not being enough. I know we can go beyond that identity.

In order to do so, I am going to challenge you to push yourself further in your healing journey. As always, you must be willing to take on the work. And, as was true for all the other pieces of recovering, you are the one to decide if you are ready and if the timing is right. In particular, make sure that you have thoroughly worked through *Part Four: Release and Renew*. It has been my personal as well as professional experience that it is almost impossible to move out of the survivor mode if there has not been a significant level of release towards the betrayer and/or the betrayal experience. When you are secure in your releasing and renewal, move ahead.

Let's continue our discussion on betrayal recovering by moving beyond the traditional mindset of survival and embracing a new identity—one which is free from the post-betrayal label and its lingering connotations. Let's grow and stretch ourselves as we embrace our final piece of recovering—*Reframe and Refine*. Before we begin, you will, one last time, assess your levels of healing in the areas of reframing and refining. Shade in the space that best describes your current reality. Then, read on.

0	1	2	3	4	5	6	7	8	9	10

Score	How Do I Feel Right Now?
0-3	I've come this far and I am pleased with my healing from betrayal. I am a survivor of this experience. I don't see any need to move beyond this place. I've been defined by my betrayal experience for so long that if I let go of this identity, then *who will I be?* How will I be? I am not sure I can do that, yet.
4-7	I've become very proud of myself for surviving my betrayal experience, and I know I have every right to feel this way. When I look in the mirror, I see a stronger, more healed person because of my hard work. I don't see anything wrong with being a "survivor"; but yet, I want to be more than that. I am just not sure how to go about it. I am somewhat anxious, but also enticed by the idea of moving beyond the survivor label.
8-10	Although it has been challenging, I have chosen to leave my survivor identity by breaking through its defining label and the connotations within. As I look back at my betrayal experience and my ensuing healing, I have reframed it so that my picture is one of goodness, honor, and value. Because I have been able to reframe my past, I no longer am defined by it. Instead, I see myself as being refined—pure, and true, and most of all—the authentic me.

Fig. 11-1: Reframe and Refine— Healing Continuum

What will your picture be?

In order to move beyond the survivor mentality, you must be willing to reframe your picture of your betrayal experience and beyond. Even with the levels and layers of healing that are in place, this is not an easy task. And, I am not suggesting, even for a moment, that you diminish or minimize how your betrayal experience impacted your life. What I am asking you to do is to take a few steps back, breathe in several deep breaths, and reflect for a few moments on your entire journey—from betrayal to the present.

As you do this, I want you to sit down, relax, and close your eyes. Imagine that you are creating a new picture, on a clean smooth canvas. Visualize this blank canvas as your past and your present. Now, slowly, reflectively, and thoughtfully, I want you to fill this canvas with healing positive images, feelings, emotions, and thoughts. Because we are all so unique in our experiences, I cannot assign you set criteria, but I will give you some prompts to think about as you create your fresh collage and reframe your journey.

From your betrayal experience until now, paint your canvas with responses to the following prompts:

- What qualities, past and present, do you admire and respect about yourself?

- What are some of your favorite memories, past and present, about your entire recovering journey?

- Who are some of the people in your life, past and present, who have cared for you, comforted you, and/or blessed you in meaningful ways?

- What are some of the specials events, places, or things, past and present, that bring you joy and hope?

- What roles in life, past and present, bring you purpose and fulfillment?

- What relationships, past and present, have brought you love and laughter, and have lightened your world?

- What symbols, rituals, or special ceremonies, past and present, enrich and enhance your life?

- Who or what, past and present, have you been willing to invest in?

- Who or what, past and present, have you learned to trust in?

- Who or what, past and present, have you believed in or found truth in?

- What feelings/ words best describe the place you are in now; what shades or colors represent your body, mind, and spirit?

As you ponder each question, if it speaks to you, visualize yourself placing your response (the emotion, feeling, image, person, or thing) onto your canvass. Make sure the symbol, or word, or picture is clear; make certain it is exactly what you want. Take time to reflect upon its meaning and its significance. Don't move on until you are ready; take as much time as you need. Take hours or days, or weeks. Give yourself this opportunity to relandscape your experience; enjoy the process as you reframe your picture.

In the introduction of this book, I mentioned a women's codependency group that I facilitated for about one year, with several follow-up sessions over the second year. At the end of our first year together, I asked each of the women to make a comparison collage that represented their past, present, and future. These collages were similar to what I am asking you to do; however, their past pictures included the damaging emotions, feelings, and images of their betrayal experiences. They worked on these for several weeks and brought them to our final meeting.

At our last session, I asked each woman to share her collage. Taking turns, each woman thoughtfully and movingly explained each part. As each one moved from the past section of her collage into the present section, the room was filled with emotion. Throats tightened and released, tears flowed, and wells of immense joy sprung from all our hearts. Shattered souls were remolded into statues of strength; fractured feelings were sculpted into structures of wholeness and fortitude; mounds of internal distrust, disbelief, and disdain of truths melted into wells of hope, faith, and purpose. We all became witness to a past reframed; we all rejoiced in the creations they had become. We all celebrated in the goodness, honor, and value that each woman unearthed in herself.

As has been true with all our work on betrayal recovering, you must do this work. If you want to move beyond the survivor mentality, you must grab hold of the canvas and start creating. Don't allow latent or lingering thought patterns or behaviors to hold you back. Sever the post-betrayal identity with its layers of containment. Free yourself completely. Feel the goodness, honor, and value in you to surface. Allow it to fill you. Allow it to move you forward.

Pause for time to work on this exercise. If it feels more comfortable for you, as you are visualizing and thinking about creating your canvas, take the time to actually make the collage. You can do so by drawing, by computer, or even the old fashioned way—cutting out pictures, words, or images. Do what suits you and what interests you.

When you are secure in your re-positioning and reframing, read on. If you need more time, take it. Do not rush this process.

What will your legacy be—define or refine?

In the *Encarta Dictionary*, the word *define* means: to characterize somebody or something; to identify somebody or something by a distinctive quality, characteristic, or feature. When we call ourselves survivors, we are defined by it. That is who we are. By reframing our pictures of our betrayal experience and beyond, we no longer see ourselves as we did before. We cease to be identified as a post-betrayal being; we are no longer labeled by a distinctive characteristic or feature in our lives. It does not adequately represent who we are and what we have become.

An acquaintance of mine, after years of her own recovering and outstanding work as a therapist, still introduces herself as a sexual abuse survivor. The label has become part of her last name, and it has become who she is. It is her identity and it is how she is known.

For me, there is a sadness in that because she is so much more.

How do you want to be? How do you want to be known? What will your legacy be? Is it to be defined by your betrayal experience, or to be refined by it?

In the *Encarta Dictionary*, the word *refine* means: to make something more effective; to improve something [...or someone..] through small [...and large...] changes that make it more effective or subtle; to make or become more elegant. Synonyms for the word *refine* add to its depth and appeal: purify, polish, perfect, hone, enhance, and cultivate. The beauty of moving beyond being defined by our survival identity is embracing the opportunity to become a more effective being and to be more elegant in the process.

Clients often ask me during the course of therapy, how will I know when my work with you is done? Of course there are many responses to this question, depending on the individual and the issues, but one thought that I share with clients is, "You won't have anything to say to me anymore. We will probably find ourselves chit-chatting about the weather, or future plans, or other more gentle topics. You might even find yourself searching for things to discuss by focusing your attention outward." Most importantly, I tell them, "You will seek ways to enhance and cultivate new ways of being, and you will want to act upon it. You will find excitement in polishing, perfecting, and honing your continued journey. You and others will be enriched in the process."

How then do you move into the refining process? As with all our other work, it is your choice based on your individual levels of healing, readiness, and timeliness. It is critical that you have done your reframing work, navigating from an unhindered and unencumbered mindset. It is equally important that you remind yourself that this piece of recovering is a process, just as is true of all the other pieces, and it comes in stages, in degrees, and in different forms. Again, because of our unique experiences and circumstances, I cannot tell you exactly what will work the best for you; however, you will utilize your customized created canvas, your psychological backdrop if you will, to guide you in your refining process. While referencing your reframed canvas, consider your previous responses and challenge yourself to move towards your desired state of wellness by taking specific actions. Some suggested actions include the following:

- Choose one or more of the qualities that you respect about yourself. How will you enhance, grow, or stretch that quality or those qualities? What actions will augment that quality in you? What will that look like?

- Choose a person or persons in your life whose presence has been meaningful or has blessed you in a specific way. How will you reconnect with them? Are there ways that you can reach out to them or show your appreciation?

- Select one of your favorite special places, events, or things that have brought you joy and hope. Revisit that place, or event, or thing. Challenge yourself to do something differently this time? What is important to keep the same or similar?

- Focus in on one of your roles in life that brings you purpose. What will you do to augment or enhance that role in ways that fulfill you?

- Focus in on one or more of the symbols, rituals, traditions or practices which hold special significance for you. What will you do to reinvest into them or to embrace them on a deeper level? What will you bring to them?

- Identify who or what you have you been able to trust in, found truth in, or been able to invest in. How will you act upon that trust, belief, or investment? How will you allow that to manifest itself in you in positive ways? Will you share that truth, investment, or trust with others in meaningful ways? If so, how?

- In reference to your canvas, choose a shade, pattern, or color (or many) that best represents the feelings/words of your body, mind, and spirit. How will you hone, brighten, or rearrange those to create a more bountiful bouquet of being?

These questions address the subtleties of our personas, and yet the magnitude of their impact and influence is far-reaching. By spending time cultivating and polishing these intricacies, we begin the delicate process of refining ourselves. We move from our intense inward reflection and recovering to an outward extension of ourselves. It is important that you move slowly, that you start small, polishing one area at a time, and that you enjoy the process along the way!

When the women in my support group were sharing the third column of their comparison collages (the future), they were challenging themselves in the refining process. One client disclosed how her role of being a single mom was so hard after her husband left her and her children. After getting through her betrayal, she now looked forward to returning to her career (something she wanted to do some day) so that she could work at home and be more available for her girls. She knew she would be stretching herself with additional course work, but she was excited about cultivating her beloved role as a mom. Another client discovered that she wanted to challenge herself by changing careers completely. Although she needed to continue her full time job, she enrolled into a Masters program and began her studies. This woman suffered tremendous betrayal in her marriage, worked through her healing, and sought to polish and to improve her nurturing skills so that she could be used effectively in a profession where she could give back. Another client who suffered betrayal on multiple fronts got to a place in her healing where she returned to a deep passion of hers—serving with a charitable foundation that did work for children abroad. When her timing was right, she slowly reconnected with her work and began to reinvest into roles and relationships that enhanced her being. As I watched these women share their refining goals and dreams, I watched them sparkle and shine—purifying, polishing, and perfecting the carefully crafted precious stones that they had become.

I want you to think of yourself as a gem—a diamond. You dug yourself out of the deepest recesses of a dark mine; you allowed yourself to be chiseled, and chipped; you chose the process of being precisely crafted and uniquely shaped into a new form. You have prepared yourself for the final touch—the polishing. As you gently cultivate and hone the intimacies and intricacies of your being, your elegance will surface. As the polishing process proceeds, feel the purity, the true value, and the authenticity of the precious stone, of you, come through.

I also want you to know that refining ourselves does not mean that we are working towards perfection. Diamonds, along with their beauty, have imperfections and blemishes; and they are still very desirable. They, too, with wear and over time, get scraped or scratched or even lost. They too need to be re-polished or renewed. At this stage in our recovering, it is important that you relax in the level of your healing and that you are excited about the process of refining.

Often times, during my years of practice as a therapist, I would get a phone call from a client whom I hadn't seen for a period of months or even years. One client referred to her calls as time for her "thirty-thousand mile check-up". Occasionally, serious matters brought her back into therapy, but more times than not, she just needed to work on her refining. Usually, in a session or two, she was back on track; and there were other times where she called in advance to cancel her appointment, letting me know that she was able to cultivate and hone the area of refining that was stretching her. Upon returning her call, there was such great joy in her voice as she relayed her process and how she was enhanced by it.

Take some time and think about an area in your life that you would like to refine. Each day, practice and incorporate attitudes, thoughts, and behaviors that are reflective of this area of cultivation. Begin now. Move slowly. Take your time. Because I am a big fan of writing, I also encourage you to journal about this process. Sometimes, the smallest of changes are the hardest to acknowledge. Whether you are thinking, meditating or journaling about your work, take the time to soak in the joys of how you are moving far beyond the post-identity of betrayal and into the refined fields of effectiveness and elegance, and of the genuine you.

End of Part Five: Reframe and Refine—Healing Continuum

Because this final section of our recovering involves a great deal of introspective reflection and thought, as well as a life-time of practice, there is no need for time constraints on the exercises. I want to encourage you to take as much time as you need, whenever you need it, and to enjoy the process. In addition, instead of re-assessing yourself after a designated period of time, use the healing continuum as a reference point for your ongoing assessment of reframing and refining.

I also need to emphasize that there will be times in your journeys where you need to suspend (for a period of time) the reframing and refining process because of life changes, transitions, and/or injuries/issues, and you need to return to a previous area of healing. This is natural and normal. Part of living out an effective lifestyle is giving oneself permission and time to embrace the stages or strategies of recovering that best suit our needs at the time.

As we conclude our discussion on *Reframe and Refine* and prepare ourselves for the Epilogue—*Reward*, I find myself not wanting to end our journey together. Because of my own care-taking tendencies and my work as a therapist, I want to reach through the pages and ask you how you are doing. Is there something more you need from me? Is there something I can help you with? It is time to say good-bye, already? Then, I remind myself.

I trust in you and in the process of recovering.

I trust that doing good work restores the good.

And, I trust in the rewards that follow.

Section IV:
Betrayal and Relapse

12   Betrayal and Relapse:
Moving from Self-Betrayal to Self-Discovery

"Deep down inside, each of us knows what our truths are.
It is forgivable to lose them... It is unforgivable not to reclaim them."
—Holli Kenley

After spending many years working and specializing in all areas of betrayal—relational, personal, professional, social, spiritual, economical, etc.—sadly, it has been my experience that most audiences can relate to and connect with this issue. And when the first edition of *Breaking Through Betrayal: And Recovering the Peace Within* was published, I was overwhelmed with how readers responded to the broadened lens from which the topic of betrayal was examined with its inclusive interpretations and its respective recovery applications. However, it was only after living through a deeply personal and painful experience of regressing into a former pattern of unhealthy behavior that I emerged with a new understanding and awareness into the issue of *self-betrayal* or what we often refer to as *relapse*.

Relapse, or self-betrayal, is not an easy topic to discuss. We don't talk about it much because it is so filled with stigma, shame, and secrecy. It is my hope, just as we did with all types of betrayal, by discussing relapse as a universal experience—one of shared suffering—we can begin to break down those barriers and embrace recovering from it together. With the understanding there are countless well-researched responsible resources on the topic of relapse as an integral part of the recovery process in behavioral and substance addiction, for the purposes of Section IV, we will expand upon its meaning and explore its ensuing implications in relationship to our recovery work with betrayal. There is much for us to learn. And although this may sound strange, as we do the hard work of recovering from self-betrayal, there is much to celebrate along the way.

Over the past several years, as I have been writing and speaking about relapse, or self-betrayal, I have been asked time and time again by inquisitive individuals, "Holli, why do you get so excited when you talk about relapse?"

And with their eyes searching mine for a morsel of optimism or hope, I respond, "This is important. By opening up our minds and having the conversation about self-betrayal, not only is it an opportunity to break down the shame, stigma, and secrecy, but relapse affords us the opportunity for self-discovery."

Holding steadily onto my words and wanting more, audiences quizzically ask, "How?"

Confidently but with compassion, my truth is shared. "First and foremost, if we are willing to pause... to take time... and to remain still, self-betrayal has many lessons to teach us. As we conduct a number of self-inventories, we learn what works for us and what does not. We discover who or what jeopardizes our truths, and perhaps most importantly, we learn why they may be vulnerable in the first place." And with a profound optimism in my voice, I conclude, "Lastly, recovery from self-betrayal provides us the opportunity for self-discovery: reclaiming our truths, restoring them, and reintegrating them into our authentic ways of being."

Watching something like hope flicker for the first time in their eyes, I welcome them to join me as we take a journey. I invite you now to do the same. Get comfortable. Give yourself time to heal. And get ready to do some meaningful and essential work as we move from Self-Betrayal to Self-Discovery.

- Part One: Redefining relapse as self-betrayal
- Part Two: Unraveling debilitating emotions and self-deprecating life messages
- Part Three: Recognizing and removing the masks of denial, disguise, and detachment
- Part Four: Recognizing and restoring areas of vulnerability
- Part Five: Recognizing and releasing the restraints of relapse
- Part Six: Reclaiming ourselves and rediscovering our truths

13 Betrayal and Relapse Part One: Redefining Relapse as Self-Betrayal

"Why did I choose to abandon all that formed the foundation of a sound mind, body, and spirit? Why - after all my work to become the real me – would I risk losing myself?"

Mountain Air

If you are starting your recovering journey with Section IV: Betrayal and Relapse, I strongly encourage you to turn to Chapter 6 – Recovering: Breaking Through the Bonds of Betrayal…and Beyond, p. 82. It is in this chapter where I explain the rationale and reasoning behind the "healing continuums" as well as how to utilize them to serve your recovering needs. In addition, if you are new to embracing a process of wellness, I also explain why it is important to pace yourself as you learn new strategies, integrate them into your recovering, and weave in elements of accountability such as reworking exercises and handling set-backs. Read these pages first. Reflect upon their significance to you. And then, get ready to begin your work.

If you have already worked the previous healing continuums or you are familiar with their purpose and how to implement them into your process of recovering, please read on.

0	1	2	3	4	5	6	7	8	9	10

As we begin *Part One: Redefining Relapse as Self-Betrayal*, assess where you are on the healing continuum. Shade in the number above which currently most describes your thinking or mindset about relapse. Then, read on.

Score	How Do I Feel Right Now?
0-3	Although I have returned to, fallen back into, or regressed into unhealthy patterns of thinking, behaving, or feeling after experiencing periods of wellness, I do not see it as a form of relapse or a self-betrayal. I think I just need to try harder and other individuals should stop judging me. Still, there is a piece of me that wonders if I am able to live a healthier life.
4-7	I've always associated relapse with issues of addiction. Now, I am beginning to understand and accept that when I choose to abandon or compromise healthy practices or return to unhealthy behaviors or relationships, I am betraying myself. It's a very painful realization, but it is one I am willing to learn more about. I am ready to embrace healing.
8-10	I have worked hard on my wellness. There have been times when I have betrayed myself by letting go of or forfeiting wellness routines or practices, or I have returned to unhealthy routines or relationships. I know I am responsible for losing my truths and I am accountable for reclaiming them. I am ready to continue growing in this area of recovery.

Fig. 13-1: Redefine Relapse—Healing Continuum

When most of us think of the topic of relapse, our minds immediately go to issues of addiction. This is completely normal! I certainly thought the same thing before becoming more fully aware of how relapse touches most of us, in one form or another. After experiencing over 25 years of my own recovering journey, I made the decision to return to my childhood environment of betrayal—a family system of addiction, emotional reactivity, and instability. I chose to return for all the right reasons and I certainly felt I had enough recovery under my belt to deal with any challenges. However, just a few weeks after my return, I quickly relapsed—regressing into a pattern of unhealthy codependent behaviors, which were destructive to my well way of being. Two years passed before I sought out additional counsel and fully re-embraced my recovering principles and practices. From this experience, relapse took on new meaning—betrayal of myself and of my truths.

Betrayal of oneself and of one's truths

As we begin to open our minds and expand our knowledge of relapse, let's return to what we learned in Chapter One—what is betrayal?

- It is an investment into someone or something met with rejection or abandonment.

- It is a profound trust in someone or something which is profoundly violated.

- It is a truth which becomes a lie or a belief which is shattered.

Thus, for any of us who has invested into any kind of program, process, or practice of a healthy way of being for a sustained period of time and/or for those of us who have invested into ourselves by implementing and integrating well ways of being into our lifestyles over a significant span of time, when we choose to fall back, return to, or regress into any type of unhealthy pattern of thinking, behaving, or feeling—we betray ourselves and our truths. Let me say it again.

After a period of wellness, when we choose to return to, fall back, or regress into any type of unhealthy pattern of thinking, behaving, or feeling, we betray ourselves and our truths.

As we think about this inclusive explanation of relapse, it is easy to see how many of us can relate to or connect with this private and painful form of betrayal—self-betrayal. And although we will examine *what we are feeling and why* in another chapter, because we *choose* to betray ourselves and our truths, deeply destructive and debilitating emotions, such as shame, accompany relapse, keeping us bound in secrecy and stigma.

In broadening our understanding of relapse as an issue of betrayal of oneself and one's truths, let's take a look at three explanations with a few examples of each.

1. Abandon, turn away, reject, or let go

2. Deny, forfeit, or compromise

3. Return to an unhealthy behavior, environment, or relationship

Abandon, turn away, reject, or let go

Relapse or self-betrayal is when we abandon, turn away from, reject, or let go of any type of recovery or treatment programs, or wellness practices. This also includes healing rituals and/or spiritual beliefs/religious practices, which have sustained us with a healthy, balanced lifestyle.

For example, many of my clients in recovery from addictions worked their 12 Step Programs for weeks, months, and even years. Tragically, because of a myriad of psychological, emotional, or physical triggers, and/or weak links in their recovery processes or over-reliance on self (with defense mechanisms at play), time and time again, clients would stop attending meetings, fail to call their sponsors, and turn away from the very sources of support which sustained their sobriety and recovery work.

Another example of self-betrayal is when we let go of or walk away from our beliefs or values. Because of the inner-personal nature of this kind of self-betrayal, we often keep it secretive for long periods of time. Over numerous years of working in a faith-based counseling center, I often heard shame-filled narratives from clients who rejected traditional practices, let go of spiritual beliefs or of meaningful healing rituals, such as meditating, journaling, or praying. Many expressed how betraying their beliefs was the beginning of losing themselves and their foundations which kept them tethered to their whole and well ways of being.

And lastly, time and time again, I remember clients who started an exercise regimen or committed to a healthy way of eating or embarked on a more balanced lifestyle, just to abandon it a few weeks or months later. Feeling embarrassed and ashamed by quitting a healthy routine, their guilt was often reflected in words such as *I should have.... I could have... if only I would have.*

Years ago, I worked with a couple who was struggling with intimacy issues. I will call them Alice and Jim. Although Jim was attracted to his wife, one of the factors Alice was constantly battling was her obesity, which contributed to her poor body image issues as well as her lack of desire. After trying several diets, Alice embraced an inclusive change in lifestyle program—incorporating exercise, balanced healthful meals, and stress reduction into her routine. Over the months we worked together, her weight melted away and her esteem soared. The entire family surrounded Alice with support, implementing the program into their lives as well. By the conclusion of our sessions together, this couple was well on their way to reestablishing healthier patterns in all aspects of the marriage. Unfortunately, about five months after our last session, Alice called to schedule a session for herself. As she briefly described her relapse—falling back into her unhealthy habits and her ensuing weight gain—words of self-condemnation quickly followed. "If only I would have... I wouldn't be where I am now. I'm such a failure.... How could I let myself down... and my family?"

Remember, betrayal is defined by an investment into someone or something met with rejection and/or abandonment. Although it is difficult to admit, when we come face to face with what it means to betray ourselves—to abandon or reject or let go of our whole and well ways of being—we begin the journey of recovering from relapse.

Deny, forfeit, or compromise

Relapse or self-betrayal means to deny, forfeit, or compromise our roles, responsibilities, and even our personas. It is a denial of cultural norms, ethnic customs, and ancestral foundations. Self-betrayal also means we forfeit or compromise long-held personal beliefs, values, and truths, which have kept us tethered to our authentic and purposeful ways of being. In very painful terms, with this kind of self-betrayal, we shatter our own beliefs; we turn our truths into lies.

In order to navigate through our days carrying out the various responsibilities many of us have, we take on different roles and adjust our personas accordingly. For example, we are not usually the same exact person at work as we are at home. We don't behave the same way around our best friends as we do with strangers. This is normal! However, there are many times where we go against who we are or what we know is true and right for us; and in doing so, we betray ourselves.

I remember a client from years ago who came in to see me regarding a relationship issue. I will call him Mathew. As we began to work together, he disclosed how ashamed he felt about denying his Jewish heritage, even to the female he was dating. Mathew shared that although he was not overly religious, as he got older, he valued the traditions and customs of his parents, discovering a deeper significance in reconnecting with his faith. Unable to reconcile his inner conflict, Matt explained how "denying his heritage was like betraying himself and his ancestors".

Some of the most heart-breaking narratives clients shared with me—both young and adult—were individuals who forfeited or compromised their beliefs or principles in order to fit in, to be liked or loved, or to get ahead. With many of my high school and young adult students or clients, I listened to their stories of caving into socially irresponsible behaviors, compromising their spiritual standards and personal expectations, only to experience horrific psychological and physical consequences along with the debilitating emotions which accompany self-betrayal. Adults, too, disclosed painful experiences of conceding their professional beliefs and ethical principles because of pressures or promises, only to forfeit their standards of integrity and honesty.

During the drastic downturn in the economy in the mid-2000s, a client—whom I will call Rob—had a very successful construction company. Rob was one of the most well-respected builders in the business and his reputation was impeccable. As the economic situation worsened, Rob saw his lifetime work slipping away. He cut some corners, a little here and then more there, trying to salvage some percentage of profit. Before long, properties were not passing inspection, liens were filed, and Rob found himself in legal and financial difficulties. As Rob sat in my office, slumped over and broken, he described how losing everything didn't come close to forfeiting his honesty and his integrity.

Again, these examples of relapse—of self-betrayal—often go unattended because of their very personal nature. When individuals have worked hard at setting and sustaining personal standards for themselves and at cultivating a reputation representative of those values, the weight of self-betrayal is heavy, filled with shame, guilt, and regret.

Remember, betrayal is a belief in something or someone which is shattered, or it is a truth which becomes a lie. When we shatter a belief in ourselves or deny a truth, we experience deep inner-personal losses of self-worth, value, and respect. Acknowledging our choice in doing so moves us forward in our recovery of them.

Return to an unhealthy behavior, environment, or relationship

Relapse or self-betrayal means a return to an unhealthy behavior, environment, or relationship. Self-betrayal means abusing the trust we have put into our wellness practices; it also means breaking the trust of people, places, and things which have supported our journeys in healthy ways; and it means shattering the trust we have put into ourselves. In short and shocking terms, self-betrayal means we violate ourselves by choosing to reenter into relationships with known toxins.

Although there is some crossover among the three explanations of self-betrayal, it is important to explore self-betrayal as returning to an unhealthy behavior, environment, or relationship because of the component of trust and its violation. With this type of self-betrayal, defense mechanisms, such as denial, disguise, and detachment play significant roles in justifying, excusing, or minimizing our choices and behaviors. Unfortunately, relapse of this kind can result in extremely damaging and dangerous outcomes.

For example, during my years as a therapist, I worked with perpetrators of domestic violence. Some of them were court-mandated; others were in therapy by choice. Either way, it was incredibly rewarding to see how both males and females worked tirelessly on their power and control issues, and on their anger. I remember one young father whom I will call Juan. He worked with me for over two years, completing all his homework assignments and making huge changes in his actions and behaviors. And I remember when Juan missed two sessions. After calling to check up on him, Juan explained how he *lost it* and almost hurt his wife. Juan admitted he violated his commitment to counseling, to his wife, and to himself. He returned the next week and resumed his hard work.

Another example of this kind of self-betrayal is with parents. Because I am a Baby Boomer, I have talked with dozens of parents who still are taking care of their adult children. I don't know what it is exactly about my generation, but we seem to have a hard time not rescuing our adult children. Although I have talked about codependency in Chapter Four, I want to mention it again because of its importance to self-betrayal. I've talked with many parents who have been rescuing their grown children for five, ten, twenty years. They are financially, emotionally, and physically depleted. At times, when parents have had enough, boundaries are set and there is a period of respite. Although this provides a bit of breathing room and time to reassess their unhealthy roles, when parents witness their adult children continuing their unhealthy behaviors, many parents regress back into their codependency. Ironically, on numerous occasions, parents have disclosed to me how deep down inside they "know what they are doing is not helping their children— and they know they are hurting themselves". Although these parents are ashamed and embarrassed to admit their truths, by doing so, they are taking the first step on the path to recovery from self-betrayal.

In my opinion, it is also important to note that returning to unhealthy relationships of *any* kind is a self-betrayal. Whether it is an abusive and controlling spouse or partner, or a friendship which is deceitful and self-serving, or a professional colleague or employer who is manipulative or exploitive, or an unethical organization or institution—when we go back to these relationships, we let go of our worth and we lose ourselves in the process. While I realize individuals return for various reasons and it is often extremely difficult and dangerous to leave, as long as we repeat the pattern of returning, we also risk compromising the same people, programs, and processes which have supported and sustained us on our journeys of wellness.

Lastly, it is vital to emphasize our explanation of relapse also includes returning to an environment which is unhealthy. We often don't want to acknowledge this. It is hard when there are certain people and places which we would like to have in our lives when these same relationships or surroundings may be very toxic to us. I shared my story at the beginning of Chapter 12, and so I know first-hand how difficult it is to distance and detach ourselves from environments which may include family members. At the same time, I know the cost of not doing so. By honestly assessing and acknowledging environments which are harmful to our recovering, we know whom or what to trust. Remember, betrayal is a profound trust which is profoundly violated. Deep down inside, most of us believe and know what is good and healthy and right for us. We must take that truth one step further. We must trust in it.

Activities – Chapter 13

Looking over the three explanations of relapse—or self-betrayal—reflect upon an experience which is representative of one or more of them.

1. Abandon, turn away from, reject, or let go of any type of recovery or treatment program, or wellness practices. This also includes healing rituals and/or spiritual beliefs/religious practices which have sustained us with a healthy, balanced lifestyle.

2. Deny, forfeit, or compromise our roles, responsibilities, and even our personas. It is a denial of cultural norms, ethnic customs, and ancestral foundations. Self-betrayal also means we forfeit or compromise long-held personal beliefs, values, and truths, which have kept us tethered to our authentic and purposeful ways of being. In very painful terms, with this kind of self-betrayal, we shatter our own beliefs... we turn our truths into lies.

3. Relapse or self-betrayal means a return to an unhealthy behavior, environment, or relationship. Self-betrayal means abusing the trust we have put into our wellness practices; it also means breaking the trust of people, places, and things which have supported our journeys in healthy ways; and it means shattering the trust we have put into ourselves. In short and shocking terms, self-betrayal means we violate ourselves by choosing to reenter into relationships or return to environments with known toxins.

When you are ready, begin journaling or writing about your episode with self-betrayal. Describe what happened and how it unfolded. Because there is typically a chain of events and/or a myriad of triggers or other predisposing factors which precipitate relapse of any kind, include their description as well. However, although these external sources of influence significantly contribute to self-betrayal, this is a time to be brutally honest with oneself by accepting ownership and responsibility for regression into unhealthy patterns of thinking, behaving, and feeling. The first step in recovery is to acknowledge your experience by speaking truths. Take your time. Pause and take a break if necessary. Return to your narrative when you feel ready.

End of Part One: Redefining Relapse as Self-Betrayal – Healing Continuum

After completing the reading of *Part One: Redefining Relapse as Self-Betrayal* and completing the Activities, reassess your current reality on the healing continuum p. 143. Then, pace yourself accordingly.

0	1	2	3	4	5	6	7	8	9	10

Score	Next Actions to Take
0-3	It is very difficult to accept that each one of us is capable of relapsing or self-betraying, especially after periods of wellness. However, it is essential to do so if we are to move forward. On a piece of paper, make two columns **Periods of Wellness**　　　　　Episodes of Self-Betrayal Fill them in. Take your time. Be honest. Validate your times of wellness. Own your times of relapse. Then, reread Chapter 13 and work the Activities. Reassess your levels before moving on. If you are feeling extremely resistant to this process, I recommend you turn to Chapter 14 - *Part Three: Recognizing and Removing The Masks of Denial, Disguise and Detachment.* Read the chapter and work the Activities. Once you are in a place of acceptance and truth, reread Chapter 13 and work the Activities. Reassess your levels before moving on. Remember, you are not alone in relapse. Many of us self-betray. Trust this truth and trust the process.
4-7	Reread Chapter 13. Work the Activities if you have not done so. After writing about your episode/s of self-betrayal, write another paragraph about how it feels to be honest and truthful. Validate your courage and honor your voice. Remember, when we speak our truths, we are free... free to move forward. Reassess your levels before moving on.
8-10	You are in a place of awareness and openness regarding your self-betrayal. Move on to Chapter 14.

Fig. 13-2: Redefine Relapse—Next Actions after Reassessment

14 Betrayal and Relapse Part Two:
Unraveling Debilitating Emotions and Self-Deprecating Life Messages

"With each new day, I too felt it was becoming harder and harder to breathe…Inhaling the insanity of it all, a heavier shroud of shame covered me, smothering my roots and suffocating my being."

Mountain Air

Part One Redefining Relapse as Self-Betrayal	Part Two Unraveling Debilitating Emotions and Self-Deprecating Life Messages
1 2 3 4 5 6 7 **8 9 10**	1 2 3 4 5 6 7 8 9 10

Before we begin *Part Two: Unraveling Debilitating Emotions and Self-Deprecating Life Messages,* assess where you are on the healing continuum. Shade in the numbered box which best describes your current reality. Then, read on.

0	1	2	3	4	5	6	7	8	9	10

Score	How Do I Feel Right Now?
0-3	The feelings I am experiencing right now are too difficult to think about, let alone talk about them! I'm so disgusted with myself. I'm so ashamed. I've worked really hard on my recovery – on my wellness – and I'm the looser who chose to mess things up again. I don't know where to start or where to begin again. I feel smothered in shame. I've pretty much given up on myself.
4-7	I'm beginning to understand how feelings of shame are very normal for anyone who experiences relapse or self-betrayal. I also am accepting that because of my choices, I can expect to feel a lot of other painful feelings such as confusion, worthlessness, and powerlessness. I want to learn more about how debilitating feelings and how damaging self-talk feeds my relapse and keeps me stuck. I am ready to get unstuck and move forward in healthy ways.

8-10	Although once in a while, I experience feelings of shame (or other debilitating emotions) and on occasion my mind will start to replay destructive self–talk, I've worked through their sources and I have the tools to manage them effectively. For the first time, I really understand the role of shame in relationship to self-betrayal, and I am learning how to take care of myself in a timely manner. I feel stronger as I tackle the work ahead of me.

Fig. 14-1: Unravel Emotions and Life Message—Healing Continuum

One of the most insidious characteristics about the nature of self-betrayal is the role of debilitating emotions and self-deprecating life messages. In recounting your relapse narratives, many of these emotions and life messages may have surfaced. This is to be expected. After all, regardless of any precipitating factors—psychological, physical, emotional, environmental, and so on—the painful truth is we *chose* to return to or regress into our unhealthy patterns of thinking, behaving, or feeling. As long as we remain silent about these toxic emotions and damaging messages, we will remain stuck. We will remain bound by them. However, by naming them, peeling them away, and processing them, we unravel their hold on us and we remove the stigma and secrecy which surround them. And although there are many emotions which will be addressed, it has been my experience and the experience of others that *shame* is critically important. Let's take a look at why.

1. What is shame?

2. What is shame's role in relapse?

3. What are the outer layers of shame? What is the inner core of shame?

4. What are life messages? Why are they important?

What is shame?

First, although there has been a great deal of discussion around shame in recent years, it remains a very private and painful topic. In examining shame and its integral relationship with self-betrayal, it is important to understand exactly what we are feeling. Let's incorporate the following acronym:

S = self
H = hatred
A = and
M = malignant
E = embarrassment
Read it again, aloud.

Self-Hatred And Malignant Embarrassment

Reading these words and soaking in their meanings clearly reinforces the magnitude of shame's debilitating role. There are times in our lives when most of us do not like ourselves for something we've done or said. We are disappointed or angry in how we have conducted ourselves. However, *self-hatred* cuts at the core of our being, slicing and dicing our sense of worth into pieces. And who hasn't had an embarrassing moment – or hundreds of them? But they are fleeting. We laugh about them and easily let go of them. But, *malignant embarrassment* feels terminal. There is no escaping it. It stays with us, encapsulating our worthlessness.

Even today, as I think back to my relapse into chaotic codependency many years ago, I can still remember my *shame*. After having over 25 years of recovery work and wellness under my belt, I felt suffocating self-hatred for letting go of my truths and tenets so quickly. And because I was a licensed therapist with years of training and experience, I was crippled with embarrassment as I struggled to hide my regression from my colleagues and other professionals. I remember saying to myself, "I feel like I am bound in my shame. I feel like I can't breathe."

By breaking apart the embedded feelings within shame—self-hatred and malignant embarrassment—and exploring their connotations, we start to unload the heaviness and weightiness carried within shame; and we can also begin to understand how and why shame contributes to the stigma and secrecy which surrounds it. In my professional work, I have found how it is difficult for most individuals who feel shame to say the words, "I feel shame." It is easier to default to "I feel ashamed" or "It was quite shameful." And for those brave enough to admit their shame; unfortunately, it is commonly received with judgment rather than compassion, forcing shame to retreat further and causing additional damage.

Several months ago, I had the pleasure of leading a workshop for therapists on relapse. After having the therapists recall an experience with self-betrayal, I then asked them to name (to write down) the debilitating emotions which accompanied their relapse. After several minutes of writing, I asked for volunteers to share their responses. One person spoke, "Self-hatred." Some voices were soft, some shaky; some were muffled, others almost muted. More individuals spoke up. "I felt ashamed." The room became thick and full. A heaviness descended upon us like an invisible blanket smothering and stifling voices. Suddenly, a quivering whisper came from the back of the room, "I was so embarrassed. It was the most shameful time in my life." And then courageously she added, "I felt shame." The audience was as motionless as statues. I paused. Then, looking around the room, I caught their eyes in mine, sensing their need for a respite. I spoke.

"Let's not forget what we are feeling right now, this moment. This is painful; this is excruciating. Thank you for acknowledging your *shame*. Thank you for sharing it with everyone. Take in a deep breath. Let it out slowly. Breathe, again." And when I saw their bodies relax and their eyes refocus, I added. "Let's remember when our clients reject their recovery programs, return to their unhealthy partners or relationships, walk away from their support systems, or abandon their ethical practices or foundational principles, they too feel what we are experiencing—*shame*. Let's imprint upon our minds how important it is to be present for them, to meet them with unconditional positive regard, and to make it safe to move ahead." Their heads nodded in unison. We all took in another deep breath and continued on.

What is shame's role in relapse?

In addition to shame's inherent cancerous connotations, a secondary but equally as important reason to highlight the emotion of shame is its cyclical relationship with relapse. Take in a deep breath and read slowly.... Shame serves to fuel and feed relapse. Further relapse fuels and feeds shame. Read it again, aloud.

> **Shame serves to fuel and feed relapse.**
> **Further relapse fuels and feeds shame.**

As we have uncovered shame's connotations, we have discovered shame is unbearable. The depth of self-hatred and the breadth of embarrassment are like steal tumors weighing us down—mind, body, and spirit. After self-betrayal, in order to seek a reprieve from the intolerable pain associated with shame, an individual returns to or regresses into the previous unhealthy patterns of thinking, behaving, and feeling in order to mitigate or alleviate that which is emotionally, psychologically, and physically unmanageable. And, as an individual descends back into relapse further, shame resurfaces and recharges, fueling and feeding additional self-betrayal.

Returning to the narrative of my client, Alice, who fell back into her unhealthy lifestyle patterns of eating, I remember how she painfully recounted this vicious cycle of self-betrayal and shame.

"Holli, Jim and I went away together for the weekend. You know, kinda like a couple's getaway? I was so excited. I was doing great on my program and I was feeling so much better about myself!" Alice hesitated and began again. "It started with the breakfast buffet... I couldn't resist all the pastries, muffins, and all the goodies... and I devoured a plateful. I tried to justify it, but I felt so ashamed. Jim didn't say anything, but I felt I let him down too." Alice's eyes lowered. "That night at dinner, I told Jim how disappointed I was in myself. He said he loved me no matter what... but when we returned home, I returned to my old habits, trying to ease my self-hatred through eating. It felt good for a few minutes, but then I hated myself even more... feeling more ashamed. So, then I would eat again.... It is just crazy-making...." Alice wiped away her tears, over-whelmed by self-contempt.

Although Alice was experiencing the deeply painful presence of self-betrayal, by acknowledging the vicious cycle and recognizing its role in sustaining relapse, she continues to gain insight into another important piece in moving forward. Understanding shame and its relationship to self-betrayal does not excuse our choices; however, additional knowledge into the trappings of relapse contributes to the release of shame as well as with other self-defeating thoughts and behaviors.

What are the outer layers and inner core of shame?

Knowing what shame feels like and understanding its cyclical relationship to self-betrayal are vital in embracing recovery. Lastly, by examining the anatomy of shame—its outer layers and its inner core—we can understand its deliberate hold on us and why its removal requires a delicate unraveling.

In both my personal and professional opinion, I believe shame's anatomy consists of both outer layers and an inner core. The outer layers serve as an *umbrella* under which all other debilitating emotions and their self-deprecating life messages take residence. Therefore, it is absolutely critical to address shame in the very initial stages of recovery. As we have discussed, it needs to be named and its role needs to be identified in sustaining self-betrayal. As shame is being named, peeled away, and processed, a myriad of other feelings and emotions typically surface. This is completely normal.

Because relapse is a form of betrayal, it is to be expected for individuals to navigate through the three States of Being—Confusion, Worthlessness, and Powerlessness—which are thoroughly discussed in Chapter 2, "What Am I Feeling and Why?" For our purposes, it is important to remind ourselves of these three states and the emotions/feelings they carry with them.

1. State of Confusion

Understandably individuals experiencing self-betrayal question themselves for not being able to sustain their well way of being. During this period of brutal self-interrogation, it is common to ask oneself questions such as the following:

- Why? Why would I do this?
- Why didn't I have enough strength to resist?
- Why can't I be like everyone else and stay well or committed to my plan?

These questions are indicative of an individual navigating through the State of Confusion. And although many individuals fall into the trap of trying to find answers to their questions in search of righting themselves from self-betrayal, doing so does not unhook us from the bonds of self-betrayal. In the State of Confusion, feelings such as sadness, moodiness, anxiousness, bouts of depression, and fatigue as well as many others are very common and must be peeled away and processed.

2. State of Worthlessness

In our self-betrayals, other painful emotions under the umbrella of shame reside in the State of Worthlessness. Increased depression, intensified anxiety, escalation of unhealthy or destructive behaviors to cope with, and an exacerbation of other symptomatology with respect to physical ailments or psychological manifestations are to be expected. Feelings of hopelessness and helplessness with an uncertainty of an individual's role, identity, and purpose are hallmarks of the State of Worthlessness. Statements such as the following need to be acknowledged, attended to, and addressed.

- I didn't realize what a total loser I was until…
- Or, I thought I was better than this… who was I kidding?
- Or, I am worthless… I don't have any hope for myself.

3. State of Powerlessness

And, thirdly, some of the most debilitating feelings and emotions festering under the umbrella of shame lay within the State of Powerlessness. Once we have entered into an episode of self-betrayal and have begun to experience the immediate as well as ongoing effects of our choices, we come face to face with two opposing forces: we feel controlled and/or changed by our self-betrayal, and we feel we cannot change or control our self-betrayal. These two realizations are accompanied by feelings of vulnerability and of volatility—presenting in a host of symptoms and manifestations: severe depression and anxiety, intensified fear and panic, increased anger or rage, unusual withdrawal or aggression, and further regression into unhealthy patterns of behaving, thinking, or feeling to cope. At times, it can feel very crazy-making as extreme fluctuations in mood, behaviors, and thoughts are representative of the State of Powerlessness.

I recall my client Alice's words as she described her feelings of powerlessness. "I don't think I will ever get a handle on this eating thing... it controls me... it has power over me." Alice's fear eased up her throat, causing her voice to shake. "I get so angry at myself... so filled with disgust. I start to feel energized... like maybe I can control this. But then, I feel completely defeated... and hopeless... I keep going back and forth... it's insane!"

As Alice and I worked together, we continued to unravel her shame by naming its destructive outer layers, carefully removing them, and processing them. This is hard work; and it requires a great deal of inner strength and, at times, external support such as professional guidance or counseling. Given the heaviness of emotions within shame and under its umbrella in conjunction with each individual's levels of vulnerability, we must keep in mind while it is mandatory to process these layers of self-betrayal, the recovery practice of doing so may, at any time, serve as the very triggers for another round of self-betrayal. This is important—read this aloud, again and slowly.

> **Although it is essential to process the outer layers of self-betrayal,**
> **the recovery practice of doing so may, at any time,**
> **serve to trigger another round of self-betrayal.**

Therefore, in our sessions, I followed Alice's pace, tenderly keeping a pulse on her levels of strength and of fragility. As we peeled away layers and layers of worthlessness—laced with self-blame, guilt, regret, and remorse—Alice also examined her destructive life messages and began releasing them as well. And whenever possible, in order to balance out this painful work and to bring in another perspective to Alice's destructive truths about herself, I asked Alice to call upon her seasons of wellness, purpose, or recovery where she felt valuable, worthy, or significant. As I listened to her and she heard herself disclose positive qualities, talents, roles, and relationships, Alice felt her shame dissipate, letting go of its hold on her and cultivating a freer space as she continued her work.

Take a moment and return to your experience with self-betrayal described in Chapter 13 – Activities. Looking over your narrative, begin thinking about the feelings and emotions which accompanied your episode with self-betrayal. Although we will address this more in the Activity section, for now, begin writing down your outer layers of shame—naming the feelings and emotions dwelling under and within the umbrella of *self-hatred and malignant embarrassment*. Take your time. Move at your own pace. Breathe.

Inner core of shame

As we continue our discussion on the anatomy of shame—its inner core—it is important to note we are moving into a very tender and difficult territory. Although this aspect of shame may not apply to everyone, for some individuals, it could easily trigger painful memories or flashbacks or highly uncomfortable physical reactions or psychological responses. You may find yourself feeling angry, or you may not understand your level of emotional reactivity. Please do whatever you need to do to take care of yourself, but of course, do not return to an unhealthy behavior. Move forward carefully and cautiously, keeping a pulse on your being.

Because of my personal experience with self-betrayal and from my professional work with many clients, I believe many individuals who are not able to sustain a well way of being by experiencing an episodic pattern of self-betrayals, or individuals who have sustained healthy ways of being for a lengthy period of time abruptly interrupted by an episode of self-betrayal, carry with them an inner core of shame.

Read this again, slowly and aloud.

**Individuals who are not able to sustain a well way of being
as evidenced by an episodic pattern of self-betrayals,**

**Or individuals who have sustained healthy ways of being for a lengthy period of time
abruptly interrupted by an episode of self-betrayal...
carry with them an inner core of shame.**

Although I cannot say this is true of all individuals, I am suggesting it is the case for most individuals, given the criteria delineated; and thus, it deserves our attention.

The inner core of shame consists of past deeply embedded injuries or injustices and/or maladaptive life messages which have not been tended to and become triggers for self-betrayal. Because of its deeply traumatic nature, the inner core of shame is typically kept out of our awareness by defense mechanisms such as denial or repression or we may have no conscious memory of them at all. Many times, although there is some level of awareness, the inner core of shame is numbed by addictions, self-medicating, or self-destructive behaviors, or by repetitive maladaptive patterns of behaving, thinking, or feeling. It might present itself in subtle ways, such as being insecure, having low self-esteem, or being introverted or shy. On the other hand, it may present itself more boldly. Such indications may be a history of unhealthy relationships—a pattern of irresponsible, abusive, or life-threatening behaviors; or individuals may struggle inter-personally and socially with narcissistic, borderline, or histrionic personalities.

Often times, the inner core of shame, dwelling within our subconscious, manifests in very serious forms of pathology, such as clinical depression, panic attacks, PTSD, or other mood/anxiety disorders. The range of personal struggle with its damaging consequences, all in an effort to mitigate the inner core of shame and lessen the pain within, is vast.

Regardless of the presenting issues, addressing the inner core of shame requires the trained guidance of a professional in order to assess the client and to intervene appropriately. Similar to healing the outer layers of shame, but even more so with the inner core of shame, while it is necessary work to root out the injuries or injustices or maladaptive life messages, doing so may easily trigger additional self-betrayal or other self-damaging, destructive behaviors. It is extremely sensitive work, for both the client and therapist, and it must be tailored very specifically to each client's levels of ego strength and fragility along with other issues of comorbidity.

As Alice and I continued our work together, I sensed she carried with her a deeply embedded injustice—her inner core of shame. After months and months of gently removing the outer layers of shame and slowly but steadily embracing additional recovering processes for self-betrayal, Alice bravely unearthed her buried childhood injury—betrayal by an older brother subjecting her to years of sexual abuse. Although her work was excruciatingly difficult, by trusting in the guidance of a professional and in the recovery process, Alice was able to root out her inner core of shame and release its hold on her. As the months continued, Alice learned how to tend to her newly cauterized wound, giving herself time to heal in all aspects of her recovery work.

The inner core of shame is hard to talk about. It is something we want to push away from awareness. It is just intolerable. However, I believe unless or until the inner core of shame is assessed, accessed, and addressed, individuals will remain at risk for self-betrayal or remain trapped in their re-occurring patterns of self-betrayals. As with recovery from any kind of betrayal, including self-betrayal, we must turn inward to uncover our truths. We must trust in the process, in our capacity to do the work, and in those trained professionals guiding us on our journeys.

This section on the outer layers and inner core of shame is a lot to absorb. Take some time and reflect upon their significance in your experience with self-betrayal. If you feel like journaling or writing down your thoughts and feelings, do so. We will address this more in the Activities. Also, consider reading *Section I: Knowledge and Awareness*.

What are life messages? Why are they important?

Throughout Part Two, I have made reference to "self-deprecating life messages" and to the importance of their unraveling as well. Life messages work in tandem with debilitating emotions; they give a voice to our past pain and to our present self-betrayals. Life messages are the thoughts we rehearse in our minds, telling ourselves about our worth and value or lack thereof. Life messages are born out of our childhood environments, and are reinforced or conditioned from all sources of influence and experience. Life messages permeate our ways of beings. Life messages can be healthy or they can be destructive. This is important. Read it again, slowly and aloud.

Life messages permeate our ways of being.
Life messages can be healthy or they can be destructive.

In my work with Alice, we addressed her self-deprecating life messages while working through the outer layers of shame and her inner core of shame. Her messages were incredibly damaging and detrimental: "I am dirty. I am nothing. I can never be like anyone else. No one cared about me. I was invisible." Over time, as we unraveled these painful messages and processed them, we slowly began replacing them with healthy life messages. By doing so, Alice continued to surface from the suffocation of shame and to begin breathing in wellness.

Unraveling our life messages is critical in our work with self-betrayal. Their sources must be identified in order to understand their inception, and we must acknowledge their role prior to a self-betrayal as well as their relationship in fueling one. For now, take some time and reflect upon your self-deprecating life messages. What do you say to yourself about yourself based on your past life experiences? What are you currently saying to yourself about your worth and value or lack thereof. For now, write them down. This can be painful. Pause. Return when you are ready. Move on to the Activities when you have finished.

Activities – Chapter 14

Let's begin breaking through the stigma and secrecy which accompany self-betrayal. Let's name the debilitating emotions and their self-deprecating life messages and peel them away. By unraveling them, we release their hold on us. Utilizing a writing process which is comfortable for you, respond to the following questions.

1. In your self-betrayal, did you experience shame? If so, what did it feel like for you? If not, describe what dominant feelings or emotions came up for you. Also, during and after a self-betrayal, what messages or self-talk do you say to yourself or do you recall others saying to you? What part does this play in your relapse?

2. We learned *shame serves to fuel and feed relapse. Further relapse fuels and feeds shame.* How has this cyclical relationship played a role in your self-betrayal? Why is this relationship important to recognize in moving forward in recovery from self-betrayal?

3. In discussing shame's anatomy, we learned about the outer layers—the debilitating emotions and their self-deprecating life messages—which fall under the umbrella of shame. First, reflect upon the three States of Being—Confusion, Worthlessness, and Powerlessness—and describe if and how each of those states plays a part in what you are feeling.

    ▪ Do you feel confused about your self-betrayal? Are you asking why? What are you saying to yourself?

    ▪ Do you feel worthless? Why? Describe what worthlessness feels like. What are you saying to yourself?

    ▪ Do you feel powerless? Why? Have you felt both vulnerable and volatile—controlled and wanting to control? What are you saying to yourself?

4. What are some of the other emotions, feelings, and messages you say to yourself during and after an episode of self-betrayal? Describe their heaviness and weightiness. What other physical or psychological symptoms do you experience during or after an episode of self-betrayal? Go slowly. Take your time.

5. We learned although it is essential to process the outer layers of self-betrayal, the recovery practice of doing so may, at any time, serve to trigger another instance of self-betrayal. Have you found this to be true for you? If so, what have you learned and how can understanding this connection help you? What positive life messages can you draw upon from seasons of wellness in your life to balance out the messages of self-recrimination? Write those down. Validate all your truths.

6. In discussing shame's anatomy, we learned about the inner core of shame—

deeply embedded injuries or injustices and their self-deprecating life messages. Because of the sensitivity of this feature of shame, I would suggest you reflect upon it and think about its relationship to re-occurring self-betrayals or how it may serve to interrupt a sustained period of wellness. If this resonates further with you, please consider consulting a professional, recovery program, or support system, and trusting yourself in their care.

7. Unraveling our life messages is critical in our work with self-betrayal. Their sources must be identified in order to understand their inception, and we must acknowledge their role prior to self-betrayal as well as their relationship in fueling it. For now, take some time and reflect upon your self-deprecating life messages. What do you say to yourself about yourself based on your past life experiences? What are you currently saying to yourself about your worth and value or lack thereof. Once you have written down your life messages, fill in the chart below. Claim any healthy life messages from prior seasons of wellness.

Life message	Source/s	Role prior to self-betrayal	Healthy life message
I am nothing	Abuse by brother	Weakens me	I am getting stronger
	Neglect by mother	Worsens self-betrayal	

Take your time. This is important work, and it is difficult work. Breathe. Take care of yourself. When you are done, take some additional time and begin releasing these emotions, feelings, and life messages. Let them go. Although we will spend additional time on this process in Chapter 16, utilize a practice which is comfortable for you in your releasing: praying, meditating, imagined rehearsal, visualization, walking or exercising, or other emotional, physical, or spiritual outlets. Move slowly. Breathe. Continue when you feel ready.

End of Part Two: Unraveling Debilitating Emotions and Self-Deprecating Life Messages – Healing Continuum

After reading *Part Two: Unraveling Debilitating Emotions and Self-Deprecating Life Messages* and spending as much time as needed (recommended two weeks) reflecting on and responding to the questions in the Activities – Chapter 13, reassess your current reality on the healing continuum p. 151.

Then, pace yourself and proceed accordingly.

0	1	2	3	4	5	6	7	8	9	10

Score	Next Actions to Take
0-3	I strongly urge you to support yourself in several ways: • Consider seeking out professional counseling or therapy. There is no shame in getting help in order to peel away the outer layers of shame and root out the inner core of shame. Recovery from self-betrayal awaits you. Take this critical step. • Consider seeing your medical doctor. There may be other issues which require evaluation, assessment, and intervention. • With either of the above, inquire about a referral for an appropriate support, recovery, or Twelve-Step group. Although recovery means we do our own work, it doesn't mean we have to do it alone.
4-7	After reflecting and responding to all the questions in Activities – Chapter 13, return to your writings. Answer the following questions: • Are there any questions which were hard for you or that you didn't answer? Why? • Do you think there are some areas which need more work, perhaps addressing the inner core of shame and/or working through self-deprecating life messages? • Does responding to any of the questions trigger you in any way or exacerbate emotional areas of vulnerability? If you answered *yes* to one or more of the questions, please consider one or more of the following: • See a counselor or a therapist. There may be other issues that need professional attention and intervention. • Get a referral for or return to your recovery, support, or Twelve-Step group.

	• Consider reading Section I: Knowledge and Awareness (chapters 1-3). Understanding betrayal more thoroughly may help in moving forward. Then, move on to Chapter 14.
8-10	• You are in a strong place of recognition and removal of debilitating emotions and destructive messages. You are breaking down the stigma and secrecy which surround shame and keep us bound in self-betrayal. • You are breaking through your negative life-messages and learning how to replace them with seasonal messages of wellness. Move ahead.

Fig. 14-2: Unravel Emotions and Life Messages—Next Actions after Reassessment

15 Betrayal and Relapse Part Three:
Recognizing and Removing
the Masks of Denial, Disguise, and Detachment

"I knew that by embracing recovering, I must interrupt and disrupt the natural flow of denial. It was time to remove this mask of relapse; it was time to let go of its hold on me."

Mountain Air

Part One	Part Two	Part Three
Redefining Relapse as Self-Betrayal	Unraveling Debilitating Emotions and Self-Deprecating Life Messages	Recognizing and Removing the Masks of Denial, Disguise, and Detachment
1 2 3 4 5 6 7 8 9 10	1 2 3 4 5 6 7 8 9 10	1 2 3 4 5 6 7 8 9 10

As we move into *Part Three: Recognizing and Removing the Masks of Denial, Disguise, and Detachment*, assess where you are on the healing continuum. Because of the nature of masks, you may feel some internal resistance nudging you away from your truths. Moving from self-betrayal to self-discovery requires courage and demands brutal honesty. You've begun the hard work. You are ready to continue. Shade in the numbered box which best describes your current reality. Then, read on.

0	1	2	3	4	5	6	7	8	9	10

Score	How Do I Feel Right Now?
0-3	When I relapse, a battle which rages on in my head. One side is telling me to face the truth while the other side is yelling at me – filling me with lies! I pretend everything is ok, but it isn't. I get mad and blame everyone and everything. And then, I pull away from my friends and family. It is crazy- making. I want to face what is going on, but I am not sure how.
4-7	I know about denial and how destructive it is, especially in recovery from relapse. However, I want to learn more and I want to understand how "pretending" and how "pulling away from healthy sources or influences" also contribute to self-betrayal or lengthen my stay in relapse. I'm not afraid of these "masks". I am ready to tackle this area of recovery. I am motivated to continue my healing.
8-10	I now have a clear understanding of all three "masks": denial, disguise, and detachment and of their respective roles in self-betrayal. I know which mask or masks I struggle with the most, how to recognize them, and what steps to take in order to remove them in a timely manner. It's empowering to know what is happening to me and why. It strengthens me in my work ahead.

Fig. 15-1: Recognize and Remove Masks—Healing Continuum

As we have discovered, naming and peeling away the layers of shame and its encompassing emotions is the first step in our recovering from self-betrayal. Although it is delicate and difficult work, it is necessary work. And, as we unravel the heaviness of our emotions and uncover our truths, we certainly become more vulnerable in the process. You may have felt this as you were working the exercises in Chapter 13. This is completely normal and to be expected. In order to protect ourselves from the discomfort and self-disdain, which accompany self-betrayal, and in the ensuing rawness of recovering our truths, we naturally default to our defense mechanisms—or what we will call "masks".

Although masks serve as a temporary tool to minimize our pain and to prevent us from further accessing our truths, the longer we adorn them, the longer we delay or derail our recovery from self-betrayal. For the purposes of our work in recovery from self-betrayal, we will identify three masks and their unique features, examine their role in precipitating and sustaining relapse, and explore ways to process their removal. As with most aspects of recovery work, equipping ourselves with knowledge about masks and owning their impact on us is critical in implementing effective intervention.

It has been my experience that with the onset of self-betrayal, the three masks present in the order of Denial, Disguise, and Detachment; however, with reoccurring episodes of self-betrayal, all three masks may be worn simultaneously. Again, sit back, get comfortable, and yet, get ready to do some hard work.

1. Mask of Denial – The Personality of Lies
2. Mask of Disguise – The Pretend Persona
3. Mask of Detachment – Pulling Away from Sources of Truth

Mask of Denial – The Personality of Lies

Most of us have heard of denial. It is a very common defense mechanism and typically carries with it a negative connotation. However, there are circumstances where denial serves in a positive role, protecting an individual in the processing of traumatic events or preventing a victim from experiencing compounded trauma. In my years as a therapist working with survivors of extreme abuse and trauma, denial often mitigated the painful process of healing and served as a barometer of ego strength, assisting both the client and myself in our work together.

At the same time, the Mask of Denial can be very destructive and damaging, especially in relapsing or regressing into any kind of unhealthy pattern of thinking, behaving, and feeling. The Mask of Denial is often referred to as the personality of lies. When we are triggered (by any source) but before we choose to self-betray, an inner voice enters our minds and starts feeding us with lies.

- One drink is no big deal.
- He loves me. I know he wouldn't hurt me again.
- If I don't help them, who will?

As soon as we entertain these deceitful thoughts, a battle begins to rage between the personality of lies and the personality of truth. Although the personality of truth may stand strong, reminding us of our support systems, years of wellness, and/or the consequences of self-betrayal, shame creeps in for considering an unhealthy response and the personality of lies takes over, assuaging the discomfort.

- It really is ok. I haven't had a drink in a year. I owe it to myself.
- He said he was sorry. I know he means it this time.
- My son and his wife will lose their house if I don't give them some money. How could I live with myself if that happens?

Once we continue to adorn the Mask of Denial without embracing and implementing effective interventions, we move further into our self-betrayal. Denial takes on a stronger role of minimizing any predictable consequences and places blame on outside forces or people. As we continue to lie to ourselves and to others, we are thrust deeper in our relapse and into its pool of shame.

As I regressed into my pattern of chaotic rescuing—slipping into the craziness of codependency—I remember the lies I told myself. "I was needed. I am the only one who can help. I'll just do this… and then no more." And, I recall how I justified those lies with more lies to others who watched my wellness slip away: "There is nothing wrong with me. I'm just tired. I'll be fine." And lastly, as I re-embraced my recovery two years later, addressing all the shame I carried with me, I remember how difficult it was to acknowledge the degree of denial and of the lies I told myself. However, increased understanding of the deceitful powers the Mask of Denial possesses and taking ownership of my lies were huge steps in its detection, recognition, and removal!

Before we move on to the Mask of Disguise, take a few moments and reflect upon your experience with self-betrayal. This is hard, so take your time. When you are ready, respond to the following questions:

- When did you first adorn the Mask of Denial? Describe in detail.
- What lies did you tell yourself or others? Name them; write them down; know them.
- As you think about your self-betrayal now and any emotions which accompany it, do you feel the Mask of Denial wanting to revisit you? What is that like for you?

Mask of Disguise – The Pretend Persona

It is natural to adjust our personas according to our environments or to adapt our personalities to accommodate our surroundings. This can be tiring, but typically is required for short periods of time. However, as we slip further into our self-betrayal, a tremendous amount of time, energy, and resources goes into wearing the Mask of Disguise, constantly portraying a *pretend persona*. Not only are lies covered up with more lies, but we are desperately trying to camouflage the deterioration and destruction going on within.

As I was slipping further into the confusion, worthlessness, and powerlessness of my self-betrayal, I pushed myself even harder in my professional life. Looking back, it was definitely a way of compensating for the extreme feelings of self-hatred and malignant embarrassment over my failure to sustain my well ways of being. The Mask of Disguise became my constant companion, hiding behind it and hoping no one would notice how I was crumbling on the inside. I remember how my biggest fear was thinking my colleagues might detect what was going on with me. Therefore, in an unhealthy attempt to camouflage my pain, I took on more responsibility within my professional organization. Holding several board positions, organizing speakers, and presenting workshops myself, in addition to my other work, I slipped further into my self-betrayal, losing any resemblance of my calm peaceful way of being. The Mask of Disguise became who I was; my false self engulfed my true self.

From my description, it is quite clear how hiding behind the Mask of Disguise moves us into a very dangerous and destructive territory. We become estranged from ourselves and our recovery truths. Tragically, the added layers of shame keep us bound in self-imposed seclusion. Sadly but most often, it isn't until the resources and energy which sustain the *pretend self* have run out or the pretend self is in ruins that an individual is ready to re-embrace recovery. However, just as with the Mask of Denial, recognizing the Mask of Disguise for what it is and understanding its role in self-betrayal assists us in arresting its placement and in its timely removal.

Although we will continue our work on masks in the Activities section, it is important to pause and reflect upon The Mask of Disguise. We must start by taking an honest inventory of what happens to each of us when we wear this manipulative mask. Answer the following questions. Take your time. This is difficult work.

- How do you present the pretend self? Who are you? What do you become?
- What lies do you tell yourself and others?
- What unhealthy behaviors do you return to in order to hide?

When you have finished, give yourself permission to learn from your responses. Instead of beating yourself up, validate your honesty and honor your knowledge. By understanding the destructive and deceptive powers of each mask, we are better prepared to recognize their seductive lure and to protect our recovering truths.

Move on to the Mask of Detachment when you are ready. Again, take your time. Take care of yourself.

The Mask of Detachment – Pulling away from Sources of Truth

As we have discussed, the three masks typically appear in the order we are discussing them—Denial, Disguise, and Detachment. However, because of their complex nature, it is important to emphasize they can present themselves almost simultaneously or move fluidly from one to the other, depending on the degree of occurrence and/or the degree of severity of the self-betrayal episode. As we tackle the third mask, the Mask of Detachment, it is also important to remind ourselves of the purpose of masks—to separate us from our truths. Certainly, as we put on the Mask of Denial, hiding behind lies and deceit, and we wear the Mask of Disguise, pretending to be someone we are not, we have already begun the separation process. However, it is strapping on the Mask of Detachment which fuels and feeds our self-betrayal by severing healthy external influences and support systems.

As I slipped into my second year of chaotic rescuing and continued immersing myself into the unhealthy dynamics of family members, I pulled away even further from my sources of support—trusted friends and trained professional colleagues. Slowly, a blanket of shame covered my being, smothering me; and at times, I felt as though I was suffocating. Embarrassed even more by my perceived lack of strength or confidence in my ability to regain my wellness, I distanced myself from anyone or anything which reminded me of what I had become. And when my husband expressed his concern over the withering away of my former self, I quickly re-attached the Mask of Denial, telling myself and him things would get better... and I just needed to try harder. Putting on the Mask of Disguise, I would pretend for a while that I was returning to my healthy ways of being, only to disappoint myself further by re-submitting to the Mask of Detachment.

Although acknowledging and understanding all three masks and their respective roles in precipitating as well as sustaining self-betrayal are extremely important, I believe the Mask of Detachment is the most critically damaging and destructive. It carries with it the most potential for derailing us from our recovering paths and for redirecting us into highly charged relapse-fed territory. By removing ourselves from healthy sources of support and by surrounding ourselves with the lies of dysfunctional individuals and the deceit of deadly influences, we abandon our lifelines to truth—and we continue to self-betray.

In order to recognize the Mask of Detachment and how it impacts each of us, it is paramount to conduct an honest self-inventory. Again, this is not easy work. Begin by answering the following questions. We will implement more exercises in the Activities section. Take your time. Take breaks if needed.

- As soon as you enter into an episode of self-betrayal, what healthy processes and/or recovery practices do you detach from? Please consider all aspects of your healthy ways of being: physical, psychological, spiritual, familial, professional, social, etc. List them all.
- What else do you do to separate and isolate from your truths?

When you finish, pause and reflect. Breathe. By identifying the three masks and recognizing their role in your journey of self-betrayal, you have begun the process of removal. You know what the masks look like and you know what they feel like. You are ready to continue the work.

In closing our discussion on masks, I want to leave you with these words. When I think back to my personal decline into self-betrayal, I did not recognize the inherent danger behind wearing masks and their sustained impact on me. I was not fully aware what I was doing was much more detrimental and destructive than altering my persona to accommodate varying situations or environments. What I did know deep down inside, was that each and every day, I was slipping further and further away from my place of peace and healthy ways of being.

Looking back now, I see by listening to and living with self-inflicted lies, pretending everything was okay when it wasn't, and removing myself from the processes, places, and people who were nurturing and supportive—all three Masks cut off my sources of truth; and thus, I could not live authentically or be at peace.

Lastly, although I've named three distinct masks, they come in many different shapes and sizes. They can appear enticing and attractive. The can be subtle and they can be seductive. Remember, it is the role of masks to move us away from what we know to be good and true for ourselves. Therefore, we must remain grounded in our recovery beliefs, tenets, or programs which serve us well. At the same time, we must also remain vigilant about when we are most vulnerable or weak and why; and how to know when we need extra encouragement, support, or counsel. In Chapter 16 – Recognizing areas of vulnerability and restoring recovery processes and wellness practices – we will address a wide range of precipitating factors.

Activities – Chapter 15

Previously in this section on masks, you were asked to conduct several self-inventories. If you have done so, return to your answers. If you have not, begin now by answering the questions for each mask.

Then, move on to Removal of Masks. Once we know what our masks look like and how our masks impact us, we can take steps to prevent their placement or assist in their timely removal. This is hard work. It is not a one-time process. It must be done again and again. It must become second nature to us.

1. **Mask of Denial – Personality of Lies**
   A. **Self-Inventory:** Why and when did you first wear the Mask of Denial? Describe in detail.
   B. **Removal:** By understanding why and when you first put on the Mask of Denial, you know your areas of vulnerability and susceptibility. Implement the following five step cognitive-behavioral exercise as soon as a message of self-deception or voice of lies enters your mind.
      i.   Call out the voice as a lie and stop it.
      ii. Remove it from your mind.
      iii. Replace it with a message of truth.
      iv. Return to a healthy decision or choice.
      v.   Repeat the process, as many times as necessary.
   C. **Self –inventory:** What lies did you tell yourself or others? Name them; write them down; know them.
   D. **Removal:** Look over your list of lies. This is important. Next to each lie, write down its opposing truth. Continue doing this until you go through all your lies. If more lies enter your mind, add them to your list and continue refuting them with your truths. Return to this list whenever needed. For example:
      Lie – They need my help. If I don't help, who will?
      Truth – They need to be responsible. I'm hurting myself by rescuing them.
   E. **Self-inventory:** As you think about your self-betrayal now and any emotions which accompany it, do you feel the Mask of Denial wanting to revisit you? What is that like for you?
   F. **Removal:** Oftentimes when we revisit or think about our self-betrayal, we experience uncomfortable feelings or emotions. The Mask of Denial may step in, minimizing our experience and setting us up for additional self-betrayal. Next to your responses about how it feels for you, write down the truths you have learned about the Mask of Denial. Take your

time. This is important. When finished, read and reflect upon your truths.

2. **Mask of Disguise – The Pretend Persona**

    A. **Self-inventory:** How do you present the pretend self? Who are you? What do you become? Describe yourself.

    B. **Removal:** In your description of the pretend self, circle the features or characteristics which concern you the most. Then, make a list of each area of concern. Next to it, write down a support source or recovery step to embrace or re-embrace. Example:

    Feature or characteristic: I start spinning, trying to help when I am exhausted and depleted.

    Support source: I stop and take a break. I review my boundaries from my codependency work and adjust what I am thinking and doing.

    C. **Self-inventory:** What lies do you tell yourself or others?

    D. **Removal:** Implement the same five-step cognitive-behavioral exercise under the Mask of Denial. Practice over and over. Have this exercise at your fingertips!

    E. **Self-inventory:** What unhealthy behaviors do you return to in order to hide?

    F. **Removal:** Next to each behavior, write down the consequences of your actions. Then, write down a healthy alternative which includes calling upon support sources or implementing recovery steps. Example:

    Behavior – I usually get angry and frustrated, snapping for no reason and pushing others away.

    Consequence – I hurt others and disappoint myself even further.

    Support source – Take time for myself. Rest, exercise, and get re-centered.

2. **Mask of Detachment – Pulling Away from Sources of Truth**

    A. **Self-inventory:** As soon as you enter into an episode of self-betrayal, what healthy processes and/or recovery practices do you detach from? Please consider all aspects of your healthy ways of being: physical, psychological, spiritual, familial, professional, social, etc. List them all.

    B. **Removal:** Next to each of your sources, explain why you detach from them and describe your feelings about doing so. Then, in another column, describe what the benefit would be if you did not detach from those sources. Example:

Source	Why I detach	Benefit of staying close
Healthy friends	Feeling ashamed	Stay connected to healthy support

C. **Self-inventory:** What else do you do to distance yourself from your truths? Describe in detail.

D. **Removal:** Next to each thought, behavior, or feeling, write down a healthy thought, behavior or feeling which counters the separation. Then, name at least one trusted individual or source of healthy support to connect with in assisting you out of your self-imposed detachment.

Why I detach	Healthy thought	Healthy support
Feel sorry for myself	Think about what I am grateful for	Spouse

After you finish, take time to honor your truths for each exercise. Validate them and your voice. If needed, rework any exercises. Take your time. There is no rushing recovery. When you are ready, move on to Chapter 16 – Recognizing and Restoring Areas of Vulnerability.

End of Part Three: Recognizing and Removing the Masks of Denial, Disguise, and Detachment – Healing Continuum

After reading *Part Three: Recognizing and Removing the Masks of Denial, Disguise, and Detachment* , work all the exercises in the Activities for a minimum of three weeks or until you feel you have solidly integrated your new truths and implemented healthy alternative behaviors into your recovery repertoire. As discussed, because all three "masks" are powerful, changing our thinking and behaving is hard work. Give yourself permission to rework any exercises at any time. When you are ready, reassess your current reality on the healing continuum p. 166. Then, pace yourself and proceed accordingly.

0	1	2	3	4	5	6	7	8	9	10

Score	Next Actions to Take
0-3	For one week, do the following: • Reread #1 Mask of Denial – The Personality of Lies. • Rework the Mask of Denial exercises: AB, CD, EF in the Activities. • Rewrite your "Removal" responses on 4x 6 index cards. When you experience the Mask of Denial starting to revisit you, pull out your cards and read them, implementing the cognitive-behavioral exercises. Replace the lies with truths. Repeat the process as many times as needed. • Do not move on to the Mask of Disguise until you feel ready. Follow the same exercises as above for #2 The Mask of Disguise – The Pretend Persona and #3 The Mask of Detachment – Pulling Away from Sources of Truth. Spend at least one week on each of the Masks, or longer if needed. Reassess your levels. Repeat the process until you are scoring at least an 8. Then, move on.
4-7	Of the three Masks, name which one (or ones) you feel are your most challenging. Then, do the following: • Write down the reasons why you struggle most with this Mask. • Looking over your "Removal" responses, identify three healthy sources of support or healthy alternate behaviors or healing truths from your responses and add any additional sources which come to mind. • Rewrite these responses on 4 x 6 cards. When you experience a Mask start to revisit you, pull out your cards, read them, and replace the unhealthy thoughts or behaviors with healing thoughts or behaviors. Repeat this process as often as needed. Do this for one week.

	• Celebrate your success in healthy ways. Change takes time. Stay strong. Reassess your levels before moving on. Repeat the process if needed.
8-10	Although we are never completely free of the Masks of Denial, Disguise, and Detachment, we can move ahead in strength by understanding them, their roles, and how they impact each of us in our recovering journeys. Continue to keep short accounts of their presence in your life and give yourself permission to rework any of the exercises whenever needed. Move ahead.

Fig. 15-2: Recognize and Remove Masks—Next Actions after Reassessment

16 Betrayal and Relapse Part Four:
Recognizing and Restoring Areas of Vulnerability

"This [memory] reminded me of the importance of conducting a fearless inventory of one's areas of vulnerability, of weakness, and of injury ... We must acknowledgement them and act upon [them]."

Mountain Air

Part One	Part Two	Part Three
Redefining Relapse as Self-Betrayal	Unraveling Debilitating Emotions and Self-Deprecating Life Messages	Recognizing and Removing the Masks of Denial, Disguise, and Detachment
1 2 3 4 5 6 7 8 9 10	1 2 3 4 5 6 7 8 9 10	1 2 3 4 5 6 7 8 9 10

Part Four
Recognizing and Restoring Areas of Vulnerability
1 2 3 4 5 6 7 8 9 10

As we begin *Part Four: Recognizing and Restoring Areas of Vulnerability,* assess where you are on the healing continuum. Shade in the number which describes your current healing reality.

0	1	2	3	4	5	6	7	8	9	10

Score	How Do I Feel Right Now?
0-3	I feel pretty good, most of the time. I'm going along working my program and then someone says something or does something, and I get so angry. Or I'll be doing fine and then, out of nowhere I think this painful thought and I can't stand it! I've heard about triggers but I don't really know what they are and why they are so important when it comes to relapse. Sometimes, I wonder if I am a total failure or if I'm just a fool. There are times when I change or fudge on my recovery routine just a little and I am ok. But, there are other times when I don't do something I should, and I feel scared because I know I am putting myself at risk for relapse. What is wrong with me? What is it that I am not getting? I want to understand what is going on and get stronger in sustaining recovery from self-betrayal, but I'm not sure how.
4-7	I've learned about triggers and I understand how they play a role in relapse. I've worked hard on addressing my triggers but I need to know more about how to manage them. I'm looking forward to learning more. Also, I think I have pretty good boundaries around my recovery work, but sometimes I slip and mess up because of other weak links in my routine. There are times when I know I am not ready – when I am vulnerable – and I make a poor decision and set myself up for self-betrayal. Why am I doing this? What can I do to become more aware my areas of vulnerability and what can I do to strengthen my recovery work? I am ready to learn and to do the hard work.
8-10	I've worked really hard identifying and working on my areas of vulnerability: triggers, weak links in my chain of events, and life changes or transitions. I have a solid understanding of how each of these impacts my wellness practices or recovery routines, and I implement specific actions in order to safe-guard my wellness. At the same time, I know I cannot become overly self-reliant and it is mandatory that I make this area of recovery from self-betrayal a priority. I'll continue growing in my self-discovery by increasing my understanding and learning additional strategies. I remain open to the process.

Fig. 16-1: Recognize and Restore Areas—Healing Continuum

In the introduction, I stated self-betrayal affords us the opportunity for self-discovery. By redefining relapse as self-betrayal, we increased our understanding of its connotations and we personalized its applications to our lives. Secondly, as we analyzed the anatomy of self-betrayal, we discovered how to recognize the outer layers of shame and how to unravel its debilitating emotions and self-deprecating life messages. We also became acquainted with the highly sensitive inner core of shame, its prevalence among many individuals, and its critical role in re-occurrence of self-betrayal. And then, we tackled the three masks of denial, disguise, and detachment. In doing so, we discovered much about our defense mechanisms and how they lure us into self-betrayal and lengthen our stay there. By identifying their features and understanding their destructive roles, we have also discovered how to implement early recognition of their unique manifestations, arrest their adornment, and arm ourselves with preventative measures. As we continue the process of self-discovery, we move into Part Four: Recognizing and Restoring Areas of Vulnerability—a critical piece in our journey of self-discovery, which will offer us a plethora of valuable insights and a myriad of restorative tools.

Although some recovery programs or counseling practices may suggest addressing areas of vulnerability earlier on in the healing process, it is my personal and professional opinion that until we own our relapse (by understanding it as a form of self-betrayal), until we are able to come out from under our blankets of shame, and unless and until we are willing to address the masks which prevent us from accessing our true selves, addressing areas of vulnerability would be premature. However, they are, without question, paramount in the protection of well ways of being and in the prevention of self-betrayal. In our discussion of vulnerability, we are recognizing and restoring three areas:

1. Triggers

2. Weak links in chain of events

3. Life changes, transitions, and other precipitating factors

Triggers

So many times over the years in my discussions with individuals about relapse, either in my professional life as a therapist or in my personal life, I have often heard questions such as, "Why doesn't she just try harder?" Or, "He has no will power. What is wrong with him?" Or, "Why can't she get her act together?" And unfortunately, I have to admit before I became a therapist and learned about relapse, I often asked myself similar questions. However, in my practice working largely with victims of abuse and trauma and in my own recovering, I became very familiar with the presence and the power of triggers. And although triggers can be incredibly damaging to our wellness and recovery work, they can also serve us in healthy ways.

If individuals have been working a recovery program or are in therapy, or have knowledge of the recovering process, they most likely are aware of their triggers. However, even with recovering experiences, many individuals do not realize their relationship to self-betrayal, and thus, do not pay close attention to them. Countless individuals, who have not had recovering experiences or who are not knowledgeable about triggers, are most likely not aware of them and to the degree with which they impact our thoughts, feelings, and behaviors. In addition, when we are triggered by someone or something, it is not uncommon for denial to surface minimizing or mitigating unpleasant feelings or emotions, and we move through the trigger without dealing with its implications or causal factors. In order to become more aware of triggers, let's find out what they are, examine their features, and discover how they play an integral role in self-betrayal.

First, what are triggers?

Triggers are messengers. Triggers send us warnings.

Read it again, slowly and aloud.

Triggers are messengers. Triggers send us warnings.

Triggers are spontaneous emotional, psychological, and physical messengers. They shake our thoughts and rattle our feelings without prior notice. Triggers send us messages that something is wrong. We are triggered when we hear or see something which doesn't feel right, or when someone says or does something which hurts us. Triggers can be mild in nature and we can let go of them easily. However, most triggers are traumatic, causing us a great deal of pain. At times, they are intolerable. When we are triggered, many times we feel angry, frightened, vulnerable, and unsafe. We want these feelings to go away. Sometimes, we will do anything to escape it, including self-betray.

Over the years, I have worked with so many amazing individuals who have worked their programs of recovery or wellness practices. It has been my experience, without fail, when a client relapsed, or self-betrayed, he was triggered by someone or something. Listening to them share their narratives without excusing or justifying their self-betrayals, time and time again, these broken individuals described how the pain of being triggered overpowered the peace of their recovering.

Helping us to recognize triggers, it is important to understand why they exist. In other words, where do they come from? Read this carefully. Triggers are symptomatic of unresolved issues or unhealed injuries. Without effective intervention, we will be re-triggered and remain at risk for relapse.

Say it again. Slowly and aloud.

Triggers are symptomatic of unresolved issues or unhealed injuries.
Without effective intervention, we will be re-triggered and remain at risk for relapse.

In Part Two: Unraveling debilitating emotions and self-deprecating life messages, I made several references to a former client whom I called Alice. Alice was a survivor of childhood sexual abuse. As Alice and I worked together for over a year, pacing her healing and keeping a pulse on her levels of fragility, Alice came face to face with a multitude of triggers catapulting her to past painful emotions, feelings, and experiences. As we worked through the triggers, Alice continued to embrace her recovering without returning to her pattern of unhealthy eating. This was incredibly hard work.

Alice's case illustrates the importance of connecting our triggers to past injuries and injustices, however minor or significant they may be. As I have shared with you, we must peel away the outer layers of shame and address the inner core. This is non-negotiable, especially when it comes to self-betrayal and sustaining recovery. By not doing so, we will be re-triggered continually, and we will remain at risk for self-betrayal.

Another important feature about triggers is related to the former characteristic, but it deserves attention. Triggers emerge from our present sources of contact; however, they emanate from our past experiences. This is important. Read it again, slowly and aloud.

Triggers emerge from our present sources of contact.
However, they emanate from our past experiences.

Because her older brother was the offender, Alice moved away years previously from her hometown where he still resided and where the abuse took place. However, Alice discovered how present sources of him easily triggered her, causing her to feel unsafe and frightened. In Alice's case, although she was mindful of eliminating any reminders of her brother, her triggers emerged from all kinds of present day sources: photos of him discovered in an old shoe box, an unexpected phone call from him with a message left on voicemail, or Alice's daughter reaching the age Alice was when the abuse began. However, through identification of her triggers and examination of their impact on her, Alice began to fortify herself better by employing timely protective and preventive strategies.

Another characteristic which helps us in understanding triggers and in restoring our recovering strategies is its ubiquitous nature. Triggers come from a multitude of sources: physical, psychological, emotional, behavioral, relational, environmental, and so on. In fact, they can emerge from any source—anywhere and at any time. Read this again, aloud.

Triggers come from a multitude of sources.
They can emerge from any source—anywhere and at any time.

In recalling my self-betrayal into chaotic codependency, I remember being triggered so easily. Triggers were everywhere—right in front of me, constantly. Moving back to my childhood home—what I refer to as my betrayal environment—I was overcome by the self-deprecating life messages which plagued me during my younger years. Whether it was driving by my elementary or middle school, or visiting old parks and playgrounds, or walking up to the home in which I grew up, psychological triggers were going off in my head like fireworks. "You are nothing. You don't matter. It's not good enough… you aren't enough." Fighting off these shame-filled messages took tremendous energy. At the same time, worn down by the intensity of it all, I relinquished my wellness.

By understanding the nature of triggers and their characteristics, we become more aware of them. And thus, through timely recognition of triggers and their role in self-betrayal, we can equip ourselves more thoroughly in addressing them and arresting their impact upon us.

I remember so well Alice's words toward the end of our sessions together. "Holli, I think there will always be triggers. I've done what I can to remove all the tangible reminders, but there are just so many other sources. However, knowing they are out there doesn't scare me anymore. I know I have the tools to work through them and move on with my life."

Although we will embrace more recovering strategies in the Activities section, the first step in addressing triggers is to identify them, describe our response, and name their sources. This is a difficult exercise and should not be rushed. Take as much time as you need. Take breaks and return when you feel ready.

Utilizing a writing format which is comfortable, make three columns.

Who or what triggers me	How I feel / What I say or do	Source / Past Experience
Childhood home	I feel sad. I don't feel valuable.	Unhappy childhood

When you are finished, move on to the next section – Weak links in chain of events.

Weak links in chain of events

Just as we have discovered what triggers are and how they impact our recovering process or wellness practices, thorough examination of our recovery routines is also critical in sustaining our well ways of being. In counseling terminology, we often refer to these patterns as our chain of events. For individuals whose recovering experience or wellness journeys are in their early stages, there is a tendency to pay very close attention to healthy routines and habits. However, as is human nature, as we become more seasoned in our ways of being, our chain of events becomes more integrated into our mindset. Nonetheless, when we self-betray, there is typically a weak link (or many) in the chain of events. Our recognition and understanding of this area of vulnerability is another important piece in moving from self-betrayal to self-discovery.

Weak links can take many different forms. However, some of the most common are the following:

- Boundary violations
- Misjudgment of levels of recovery, wellness, or preparedness
- Lack of support or feelings of isolation

Let's get started with our first area.

Boundary violations

Boundaries are the personalized measures which we have put into place in order to safeguard our wellness. Boundary violations occur when we choose to go against any protective measures which have been implemented. This would include going to places or socializing with certain individuals, knowing they jeopardize our recovery. This also means putting off going to support meetings or avoiding healthy practices which we know sustain our well ways of being. This includes inviting in any unhealthy source which we know is contrary to what we have been embracing and/or placing ourselves in at-risk environments.

This is important. Boundaries are not about pushing others away; boundaries are about creating a protected space, which allows us to honor our healthy ways of being. Crossing over boundaries or violating them weakens the links in our chain of wellness and makes us vulnerable for self-betrayal.

Misjudgment of levels of recovery, wellness, or preparedness

Many times we think we have enough recovering experience under our belts to step out of our comfort zones. It is not wrong to want to take risks, if we do extra work ahead of time in order to be adequately prepared for what might come our way. When we misjudge our levels of strength or growth, we can be easily triggered. Feeling vulnerable or frightened, we self-betray.

In working with victims of abuse and trauma, there were circumstances where survivors were required to face their betrayers, most often due to legal proceedings. Before my clients attended court, we spent as many sessions as needed reinforcing their recovery strategies especially in the management of triggers. It is not a sign of weakness to admit we are not ready to do something or to go someplace. It is a sign of strength that we have the self-awareness not to. Let me say that again.

> **It is not a sign of weakness to admit we are unready to do something.**
> **It is a sign of strength that we have the self-awareness not to.**

Therefore, it is mandatory to keep an honest pulse on our levels of recovery, wellness, or preparedness. Misjudging our levels places unnecessary tension on our links creating areas of vulnerability and setting us up for self-betrayal.

Lack of support or feelings of isolation

Early on in recovery or in acquiring a healthy way of being, we tend to reach out for support. Not only does the camaraderie make it more fun and enjoyable, but there is incredible comfort in knowing how others understand and travel a similar journey. As we become more seasoned and feel more confident in our levels of growth, we often tend to withdraw or pull away from social systems of support. Again, there is nothing wrong with this. However, when we face a vulnerable period or if we are experiencing a series of challenging triggers, feeling like we have no one to call or no one to come alongside us can set us up for self-betrayal. Although independence is good, when we are talking about sustaining wellness, there is strength in numbers. This is important. Read it again, slowly and aloud.

> **Although independence is good, when we are talking about wellness,**
> **there is strength in numbers.**

One of the things which I really admire and respect about several of my close friends who have been in AA or NA for dozens of years is how they never think twice about calling their sponsors or attending extra meetings if they even sense a rough patch is coming their way. Although my friends do the hard work, their fellowship with others is an integral part of their journeys. Having a lack of support or experiencing feelings of isolation contributes to the weakening of our links. Having the links of others to join in with ours redirects us to our wellness paths.

As we get ready to move on to our last area of vulnerability, it is important to note how we included triggers in the examples above. There is an important relationship between triggers and weak links in our chain of events. Triggers can and will test the strength of our recovery links. Weak links in our chain of events will make us more vulnerable to triggers. Read it again, slowly.

<blockquote>

Triggers can and will test the strength of our recovery links.
Weak links in our chain of events will make us more vulnerable to triggers.

</blockquote>

In our process of self-discovery, it is mandatory to know both.

Before we move on to our last area of vulnerability, take some time and reflect upon your recovery routines and healing habits. Returning to your choice of format, respond to the following questions. Take your time. We will add to this exercise in the Activities section

- What does your chain of events look like? In other words, what is your recovery routine or what are your wellness practices?

- What weak links do you detect in your chain of events with regards to boundary violations, misjudging levels of recovery or wellness, or lacking support?

Call out these areas of vulnerability. Write them down. Know them.

Life changes, transitions, and other precipitating factors

As we continue discovering more about ourselves and our experiences with self-betrayal by exploring areas of vulnerability, I find there is hope in uncovering reasons and explanations behind our choices and their ensuing consequences. As I have said, we are not here to excuse our self-betrayals; we are here to bring understanding to them. And, understanding fuels recovery.

The last area of vulnerability covers a wide range of concerns: life changes, transitions, and other precipitating factors. As with the other areas of vulnerability, becoming more aware of them and their impact on us strengthens our process of self-discovery.

Life changes

As we go through life, we constantly experience change. Some of us handle change easily; others don't. Some changes come along naturally and are to be expected. Others happen randomly and often are catastrophic in nature. Two factors are important. First, we need to know ourselves and understand how we handle change. Secondly, based on our self-awareness regarding change, we need to be adaptable, adjusting our recovery routines and wellness practices accordingly. For example, if we know a change is on the horizon and we know it causes added stress on our links, we implement additional strategies or increase certain routines in order to move through it. If a life change is unexpected, we again restore our recovering with added support or self-care exercises. Although we cannot prepare for everything, especially traumatic events, becoming familiar with our levels of vulnerability in this area serves as a source of added strength during unsettling times.

Transitions

There is a slight difference between life changes and transitions, but it is important and should be addressed. Transitions, as opposed to life changes, are natural occurrences. We expect to move from one stage to another, and we can plan and prepare for them. Sometimes, they unfold without much notice or disruption. As with life changes, some individuals handle them well; others do not. Again, it is important to know how you navigate them and what you need to do in order to move through them without self-betraying. Although transitions can be painless, they can also bring about a host of intolerable feelings: depression, anger, loss, anxiety, worthlessness, and hopelessness. The heaviness of these emotions and feelings can wear on our links and erode their sustainability. Becoming aware of this kind of weakening helps us to shore up our recovery routines and healthy habits, making us less vulnerable.

Because my friends and I are at the age where our parents are becoming quite elderly, it has not been uncommon for many of us to experience their passing. Even though we know this is to be expected and it is a natural transition during this stage of life, we still feel tremendous loss and sadness. We each know ourselves, attend to our links, and move forward in our grief, honoring our well ways of being.

Other precipitating factors

We have covered several areas of vulnerability. At the same time, it is important to recognize there may be other precipitating factors which contribute to an individual choosing self-betrayal. Some of these factors may be chronic or reoccurring; others may be acute or short-term in nature. Regardless of their longevity, their presence adds tremendous tension on our links and, over time, erodes them, placing us at heightened risk for self-betrayal. Because there are many, we will name some of the most common. Please remember, whatever yours may be, identify them and become acquainted with them as you continue to uncover your areas of vulnerability.

- Physical or mental illness
- Underlying past issues of abuse or trauma
- Family of origin issues
- Unhealthy, abusive, or violent relationships
- Environments of neglect, abuse, or hardship
- Other pathology or psychosis

Depending upon the severity of other precipitating factors, it is very probable that the guidance of a professional or support program would benefit the individual. Many serious factors are accompanied by other complex manifestations or complicated pathology. They also carry with them the outer layers of shame, and most often, the inner core of shame. As we discussed in Part Two, addressing these more sensitive aspects of self-betrayal along with issues of comorbidity requires the assistance of a skilled therapist or substantial recovery process. If we are to move out of self-betrayal to self-discovery, we must be willing to learn what is keeping us there.

Pause for now and reflect. We have covered some challenging material. When you are ready, spend some time thinking about life changes, transitions, and other precipitating factors. Write down examples of areas in which you felt vulnerable, where you recognize their impact on your recovery or wellness. For now, list them. We will continue with this in the Activities section.

If you are feeling a heaviness right now, relax and breathe. Self-discovery is hard work. Facing our self-betrayal is never easy; however, anything worthwhile rarely is. As we move forward—Recognizing and Releasing the Restraints of Relapse—the weightiness of self-betrayal will start to lift... as our truths continue to surface.

Activities – Chapter 16

Previously, in Part Four, we began several exercises in recognizing areas of vulnerability. If you have completed them, move on to the restoring exercises. If you have not, please do so now.

    1. **Triggers**

        A. The first step in addressing triggers is to identify them, describe our response, and name their sources. This is a difficult exercise and should not be rushed. Take as much time as you need. Take breaks and return when you feel ready. Also, because triggers are fluid and can change over time, add to your list as these changes occur.

            Utilizing a writing format which is comfortable, make three columns.

Who or what triggers me	How I feel / What I say or do	Source / Past Experience/
Childhood home	I feel sad. I don't feel valuable.	Unhappy childhood

        B. Our first restorative step, as we discussed earlier in Part Four, is to attend to the underlying issues or causal factors of our triggers. Not doing so can and will catapult us back into previous unhealthy patterns of thinking, behaving, and feeling. Looking over your sources of triggers, take an honest assessment of their levels of injury and of recovery from them. Consider seeking our professional guidance or group support. We must heal the wounds of our past in order to move forward.

        C. Our second restorative step, after working through underlying issues or injuries, is to take an inventory of your environment and of those people, places, and things that are triggering you.

            i. Assess your degree of exposure to them; adjust boundaries and set stronger ones if needed.

            ii. Assess your expectations of yourself; what you can handle or what you cannot. Reset expectations to meet your wellness needs; not those of others.

iii. Assess your needs for additional support. Attend a meeting, call a sponsor, or see a professional. There may be some residual recovering which needs attending to.

Note: There are additional exercises in Chapter 9 – Subsection Two: Boundary Work – Bracing Yourself with Supportive Structures, which may be helpful, especially "Boundary-based decision making" and "Betrayal-proofing your relationships".

D. The third restorative exercise is really important. I call it the "trigger thermometer exercise"; there are several steps to this "trigger teaching tool".

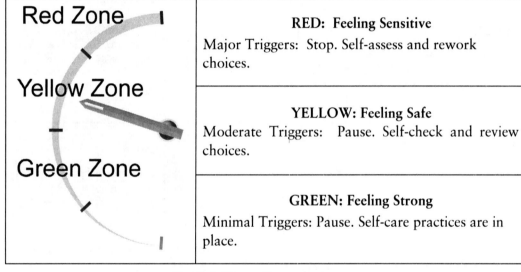

Red Zone	**RED: Feeling Sensitive** Major Triggers: Stop. Self-assess and rework choices.
Yellow Zone	**YELLOW: Feeling Safe** Moderate Triggers: Pause. Self-check and review choices.
Green Zone	**GREEN: Feeling Strong** Minimal Triggers: Pause. Self-care practices are in place.

Fig. 16-2: Trigger Thermometer

i. Imagine there is a trigger thermometer within your being. Each and every day (or even throughout the day), take a reading on how you are feeling—your levels of sensitivity, vulnerability, or strength in your recovering or wellness journey.

ii. After taking an honest assessment, make a mental note of your level. Are you feeling strong, just ok, or vulnerable?

iii. If you are in a place of strength, you understand your triggers may have a minimal impact on you. Of course, it depends on the trigger and its relationship to you. If you are feeling slightly vulnerable or at risk, you must immediately communicate to yourself that your triggers can and will impact you severely; in fact, they could redirect you into self-betrayal.

iv. Lastly, by knowing what is going on with your levels of strength or sensitivity, you have the knowledge and the power to make healthy choices about what to do, where to go, and when and how to go about your day. You are taking care of you!

E. Another restorative exercise is one I've utilized with survivors of abuse and trauma. I often refer to it as a "trigger's ally" because it can become a reliable companion in our work arresting triggers. The four-step exercise is as follows:

  i. Step One – STOP. As soon as you feel triggered, stop whatever you are doing or feeling. In fact, say the word "STOP" aloud.

  ii. Step Two – CALM YOURSELF. Immediately, take in some deep breaths. If you can move away from the trigger, do so. Sit down and relax. Keep breathing. Continue to calm yourself.

  iii. Step Three – CLAIM YOUR PRESENT REALITY. Recall your present healing reality. Tell yourself you are in a well place; you have worked hard; you are safe and healthy; and you have the right to take care of yourself. Repeat as needed.

  iv. Step Four – CHOOSE AN ALTERNATIVE HEALTHY BEHAVIOR. If you are still feeling triggered, there are several healing options: exit the environment of the trigger; call a friend, sponsor, or counselor; set or reset a boundary; reclaim your voice and state what you need; set and adjust expectations and then maintain them.

  Remember, triggers can be relentless. If the trigger returns, repeat the exercise.

2. **Weak links in chain of events**

A. It is critical we recognize the weak links in our chain of events. Take some time and reflect upon your recovery routines and wellness practices. Respond to the following questions.

  i. What does your chain of events look like? In other words, what is your recovery routine or what are your wellness practices?

  ii. What weak links do you detect in your chain of events with regards to boundary violations, misjudging levels of recovery or wellness, or lacking support?

  Call out these areas of vulnerability. Write them down. Know them.

B. The first restorative exercise is to assess and adjust weak links in your boundaries. Utilize this three-step process.

  i. Identify and list your boundaries—the protective measures you implement to safeguard your wellness practices.

     ii. Next to each one, describe whether it is a strong boundary or a vulnerable one.

    iii. If it is a strong one, great. If it is vulnerable, name two actions you can implement or changes you need to make to strengthen it. Do this now. Do not procrastinate. Then, take action on them. This is where your hard work pays off.

  C. The second restorative exercise is to maintain an awareness of weak links with regard to your levels of wellness and lack of support. Utilizing the "trigger thermometer" in the above exercise, honestly assess your levels as you begin your day, and as you go throughout your day. If you are feeling strong, move ahead. If you are feeling vulnerable, implement the following three steps.

     i. Identify the sources of vulnerability (triggers, missing a meeting, re-surfacing of shame or other painful emotions, feeling isolated, etc.).

    ii. Next to each source, identify and implement at least two actions to strengthen the weak link. Do this now. Then, act upon it.

    iii. Call for support and connect with those who embrace wellness. Continue to keep a pulse on how you feel.

3. **Life changes, transitions, and other precipitating factors**

  A. If you have not already done so, spend some time thinking about life changes, transitions, and other precipitating factors. Write down examples of areas in which you felt vulnerable, where you recognize their impact on your recovery or wellness.

  B. In order to restore these areas of vulnerability, implement the following exercise.

     i. For each example, write down a more detailed explanation of the life change, transition, or precipitating factor. Describe more fully how it impacted you: your triggers, feelings, emotions, and behaviors. With complete honesty, describe how it weakened your links and contributed to self-betrayal. Learn from your past. Learn about yourself.

    ii. Then, plan for the future. Write down a step-by-step plan for how you would handle the change, transition, or other factors differently next time. Turn to your recovery lifelines and wellness repertoire. Implement what works for you. Know what doesn't. Be very specific and realistic. Assess and adjust plans as needed.

The work of recognizing weak links and restoring areas of vulnerability is not easy. However, by doing so, we learn more about ourselves – what works for us, what doesn't, and why. It feels good to understand. It strengthens our resolve and lightens our spirits. It readies us for the process of releasing.

End of Part Four: Recognizing and Releasing Areas of Vulnerability - Healing Continuum

After completing the reading in *Part Four: Recognizing and Restoring Areas of Vulnerability,* work all the exercises for a minimum of three weeks or until you feel you have an honest and detailed recognition of your areas of vulnerability and you have solidly implemented the restorative exercises into your recovery routines. These cognitive-behavioral exercises must become second nature to you. You should be able to call them up and act upon them in a moment's time. When you are ready, reassess your current healing reality on the healing continuum p. 178. Then, pace yourself and proceed accordingly.

0	1	2	3	4	5	6	7	8	9	10

Score	Next Actions to Take
0-3	There may be some strong resistance going on in facing your triggers, weak links in your chain of events, or other precipitating factors. This can be very painful work and often the Mask of Denial will step in to minimize our feelings of shame and to mitigate unresolved injuries or issues. Please consider seeking out professional sources of guidance or therapy to assist you in this process as is recommended in Restorative exercise B. If you feel ready to do the work but feel a bit over-whelmed, slow down the process by implementing the following steps for one week: • Reread the section on Triggers. • Rework #1 Trigger exercise A and then C. • On a 4 x 6 index cards, identify and write down 2 boundaries and 2 expectations you want to set for yourself and 2 sources of support. • Review your cards every day and be prepared to implement your boundaries, expectations, and support, if and when you feel triggered. • Repeat the process until this becomes second nature to you. • Do not move on to the next exercise until you feel ready. Follow the same steps as above for #1 Trigger exercises D and E (each one for a minimum of one week). Therefore, you will be spending a minimum of three weeks on this exercise. When you feel ready, move on and repeat the same process for the following: • Weak links in chain of events exercises A,B, and C. • Life changes, transitions, and other precipitating factors exercises A and B. Do not rush this process. Take the time you need as you continue to learn about your areas of vulnerability and how to grow stronger in your self-discovery. When ready, reassess your levels until you are scoring at least an 8.

	Then, move on.
4-7	Of the three areas of vulnerability – triggers, weak link in chain of events, or life changes, transitions, and other factors – name which one you feel is your most challenging. Then, do the following: • Reread the section on that area of vulnerability. • Rework all the exercises for that area, spending at least one week or more on each of the restorative exercises before moving on to the next. • For each of the responses to the restorative exercises, write down your specific recovery actions on 4 x 6 cards. When you feel vulnerable in any area, pull out your cards, read your restorative responses, and act upon them. Repeat the process as often as needed. • Acknowledge your success. Validate what is working for you and why and what isn't. Feel the process of self-discovery take hold within you. Reassess your levels before moving on. If needed, repeat the process with any of the remaining areas of vulnerability. Trust the process. Take your time. Move ahead when you have scored at least an 8 and you feel ready.
8-10	I am fortified in my recovery work by continuing to learn about my specific areas of vulnerability. By making my awareness of them a priority and by integrating recovery tools into my repertoire, I can move ahead in strength, not fear. At the same time, I will not become complacent. I understand my areas of vulnerability can shift and change over time. I am committed to revisiting my responses and reworking exercises as needed. I am embracing this process of self-discovery and ready to move ahead.

Fig. 16-3: Recognize and Restore Areas—Next Actions after Reassessment

17 Betrayal and Relapse Part Five:
Recognizing and Releasing the Restraints of Relapse

"With the insanity of the past many months gnawing at my consciousness, I began exploring the restraints of relapse—the trappings which contain us in our descent from recovery."

Mountain Air

Part One Redefining Relapse as Self-Betrayal	Part Two Unraveling Debilitating Emotions and Self-Deprecating Life Messages	Part Three Recognizing and Removing the Masks of Denial, Disguise, and Detachment
1 2 3 4 5 6 7 8 9 10	1 2 3 4 5 6 7 8 9 10	1 2 3 4 5 6 7 8 9 10

Part Four Recognizing and Restoring Areas of Vulnerability	Part Five Recognizing and Releasing the Restraints of Relapse
1 2 3 4 5 6 7 8 9 10	1 2 3 4 5 6 7 8 9 10

As we begin Part Five: *Recognizing and Releasing the Restraints of Relapse,* assess where you are on the healing continuum. Shade in the number which describes your current healing reality.

0	1	2	3	4	5	6	7	8	9	10

Score	How Do I Feel Right Now?
0-3	I think I've been angry at myself for so long, I don't know how to feel any different! There are times when I try to let go of my self-blame and self-pity, but I'm almost afraid of how I might feel! When I admit those feelings, I feel even worse. It's a crazy cycle! I'm not a big believer in forgiveness – of myself or of others - but I'm wondering if there is some other way to let go of all this heaviness I carry around? I've worked hard in other areas of my recovery from self-betrayal, and I want to move forward. I want to feel free.

4-7	I've struggled on and off with releasing my restraints. It seems as though I let them go and I am ok for a while. Then, almost without my awareness, they creep back into my being and I find myself filled with regrets or self-blame or I start getting angry at others. What is it I'm not doing and how can I move forward in healthier ways? The "gifts" of releasing? I'm not sure what that means? I'd like to know more.
8-10	I've learned that recognizing and releasing the restraints of relapse is an on-going process. It is one I have integrated daily into my recovering routine. I am aware of my most problematic restraints and I have a comfortable safe process by which to release them. Most importantly, I have begun to receive many gifts of releasing and I've learned how to acknowledge them as well as honor them as an integral part of my healing journey.

Fig. 17-1: Recognize and Release Restraints—Healing Continuum

In most recovery programs or wellness routines, there is a timely practice for letting go of past emotional and psychological burdens. Commonly, this practice is encouraged earlier on in the process. Although I have left Part Five: Recognizing and Releasing the Restraints of Relapse until now, its principles can be implemented at any time during the self-discovery process. At the same time, I have found our acknowledgment of the need for releasing and our appreciation for its multitude of gifts serve our journeys more effectively after we have cleared away the contagions of debilitating emotions, destructive masks, and detrimental areas of vulnerability. In addition, placing the process of releasing before Part Six: Reclaiming Ourselves and Rediscovering Our Truths prepares and positions us to do so. Let's get started.

1. Recognizing the restrains of relapse

2. Releasing the restraints of relapse

3. Gifts of releasing

Recognizing the restraints of relapse

When I think back to my self-betrayal, there was no one who beat me up more than I did! I did a really good job of it! This is another part of the insidiousness of relapse. We are responsible for choosing it; thus, we are to blame for it. However, we are also accountable for releasing ourselves from it. If we choose not to, no one else is to blame for that either.

Because there are so many different kinds of self-betrayal and we are all so unique, each experience carries with it a wide range of "restraints of relapse". Restraints hold us back. Restraints shackle our recovery. This is important. Let's say it again, slowly and aloud.

Restraints hold us back. Restraints shackle our recovery.

Although many of us can feel or sense their restrictive presence, it is important to get acquainted with restraints. Don't second-guess them. Restraints can be deceptive, luring us into unhealthy territory. Name them and know how they feel.

Restraints come in many forms. Some of the most common are the following:

- Toxic emotions
- Negativity
- Unhealthy influences
- Self-recriminating life messages
- Pity parties or poor-me scenarios
- Holding onto un-forgiveness
- Overreliance on self

Although I remember experiencing most of these restraints of relapse to some degree, I struggled mostly with the toxic emotions of anger and regret. Even as I was moving through my recovering process, I felt angry over my choices. And then, because I waited almost two years before seeking out professional guidance, thereby lengthening my stay in self-betrayal, I had a hard time letting go of the waves of regret, which continued to wash over me. By pausing, taking the time to identify my restraints, and reflecting on their contrary nature, I was ready for their release.

Before we move forward with releasing, it is critical to take an honest inventory of your restraints. Returning to your writing format, complete the following exercise.

- Begin naming your restraints. Who or what is holding you back?

- Who or what do you need to let go of?

Take your time. Breathe. Take breaks when needed. Begin again. We will continue with additional exercises in the Activities section.

Releasing the restraints of relapse

I like to use the word "releasing" for several reasons. First, it means "letting go". We no longer will hold onto someone or something which is not serving us in healthy ways. Secondly, with *"ing"* on the end, it is an action verb. This means releasing takes work. And thirdly, the applications of releasing are numerous: removing, letting go, forgiving, cleansing, purging, washing away, casting out, and so on. "Releasing" affords us the freedom to choose an application which suits our personalities and our processes.

Once we are comfortable with an application, we move on to selecting a process which also fits with our recovery routines, wellness practices, and foundational principles or spiritual beliefs. This is important for two reasons. First, releasing is personal. Finding a venue which is safe is critical. Secondly, releasing is profoundly inner-personal. Choosing a process which honors you and your voice is paramount. Thirdly, releasing is your partner in recovery. Making it your companion, like a reliable friend, supports and strengthens your spirit.

Therefore, consider any of the following processes; then, choose one or more to serve you.

- Turning to your Higher Power, Source, God, faith or belief system
- Meditating or praying
- Journaling, writing, or utilizing any type of creative expression
- Walking, hiking, or integrating other healthy physical expressions of release
- Embracing healing rituals, cultural practices, or traditional customs
- Spending time in environments of nurturance, peace, and renewal
- Connecting with others with whom you feel safe and trust in the process

When you are ready, take a few moments and journal about your process of releasing. Describe what works for you and why it does. Take your time. Reflect on your responses. We will continue in the Activities section.

Gifts of releasing

One of the wonders in moving from self-betrayal to self-discovery is how recovering rewards us. Throughout each part of the recovering process, we have received the gifts of awareness and understanding; and we have embraced recovering tools and strategies, reclaiming ourselves along the way. Part Five: Recognizing and Releasing the Restraints of Relapse is no different.

However, it has been my experience and the experiences of many others, when releasing the restraints of relapse, the gifts are beautiful and bountiful! As is true with so many things in life, when we finally let go of anyone or anything which holds us back, not only we are freed from it, but we are free to move forward—free to receive the gifts awaiting us.

By finally letting go of my firm hold on regret and anger, I changed completely. My spirit felt cleansed and my perceptions were clarified. I saw life through a lens of compassion and gratitude. Starving for more, I released residual restraints of disappointment and sadness. In letting go, I received their respective gifts while honoring the process and maintaining an attitude of humility.

Before moving on to the Activities section, take as much time as needed and reflect upon your gifts of releasing. If this is premature, for now, reflect upon other gifts you have received in your recovering from self-betrayal. Return to your format, writing down what gifts you claim. Do not rush the process. Move at your own pace. Stay the course. Take time to honor your recovering. You have prepared yourself well while paving the path for Part Six: Reclaiming Ourselves and Rediscovering Truths.

Activities – Chapter 17

Previously in Part Five, we began several exercises in recognizing and releasing the restraints of relapse. If you have completed them, continue on with the remaining exercises. If you have not, please do so now.

1. **Recognizing the restraints of relapse**
    A. Take an honest inventory of your restraints. Returning to your writing format, begin naming your restraints. Who or what is holding you back? Who or what do you need to let go of? Take your time. This is important.
    B. Next to each restraint, answer three questions:
        i.   Why you are holding onto it?
        ii. How is it hurting you?
        iii. What would happen if you let go of it?

The act of releasing comes in our own time. However, as you reflect upon your responses, remember, the longer you hold on to your restraints, the longer they will hold you back.

2. **Releasing the restraints of relapse**
    A. Take a few moments and journal about your process of releasing. Describe what works for you and why it does. Take your time.
    B. Look over your list of restraints. Work through them one at a time, utilizing your process for releasing. Take as many days or weeks as needed. I would recommend not moving on to a second or third restraint until you feel at peace with the release of the prior one. However, you know yourself best and what works for you. Trust in your process.
    C. As restraints revisit you, confront them and release them in a timely manner. Do not beat yourself up. This is normal. You have the tools under your belt! Grab hold of them whenever you need them!

3. **Gifts of releasing**
    A. Take as much time as needed and reflect upon your gifts of releasing. If this is premature, for now, reflect upon other gifts you have received in your recovering from self-betrayal. Do not rush the process. Move at your own pace. Stay the course. Take time to honor your recovering. Return to your format, writing down what gifts you claim.
    B. Next to each gift, answer the following questions:
        i.   What are you feeling?
        ii. How has this gift changed or transformed you?
        iii. How will this gift serve you moving forward?

Release your restraints and claim your gifts, often. As you do, be mindful of the discoveries which unfold and embrace the strength within their healing truths.

End of Part Five: Recognizing and Releasing the Restraints of Relapse – Healing Continuum

After completing the reading in *Part Five: Recognizing and Releasing the Restraints of Relapse,* work all the exercises for a minimum or three weeks or until you feel you have taken a thorough inventory of your restraints, you are releasing them in a timely and meaningful manner, and you are embracing the gifts which emerge from their removal. When you are ready, reassess your current healing reality on the healing continuum p. 193. Then, pace yourself and proceed.

0	1	2	3	4	5	6	7	8	9	10

Score	Next Actions to Take
0-3	Releasing the restraints of relapse can feel foreign and it can feel frightening. As strange as it might seem, even unhealthy feelings, emotions, or behaviors can make us feel safe. They are what we know. Slow down the process. Take your time and rework the exercises in the Activities in the following manner: • Spend two weeks or more on #1 – A and B. Reflect and write a little each day. Pause and take breaks when needed. Complete your inventory. • Spend two weeks or more on #2 – A, B and C. Choose one restraint and work on releasing it. Go slowly. Take more time if needed. Do not move onto another restraint until you feel comfortable with this process. • For now, don't force the "gifts" to come. Work on your releasing and when the time comes where you feel the "release take hold" and the "gift emerge", return to your writings and notate it. Breathe. Relax. Continue your releasing. Make it a priority. By removing the old, we make room for the new. Reassess your levels when the process of releasing becomes a safe and a natural part of your recovery repertoire. Move forward when you feel free to do so.
4-7	Sometimes we get lazy or we become overly confident in our recovering routines. As with all aspects of recovery from self-betrayal, recognizing and releasing our restraints must be a priority as well. Also, restraints can shift so we must be mindful of their changing presence. Implement the following practices: • Once a week, revisit your inventory of restraints - Activities #1 - A. Add to the list or make any changes. Then, reflect upon them. Add to or reword your responses in #1 – B. Really get to know your restraints. Understand them.

	• Once a day, set a time for releasing. Keep this time. Safe-guard it! This is mandatory. Follow the practice in Activities #2 – A, B, and C. If needed, slow it down. Go at your own pace, but keep going.
	• When you are ready or you feel the change which comes from releasing take hold, begin paying attention to the "gifts". They may be subtle at first, but they will surface. Honor them. Validate them. Give them a voice by writing them down.
	When this process is solidly integrated into your routine, reassess your levels. Move on.
8-10	Continue your practice of recognizing your restraints. Revisit your list of restraints if you feel new ones emerge or old ones resurface. Continue releasing your restraints in a timely and purposeful manner. Continue receiving your gifts. Honor them. Let them speak in you and through you as we move forward in our process of self-discovery.

Fig. 17-2: Recognize and Release Restraints—Next Actions after Reassessment

18 Betrayal and Relapse Part Six:
Reclaiming Ourselves and Rediscovering Our Truths

"Don't stay too long in the shame-filled grounds of relapse.
Fertile soil awaits your return and your recovering."

Mountain Air

Part One Redefining Relapse as Self-Betrayal	Part Two Unraveling Debilitating Emotions and Self- Deprecating Life Messages	Part Three Recognizing and Removing the Masks of Denial, Disguise, and Detachment
1 2 3 4 5 6 7 8 9 10	1 2 3 4 5 6 7 8 9 10	1 2 3 4 5 6 7 8 9 10

Part Four Recognizing and Restoring Areas of Vulnerability	Part Five Recognizing and Releasing the Restraints of Relapse	Part Six Reclaiming Ourselves and Rediscovering Our Truths
1 2 3 4 5 6 7 8 9 10	1 2 3 4 5 6 7 8 9 10	1 2 3 4 5 6 7 8 9 10

We began our journey with a painful truth about self-betrayal.

**Relapse is about losing who we are
and forfeiting our potential for who we are meant to be.**

We continue our journey with a profound truth about self-betrayal.

**Relapse gives us the opportunity to claim lessons from the past
and to reclaim ourselves and our truths.**

In this journey of moving from self-betrayal to self-discovery, we have bravely dug out our truths buried deeply within dark places; we have courageously unearthed their capsulation; and we have delicately but deliberately attended to the pulling out of shame-filled roots, the pruning away of unhealthy branches, and the processing of their purposeful disposal. As with any path of recovering, it is not only in the preparatory stages of our work or during the step-by-step procedures themselves, but it is within the entire journey where we are cultivating an inner landscape readying it for renewal and regrowth.

Doing the hard work of moving from self-betrayal, it is paramount to pause during the process and take stock of how each step of awareness, recognition, and application contributes to self-discovery. And, it is in Step Six: Reclaiming Ourselves and Rediscovering Our Truths where we will take time to be still, further acknowledging and embracing what we have learned, and embedding those lessons into our journeys ahead. It is time to draw from our compost pile of healing nutrients and to cultivate our spirits in our ongoing process of self-discovery.

Before you begin Part Six: Reclaiming Ourselves and Rediscovering Our Truths, pause once again and assess where you are on the healing continuum. Take your time. Breathe. Shade in the number which describes your current healing truths.

0	1	2	3	4	5	6	7	8	9	10

Score	How Do I Feel Right Now?
0-3	Did I really face my self-betrayal? Did I do the hard work? Am I deserving of self-acknowledgment? What is like to claim my truths - to honor my work and my voice? I am scared, but I think I'm ready to find out…
4-7	I'm a little nervous. I start to doubt myself and I wonder if I really did all the hard work. I know my recovering journey is not over. But, my truths are there. I can feel them… sense them… I want to know them. I am ready to claim them.
8-10	I believe and know by working my recovering program and trusting the process, moving out of self-betrayal affords me the opportunity for self-discovery. As I claim lessons from my past and reclaim myself, my truths grow stronger every day and take firm residence within my being. Although my recovering journey continues, I want and need to take time to honor where I've been and where I am.

Fig. 18-1: Reclaim and Rediscover Truths—Healing Continuum

Let's gets started as we harvest three areas.

1. Replacing the old with the new
2. Rebuilding boundaries and fortifying them
3. Restoring self-work and self-worth

Replacing the old with the new

One of the beauties of self-discovery is the ongoing development of an awareness to truth and of an awakening to self. As we work each step, these discoveries emerge and take hold. Although there is prior recognition of them during our process, accompanied by restorative properties, it is important to re-identify them, clarifying their significance to our recovering. And, because our mindset has moved out of the shadows of shame, our thoughts are purposely positioned for their reclaiming.

Take your time and work through the following questions. Refer back to your writings in the previous sections, drawing upon your discoveries and adding to them.

1. **Part One: Redefining Relapse**

   A. Return to your narrative from Part One. As you reread it now and reflect upon your self-betrayal, what comes to mind? Do you view it differently? The same? How and why?

   B. How has redefining relapse as a universal experience—one of shared suffering—changed your perspective or your attitudes about it? Explain in detail.

   C. What have you learned about yourself in approaching relapse as an opportunity to move from self-betrayal to self-discovery? Take your time. Validate your words. Honor your voice.

2. **Part Two: Unraveling Debilitating Emotions and Self-deprecating Life Messages**

   A. Recalling the debilitating emotions which accompany self-betrayal is painful work. What emotions were most difficult for you to work through? What have you learned about them? If they resurface, how will you deal with them in a timely way?

   B. What did you learn about shame—the outer layers and the inner core? How has shame played a role in your self-betrayal? Describe in detail. How can you use your new knowledge to arrest its presence in the future?

   C. In an episode of self-betrayal, we flood ourselves with self-deprecating life messages. How have yours played a role in self-betrayal? Drawing from previous healthy seasons in your life and from your current recovering, what positive life messages can you tell yourself now? Write them down; claim your truths.

3. **Part Three: Recognizing and Restoring the Masks of Denial, Disguise, and Detachment**

   A. What did you learn about the three masks? How can your new insights help you in moving ahead?

   B. Which mask is most detrimental to you? Why and how so? If there is more than one, explain as well. How does knowing this help you?

   C. What truths about yourself and your recovery will you claim when the personality of lies, pretend persona, and/or pulling away from truths start to surface? How will you implement them? Take your time; this is important.

Rebuilding boundaries and fortifying them

Boundary work is a part of most recovery work and is an integral part of sustaining it. As I shared, "Boundaries aren't about pushing others away; boundaries are about putting a safe space around us in order to do our work." Boundaries also communicate to us and to others that our wellness is important, and we are important.

Another important discovery in our work is finding out what boundaries are weak, which are strong, and where we need fortifications. Referring back to your work in Part Five: Recognizing and Restoring Areas of Vulnerability, continue describing how you have cultivated healthier ways of being. Continue claiming more of your truths.

1. **Recognizing and restoring areas of vulnerability**
   A. What have you learned about triggers? What is the most important feature about triggers in its application to your wellness? What new steps will you take to arrest your triggers in a timely way?
   B. In reviewing your chain of events and the concept of weak links, what discoveries did you make? What new boundaries have you implemented? What old ones need shoring up? How will you communicate these new truths, to yourself and to others? Think through this section carefully. Honor your discoveries. Celebrate your truths.
   C. What have you discovered about yourself in handling life changes, transitions, or other precipitating factors? Instead of looking at them as areas of weakness, how can you now claim these truths to serve you in healthy ways? Take your time. This is important.

Restoring self-work and self-worth

As I stated in the introduction, one of the reasons I get so excited when talking about relapse is because it affords us the opportunity for self-discovery—to reclaim lessons from the past and to reclaim ourselves and our truths. Self-betrayal is not a permanent placement; self-betrayal positions us for the restorative resurrection of our work and worth. Our restoring of self-work and self-worth is evidenced in how we live out our recovering—one day at a time; one step at a time; sometimes, one breath at a time. It is demonstrated in our implementation of truths and in their representations of us, through our thoughts, feelings, and behaviors.

First, by referring back to Step Five: Recognizing and Releasing the Restraints of Relapse, reflect upon your responses and add to your truths. Claim them now.

2. **Recognizing and releasing the restraints of relapse**
   A. What discoveries did you make regarding your restraints and their role in your self-work and self-worth?
   B. What new truths have you claimed in the releasing of your restraints? Describe them fully. Celebrate these discoveries.
   C. What gifts have replaced your restraints? How have they impacted your self-work and self-worth? In describing them, rejoice in their presence. Pause and honor these truths.

Secondly, take in a deep breath as you begin the next section. Give yourself permission to spend as much time as you need. Take breaks. Return and begin again. This is important.

Think about your life. Think about all the journeys you have taken. Think about the seasons of wellness in your life. Pause. Reflect and remember. Whether the seasons of wellness have been bountiful or whether they have been scarce, each one brings with it past experiences of survival, of sustainability, and of strength. We are here now. And, it is important to recognize them and reclaim them. It is vital to integrate these seasonal truths into our current self-work and self-worth.

3. **Reclaiming ourselves and rediscovering our truths**

    A. In previous seasons of wellness, where did you learn resiliency? From whom or what? How have those lessons helped you and how will they continue to help you in your process of self-discovery?

    B. During seasons of recovering, how did you learn to differentiate between danger and safety? Who or what jeopardized your truths and who or what did not? What powerful truths will you commit to carrying with you in strengthening your self-work and self-worth?

    C. In previous seasons of sustained healing, where, when, and from whom or what did you learn the difference between trust and mistrust—in yourself and in others? How have those lessons augmented and enhanced your self-work and self-worth? How can they continue to do so?

    D. During prior seasons of self-discovery, when did you learn the difference between the hard work of recovery versus the consequences of complacency? How will you integrate those truths into your process of self-discovery? How will you allow those truths to strengthen your self-work and supplement your self-worth?

Take as much time as needed in responding to these questions. Reflect on your responses, rewrite or revise as needed, and revisit them often. These truths provide the fertile soil from which our self-discovery will grow and flourish. These truths are ours for the taking. Reach out and claim them. And, if and when you start to doubt yourself, pause. Be still. Give yourself permission to go back and rework any parts or sections of recovering from self-betrayal to self-discovery. There is no weakness in doing so; recovery strengthens and sustains us in truth.

Trust in the process.

Believe in yourself.

Continue to live it out.

End of Part Six: Reclaiming Ourselves and Rediscovering Our Truths – Healing Continuum

In closing, I leave you with a few final reflections. Throughout Section IV – Betrayal and Relapse, I have shared parts of my journey of self-betrayal with you. In the winter of 2011, after struggling for almost two years, I reached out to a professional to assist in my recovering. Just as I have recommended, because I was not able to access or address my inner core of shame, I knew I needed a trusted therapist to guide me through the process. And although I thought I would keep my self-betrayal experience a private matter, I chose to submit my journals for publication. After much revision and editing, *Mountain Air: Relapsing and Finding the Way Back…One Breath at a Time* was published in 2013 by Loving Healing Press, Inc.

Not a day goes by where I don't reflect upon my journey from self-betrayal to self-discovery. One of the most important lessons I have learned is amidst the hard work of recovering and within the humility of releasing my past, I constantly receive the grace and strength to move forward. And although I would never recommend choosing self-betrayal, my life has become more meaningful and purposeful because of lost truths recovered and because of new truths claimed. For the past four years, I have continued to live them out.

Each day, in my quiet time, I ask myself four questions. I reflect on them. I embrace them as my personal healing continuum, and I utilize them as my ongoing source of accountability. I pause. And, I continue on my path of self-discovery. I pose them to you now.

- What are your truths?
- How have you already claimed them and how will you continue to do so?
- How have you and how will you continue to integrate them into your authentic self?
- How will you continue to be true to yourself?

Live out your self-discovery—one breath, one step, one day at a time.
Live out your wellness, allowing your truths to speak for themselves.
Holli

Epilogue

"Feel how that [your] activity enriches not only your life, but that of countless others."
—Eckhart Tolle

Reward

Addressing recovering from betrayal, betrayal in relationship to codependency and grief, and self-betrayal requires much from both reader and author. For me, however, taking this journey with you has been a privilege. The driving force behind this endeavor has been to bring a fresh insight into the topic of betrayal along with healing approaches for those of us impacted by its invasion into our lives. Helping others is not only my call in life on a professional basis, but it is also an integral part of my being. The rewards I have experienced, along the way, far surpass any I could have planned or hoped for. That is the beauty of giving back to others.

As I think about my personal journeys with betrayal and recovering from self-betrayal, multiple rewards come to mind. However, the one reward which has impacted me the most and continues to influence my choices in life the most significantly is the emergence of a newly uncovered emotion—courage. Having dutifully executed the role of a peacemaker in my personal relationships, I wasn't one to speak up or speak out against others; I was never one to rock the boat. For the majority of my youth and young adult life, it was more important to me to ensure other peoples' places, positions, and points of view were respected, even if it meant mine were not.

Embracing recovering from the betrayal injuries in my life has slowly, but ever so constantly, deposited the seeds and nurtured the buds of courage within me. Over time, and with continual recovering, I have learned to speak up about my truths and to challenge perceptions based on false images and secretive pasts. On various levels, I have learned to confront what is hurtful and damaging to me. I have learned to do so with a bold spirit, blending it with mutual respect, and consideration. Although there is much ground for the roots of courage to spread and take hold, I am grateful to claim it as one of my rewards. I no longer see myself as just a peacemaker, but a risk-taker as well.

In your recovering journey, I challenged you on many levels. With each phase of your recovering readings, activities, and continuum, I wanted to inform you, encourage you, and equip you with effective tools and strategies designed to move you away from your injured state and move you toward your desired state of wellness. In addition, I purposely created a mood of tension and accountability within the process by asking you to conduct personal inventories and to assess your levels of healing and growth along the way. However, it was you who did the work. Each step of the way, you took on the challenge. You took the initiative; you made the time; and you chose to reinvest one more time, into you. By choosing to take this journey, you gave yourself the most priceless gift possible—the gift of recovering. It is a gift filled with rewards; it awaits your claim and your calling.

As you think about your entire journey, what rewards will you claim? They may be personal, relational, or professional. They may be external or internal. They may be extrinsic or intrinsic. They may be tangible or they may be abstract. No reward is too small or too insignificant. Each one matters. Each one is well-earned and well-deserved.

On a professional level, I have experienced another intrinsic reward which has taken on a life of its own. It is the motivation and drive behind writing the first edition—and then the second edition—of *Breaking Through Betrayal: And Recovering the Peace Within*. It is a force within me I cannot explain or control! My passion to bring relief and recovery from betrayal injury to others is fueled by unexplainable energy, focus, and discipline. Each time I sit down to write, I take a moment to acknowledge this reward and I am amazed by its presence.

Whether it is in our professional lives and/or our personal journeys, it is important to take time to immerse ourselves into the depths of affirmation and acknowledgment that come our way. Whatever your rewards may be, allow yourself the privilege of soaking in their worth and value. Give yourself permission to bask in the rays of their influence and impact on you. Smile, cry, pray, and laugh. Let your emotions flow as you fully embrace what your investment has returned to you and how it is reflected in you.

Once again, pause and take some time to ponder your rewards. Make a mental note or even a written notation acknowledging the budding rewards which continue to blossom and reseed within you. Feel their transformation as you continue to breathe life into them and into you. Enjoy the process.

I am sure you know by now I could not leave you without one more task at hand, one more stretching piece of recovering! Our journey would just not be complete!

Although we experience historical periods of peace and prosperity, over the past decade, our country along with so many others has endured some of the most astounding and astonishing betrayals of our time. I have to believe that each one of us must know someone, and sadly probably many more, whose lives have been devastated, if not destroyed. Betrayal, disguising itself in all forms, has left people bankrupt emotionally, physically, financially, professionally, socially, relationally, and so on. Each day the fallout continues within our governments, our communities, and our families. Each day, another person is robbed; another person's life is re-landscaped, just as was ours.

In our recovering, I believe we not only have an opportunity, but we have a calling to reach out to others. You might be thinking, "What do I have to offer? Although I am in a strong healing place, I don't have the skills or the time to help someone else. What can I do?" I can't tell you exactly how and where your innate special abilities and talents will take you, but I will tell you that you hold in your possession a unique and powerful gift—knowledge and experience of betrayal recovering. You know what betrayal feels like, and how it rears and displays its ugly manifestations in your life. And, you have in your recovering bank the insight that release from its bondage takes tremendous investment, but it is reachable and it is real.

When I closed my private practice several years ago, to take time off to write the first edition of this book, I never anticipated how difficult it would be to terminate the relationships I had built with many clients over the years. During the two to three weeks of the termination sessions, I was a basket case, as were my clients! Of course, we planned and prepared for our last sessions together. Mostly, we spoke of their healing places and recovering plans. But, we ended with words of mutual gratitude, respect, and closure. Although some clients gave me small mementos (within the ethical guidelines) as parting gifts, others spoke or wrote their words. One client, who battled betrayal on multiple fronts, and who courageously worked her recovering program, wrote me a tender message. Her words, still with me today, are both rewarding and humbling:

> "Dear Holli,
>   Goodbyes are painful! Three and a half years ago, when my neighbor gave me your name, it was a God thing. You are a gift God gave me in the darkest hours of my life. You have gently, lovingly, but firmly guided me through trying to find out who I really am. I have shared with you my most intimate thoughts and feelings and you always gently guided me in the direction of healing. I know I have made it because you cared about me..."

In closing, I challenge you to find your calling, your venue for continued change and recovering. Care about someone or something. Stand up against betrayal when it calls to you. Act upon it. Show someone you can be believed and you can believe in them. Demonstrate trust in someone or something and make it profoundly evident that you can be trusted. Live out your willingness to invest into someone or something and prove without a doubt you are worthy of their investment. Listen, empathize, and comfort. Whatever form it takes, each act of giving back will give others hope.

It is hope which keeps us going; it is hope which tells us that betrayal will not win out. We must be the messengers, in whatever form betrayal calls to us. Take some time but do not waste time; betrayal abounds as we speak. Seek out your venue and share your gifts with others. Allow your wellness and wholeness to spill out and to speak for you. It is time.

As we both continue our journeys, I want you to know:

- I ask this of you because I believe in you and in the recovering process.
- I ask this of you because I trust in you and in your level of wellness.
- I ask this of you because I know the rewards of investing into you.
- I ask this of you because others await your calling, just as you did mine.

Believe and Be Well.

About the Author

Holli Kenley is a Licensed Marriage and Family Therapist in the state of California. She holds a Masters Degree in Psychology with an emphasis on Marriage, Family, and Child Counseling. She first became interested in promoting the wellness of others in the early 1990s by volunteering time leading support groups for women struggling with Premenstrual Dysphoric Disorder (PMDD). This experience was the motivation behind her first book—*The PMS Puzzle*—as well as the impetus to return to graduate school, to become a licensed therapist.

Prior to and during her work as a therapist, Holli was a California middle and high school Humanities teacher. For nearly thirty years, Holli sought not only to teach students but to reach out to young people as they often navigated through painful and challenging life experiences. Much of who Holli is, as a person and a therapist, has been shaped largely by her role as a teacher.

For two decades (both as an intern and a licensed clinician), Holli has worked in a variety of settings: a women's shelter and transitional housing, a counseling center, and in private practice. Counseling with adolescents, teens, young and older adults, Holli's areas of special training and interest include trauma, abuse, addiction, codependency, and grief/loss. It is because of these presenting issues along with Holli's passion for clients to move out of their fragile states and into a place of purposeful authenticity that she authored her second book—*Breaking Through Betrayal: And Recovering the Peace Within*.

Holli has written this book for anyone who has come face to face with betrayal of any kind and in any form. She invites the reader to take a journey with her: to break through the devastation of betrayal in one's life through compassionate understanding and processing of one's vulnerable position. Then, by providing the reader with Cognitive-Behavioral tools and strategies, benchmarks for assessment, and timelines for individualized pacing, Holli engages the reader in an empowering process tailored specifically for recovery from betrayal injury. Her purpose is simple—to bring relief, release, and renewal from the bondage of betrayal.

Holli currently works in the field of psychology as an author, speaker, and workshop presenter. Because of her own life experiences and the recovery that she has embraced throughout her personal journey, Holli has a deep desire to impart her healing strategies to others. In her words, "I believe, know, and trust that wellness awaits each of us. We choose the time."

After spending over twenty years living in Southern California, Holli and her husband have moved to the mountains of Arizona.

Try These Other Empowering Titles from

Holli Kenley, M.A., Marriage and Family Therapist

Mountain Air: Relapsing and Finding the Way Back...One Breath at a Time

Betrayal-Proof Your Relationship: What Couples Need To Know & Do

Cyber Bullying No More: Parenting A High Tech Generation

Another Way: A Novel

Available at **www.amazon.com/author/hollikenley**

To find out more about Holli's work or to contact her for workshops, conferences, or speaking opportunities, please visit her website www.hollikenley.com.

Follow on Twitter https://twitter.com/HolliKenley

Stop by her Facebook page www.facebook.com/AuthorHolliKenley

Bibliography

Beattie, M. (2011). *Codependent no more: How to stop controlling others and start caring for yourself.* Center City, Minn.: Hazelden.

Films Media Group. (2010). TEDTalks: *Brene Brown--The Power of Vulnerability.* TED.

Grossman, D., & DeGaetano, G. (2014). *Stop teaching our kids to kill: A call to action against TV, movie, and video game violence.* New York : Crown

In Gurman, A. S., In Lebow, J., & In Snyder, D. K. (2015). *Clinical handbook of couple therapy.* New York: Guilford Press.

Hedva, B., & Hedva, B. J. (2013). *Betrayal, trust, and forgiveness: A guide to emotional healing and self-renewal.* Berkeley: Celestial Arts.

Herzanek, J. (2010). *Why don't they just quit?: What families and friends need to know about addiction and recovery.* Boulder, CO: Changing Lives Foundation.

Kenley, H. (2013). Mountain air: *Relapsing and finding the way back... one breath at a time.* Ann Arbor: Loving Healing Press.

Kenley, H. (2011). *Betrayal-proof your relationship: What couples need to know & do.* Ann Arbor: Loving Healing Press.

Maltz, W. (2012). *The sexual healing journey: A guide for survivors of sexual abuse.* New York: William Morrow.

Nichols, M. P. (2014). *Family therapy: Concepts and methods.* Harlow: Pearson.

Pretzer, J. (2013). *Clinical applications of cognitive therapy.* New York: Plenum Press.

Salvador, M., & Vetere, A. (2012). *Families and family therapy.* London: Routledge.

Santrock, J. W. (2014). *A topical approach to life-span development.* Boston: McGraw-Hill.

Sheff, D. (2009). *Beautiful boy: A father's journey through his son's addiction.* Boston: Houghton Mifflin Harcourt.

Sheff, N. (2009). *Tweak: Growing up on methamphetamines.* New York : Atheneum Books for Young Reader

Taughinbaugh, C. (2014). *Parents to PhDs: 28 interview with parents who share heartache, wisdom, and healing through first-hand experiences.* (Kindle ed.). Amazon Digital Services.

Taughinbaugh, C. (2011). *101 natural highs for an amazing drug-free life.* (Kindle ed.). Amazon Digital Services.

Tolle, E. (2009). *A new earth: Awakening to your life's purpose.* London: Penguin Books.

Watson, D. L., & Tharp, R. G. (2014). *Self-directed behavior: Self-modification for personal adjustment.* Monterey: Brooks/Cole.

Wincze, J. P., & Weisberg, R. B. (2015). *Sexual dysfunction: A guide for assessment and treatment.* New York: Guilford Press

Index

CPSIA information can be obtained
at www.ICGtesting.com
Printed in the USA
FSOW02n0333100216
16643FS